Fostering Autonomy

Fostering Autonomy

A Theory of Citizenship,
the State, and Social Service Delivery

ELIZABETH BEN-ISHAI

The Pennsylvania State University Press
University Park, Pennsylvania

LIBRARY OF CONGRESS CATALOGING-IN-PUBLICATION DATA

Ben-Ishai, Elizabeth, 1981–
    Fostering autonomy : a theory of citizenship, the state, and
social service delivery / Elizabeth Ben-Ishai.
        p.   cm.
Includes bibliographical references and index.
Summary: "Building on a feminist conception of individual
autonomy, explores the obligation of the state to foster autonomy
in its citizens, particularly the most vulnerable, through social
service delivery. Draws on both successful and less successful
examples of service delivery to generate a theoretical account of
the autonomy-fostering state"—Provided by publisher.
ISBN 978-0-271-05217-5 (cloth : alk. paper)
ISBN 978-0-271-05218-2 (pbk. : alk. paper)
1. Citizenship—Social aspects.
2. Autonomy.
3. Public welfare.
4. Social service.
5. Feminist theory.
6. Feminism.
7. Political science.
I. Title.

JF801.B4546   2012
323.601—dc23
2011036764

The Pennsylvania State University Press is a member of
the Association of American University Presses.

It is the policy of The Pennsylvania State University Press
to use acid-free paper. Publications on uncoated stock satisfy
the minimum requirements of American National Standard
for Information Sciences—Permanence of Paper for Printed
Library Material, ANSI z39.48-1992.

For ERIC

Contents

....

Acknowledgments

....

I became interested in the concept of autonomy, and particularly relational autonomy, as an undergraduate at the University of Toronto, when I took a class on feminist legal theory with Jennifer Nedelsky. Her course and her scholarship fueled my interest in feminist political theory and motivated me to pursue a Ph.D. in the field. As is evident in the pages that follow, her work continues to inspire me.

Don Herzog, Mika LaVaque-Manty, Elizabeth Wingrove, and Mariah Zeisberg generously offered their time and knowledge both during the early stages of the writing process and as I revised the manuscript. Don pressed me to clarify my ideas and tighten my arguments. Elizabeth has provided me with brilliant feedback, challenging me in ways that were motivating and encouraging. Mariah frequently managed to capture the essence of this project so precisely that, upon speaking with her, I was better able to understand it myself. In addition, Stephen Darwall offered a supportive and helpful perspective.

Mika read endless drafts of chapters and related papers, spent hours upon hours discussing the ideas that eventually found their way into this book, offered moral support and encouragement when I needed it (which was often), and, most of all, provided the intellectual insight without which this project could not have been completed. As if this were not enough, an accomplished runner, Mika provided me with advice as I trained for a marathon during grad school. Combining scholarly and athletic expertise, more than a few of our conversations about the material in this book took place on runs through the streets and trails of Ann Arbor. I am grateful for his continued mentorship and friendship.

I received support to complete this book from the University of Michigan Department of Political Science, Rackham Graduate School, and the Institute for Humanities. Albion College provided support for me to continue this research and also to present it at various conferences.

Over the past five years, I have presented stand-alone versions of almost all the chapters of this book at conferences, including the American Political Science Association, Western Political Science Association, Association for Political Thought, and Canadian Political Science Association meetings. Audiences and discussants at these conferences helped me develop this project immensely. I presented several of the chapters of the book to graduate students and faculty at the University of Michigan Political Theory Workshop; these presentations and the feedback they garnered were helpful. Fellows at the Institute for Humanities at UM offered valuable feedback on chapter 6 of the book. Different versions of two of the chapters have been published elsewhere. A version of chapter 3 was published as "The New Paternalism: An Analysis of Power, State Intervention, and Autonomy," *Political Research Quarterly*, December 22, 2010. A version of chapter 5 was published as "The Autonomy-Fostering State: 'Coordinated Fragmentation' and Domestic Violence Services," *Journal of Political Philosophy* 17, no. 3 (2009): 307–31. The book has benefited form the comments of anonymous reviewers and the editors at both these journals.

My colleagues in the political science department at Albion College—Dyron Dabney, Andy Grossman, and Bill Rose—have provided a pleasant and supportive environment within which to work. Teaching courses on feminist theory and social welfare policy at Albion has been helpful in clarifying my thoughts on this project; I am thankful to the students who signed up for those classes. My "carpool buddies" made completing this book while teaching a heavy course load and commuting an hour each way not only tolerable, but even fun. I am thankful for the companionship and good humor of Holger Elischberger, Scott Melzer, and Helena Mesa. Michael Dixon and I began teaching at Albion at the same time, in 2008, and his friendship and commiseration made the adjustment process much more bearable.

Sandy Thatcher took this project on as he was preparing to retire from Penn State University Press. I am grateful for his willingness to work with me and for his thoughtful choice of reviewers. The detailed and perceptive reviews I received from Catriona Mackenzie and Julie Ann White, both scholars whose work I admire greatly, were enormously helpful. I was fortunate to work with Sandy up until his departure, after which Kendra Boileau took the reins and continued to offer support for the project.

I am thankful to my friends at the University of Michigan and in Ann Arbor, who offered me both support and (necessary) distractions as I worked on the book. Thanks to Megan Biddinger, Ross Bowling, Derek Caveney, Tyler

Cornelius, Anne Davis, Deniz Erkmen, Ryan Gittins, Matt Ides, Ursula Lawrence, Cathy Miller, Kathleen Tipler, Urmila Venkatesh, and, most of all, Roisin O'Mara. My running friends back in Toronto provided support and inspiration, athletic and otherwise.

My father, Israel Ben-Ishai, offered his unfailing support, possibly embodying the notion of "fostering autonomy" better than anyone. He has always allowed me to find my own way—even when I took the difficult and less enlightened one—and believed in me. My sister, Stephanie Ben-Ishai, has been a role model in her dedication and success as a scholar. She has offered me intellectual and professional support as well as friendship. My mother, Ilana Klein, has always been a model of persistence and perseverance, which I have tried to follow as best I can.

Last, but not least, I thank my partner, friend, travel buddy, "activity partner," and intellectual companion, Eric Eide. His love, even when expressed from India via spotty Internet connections and Skype, is what sustained me while I worked on this project. Eric has read and discussed many parts of this project with me, which has surely made this a better book. Perhaps as important have been all of the moments I have spent with Eric *not* working on this book. Our travels around the world, from trekking in Chilean Patagonia to scuba diving in Indonesia, and our quieter moments closer to home have made me a happier and better person. I look forward to our future adventures.

1 INTRODUCTION

Can the state foster autonomy in addicted drug users without requiring abstinence? When these users participate in the *delivery* of state-funded services for which they are also *recipients*, how can we understand the role of the state? Is a battered woman who *chooses* to remain in an abusive, even potentially lethal, relationship acting autonomously? What, if any, is the role of the state in intervening in her decision-making process? Do harsh sanctions, including the loss of all benefits, levied by a paternalistic state on welfare recipients who fail to meet rigid work and conduct requirements facilitate autonomy competency? Do legal citizenship requirements set the boundaries of the state's obligations to members of its community, or does social service delivery in the context of a globalizing world blur such distinctions? Can autonomy and coercive relations of domination coexist? This book begins to reconcile the sometimes-paradoxical claims surrounding the role of the state in fostering autonomy through social service delivery, often in our most vulnerable citizens—citizens that conventional theories of autonomy largely fail to accommodate.

Despite the complexity of these questions, I argue that the state does indeed have an obligation to foster autonomy, wherever possible, in its individual citizens. Moreover, I suggest that despite the apparent tensions that emerge in practical and theoretical attempts to engage in autonomy-fostering practices, it is possible—and desirable—for the state to endeavor to do so. Such an obligation exists in states that lay claim to standards of equal citizenship rights for all members of the community—liberal democracies that are founded on particular notions of justice and inclusion. Simply by focusing on this particular attribute—autonomy—this study makes two claims. First, I participate in the project of "reclaiming" autonomy from its conventionally individualistic context. That is, I argue that autonomy ought to be valued. Though feminists and other critical scholars have sometimes seen this concept as exclusionary, a growing number of theorists have reconceived of autonomy in a way that, I am convinced, highlights its importance. Second, I suggest that autonomy is a capacity that *can* be fostered. This claim follows from the first as it is related to the reconceived notion of autonomy as *relational*; in this conception, autonomy develops not in isolation but out of enabling social relations.

With these initial claims in mind, in the chapters that follow I draw on empirical examples of social service delivery models in order to develop a theory of the "autonomy-fostering state." Moreover, I consider the implications of such a theory for our conceptions of autonomy, citizenship, service delivery practices, and the state itself. In this introductory chapter, I lay out the theoretical starting points for my consideration of each of these interrelated concepts and anticipate how they will come to life in the context of the "case studies" I discuss below. The theory of autonomy I offer is closely tied to citizenship, as I claim that the capacity for autonomy is a central requirement for access to and exercise of the rights and status associated with citizenship—that is, citizenship is in many ways the political realization of autonomy. My theory of the state also follows from the account of autonomy I put forth. I suggest that given a notion of autonomy as socially constituted, the state-citizen relationship must be seen as a pivotal site at which such constitution occurs. I turn to service delivery because it is for many the primary site at which interaction with the state takes place. Moreover, my concern with the autonomy of vulnerable and marginalized people makes service delivery particularly illuminating. This project, then, contributes to theories of autonomy and the state in two different but related ways. First, I offer a normative account of what the autonomy-fostering state might look like. Second, following from this account, I offer a set of analytic tools that help us to better make sense of the contradictions and tensions that emerge from the practices of existing liberal-democratic states.

Autonomy

Feminist political theorists have rightly been concerned with problems of autonomy for some time. The broadly conceived feminist project of overcoming gender oppression (understood in a far-ranging array of ways) is necessarily connected to the notion of individual autonomy. Where such oppression has denied women—and those ideas, institutions, and relationships gendered "feminine"—proper respect, recognition, and access to resources, it has often also (or consequently) denied them the opportunity to develop and exercise autonomy. By autonomy, I mean the capacity to live one's life according to one's own plans—that is, the capacity for "self-government." Despite the relevance of autonomy to feminism, feminists have also been concerned about the implications of such notions of self-government, which are sometimes criticized for being overly individualistic; for referencing only atomistic, unencumbered, and independent individuals, categories that have conventionally excluded most women; and for ignoring the inherent sociality of human beings. In response to these claims, many theorists, feminist and otherwise, have argued that autonomy is a "relational" concept.[1]

Given that humans are socially embedded creatures, autonomy cannot be theorized as though such interdependence does not exist. Instead, we must navigate the path between acknowledging the "constitutiveness of social relations" and the "value of self-determination."[2] Autonomy can be understood, then, "as an acquired set of capacities to lead one's own life"—that is, acquired in the context of our various relationships.[3]

Thus the capacities associated with autonomy "do not merely emerge naturally, but must be developed through various processes involving educational, social and personal resources."[4] Given the importance that liberal societies often place on protecting the vulnerable, "[they] should be especially concerned to address vulnerabilities of individuals regarding the development and maintenance of their autonomy."[5] Joel Anderson and Axel Honneth identify three "relations-to-self" that are central to autonomy-competency and therefore require particular social supports: self-respect, self-trust, and self-esteem.[6] Catriona Mackenzie further elaborates why these relations-to-self are so crucial: "Because our practical identities are complex and dynamic, deliberating about what we ought to do involves self-interpretation—working out which of our desires should constitute reasons for us, which commitments are most important, which emotional responses we should attend to, how to reconcile inner conflicts arising from the obligations of different social roles, and so on."[7] The three relations-to-self referenced by Anderson and Honneth constitute or shape practices of self-interpretation. In turn, it is relationships of recognition that are central to establishing enabling relations-to-self; where such recognition does not exist, one's autonomy is threatened. That is, "one's autonomy is *vulnerable to disruptions in one's relationship to others*."[8] This attention to the vulnerability of our capacity to act autonomously brings into focus the relations of power so pivotal in determining what contexts will be most conducive to developing autonomy-competency. The trajectories of power that we find in given social contexts are important for our understanding of the types of relationships that *constrain* relations-to-self, and therefore the development of the capacities required for autonomous action.

For example, Marilyn Friedman discusses autonomy in relation to male dominance. She points out just how damaging and contraindicated relations of dominance are to autonomy. One response to the experience of being dominated, Friedman explains, is to "abandon wants and values that dominance relationships prevent [the dominated] from realizing. A dominated person may try to convince herself that she never really wanted those things in the first place."[9] In addition, Friedman notes, a chronically dominated person may come to rely on certain structures and institutions for protection. She may subsequently be reluctant to criticize these sources of protection: "My capacity for critical thinking would be constrained by my need for protection."[10] The likelihood of, first, abandoning one's desired means or ends or, second, losing the opportunity or capacity to level criticisms at dominant institutions in society—which happen to afford some of us protection from some kinds of domination—represents a serious assault on the opportunity to develop and exercise the capacity to act autonomously. Where the state delivers social services in such a way that leads those dependent on it to be embedded in relations of dominance, autonomy is threatened.

This relational conception of autonomy and its underlying analysis of relations of power are central to my argument in this book. Indeed, it is such an understanding of autonomy that makes the possibility of fostering autonomy coherent. Using existing accounts of relational autonomy as a starting point, in the chapters that follow I use the empirical examples that serve as case studies to present a richer account of the specific social relations that enable and hinder autonomy, and the empirically situated problems or discontinuities that suggest a need for greater nuance in our theories of autonomy. For example, one chapter on services for domestic violence survivors draws our attention to, on the one hand, the complexities of the effects of oppressive socialization on autonomy, and on the other hand, the contextual nature of autonomous action. Further, in a chapter on the "new paternalism," the relationship between autonomy and paternalism is complicated in light of a more nuanced conception of paternalism that takes into account power relations. Another chapter on immigration provisions under welfare reform complicates even further the relationship between citizenship—in this case legal citizen-ship—and autonomy. Though it is *social* citizenship that most often crops up in discussions of social welfare service delivery, *legal* citizenship, too, plays an important role in granting access to autonomy. But legal citizenship is not of-ten a product of autonomous decision making, instead emerging as a product of birth. Migration decisions, in turn, can be considered autonomous, but only when conceived of relationally—as a product of vast global economic inequal-ities that shape the life prospects of individuals. Such a relational account of migration decisions better situates claims to responsibility, both individual and collective, that arise in debates over immigrant welfare claims.

In order to better grapple with the problems of autonomy that emerge from my analysis of empirical examples, I offer elements of a theory of autonomy that differ from other theorists' accounts. I do this first, in my treatment of the debate over procedural versus substantive accounts of autonomy, and second, in my use of both the ascriptive and capacity-related notions of autonomy. The debate between procedural and substantive accounts of autonomy has preoc-cupied autonomy theorists for some time. Theorists who understand auton-omy as "content-neutral" or "procedural" argue that "the *content* of a person's desires, values, beliefs, and emotional attitudes is irrelevant to the issues of whether the person is autonomous with respect to those aspects of her moti-vational structure and the actions that flow from them."[11] That is, what mat-ters for autonomy is not the substance of the autonomous belief or action, but rather the way one arrives at this belief or action. There are no particular val-ues that the autonomous individual must adopt in order to count as such. The key to autonomy for proceduralists is some form of self-reflection, indicating that actions are taken in accord with certain values held by the individual, rather than impulsively or according to values one does not perceive to be "one's own." Marilyn Friedman explains: "That something matters deeply to a person when she attends to it, and that this concern partly directs her choices and actions, imparts a special significance to her behavior that it is appropri-ate to call determination by herself as the self she is."[12]

But such a conception of autonomy is limited, many theorists have noted, by the pervasive existence of oppressive socialization and the ensuing inter-nalization of values that serve to *limit* one's autonomy. This does not mesh well with the high value that proceduralists place on the individual's perception of herself as engaging in critical self-reflection that enables her to make choices and take actions that are "her own." In response to such objections, theorists of procedural relational autonomy note that what is "her" own will always be a product of social relations: we cannot dismiss perception of self-reflection out of hand simply on account of socialization, since indeed one cannot be "outside" socialization. But Paul Benson highlights an important problem with this response: "Certain forms of socialization are oppressive and clearly lessen autonomy. In some prominent cases, the general means by which oppressive socialization operates are no different than those through which benign socialization takes effect."[13] Thus, unless we are willing to concede that, because both fall under the rubric of "socialization," decisions made under the constraints of oppressive socialization are equally autonomous to those taken within the context of enabling socialization, critical reflection may not be a sufficient means for discerning between autonomous and nonautonomous behavior.

In contrast, substantive views of autonomy require that it be consistent with certain conditions that go beyond the procedural requirements of self-reflection. While some strong substantive theories require that autonomous individuals have the capacity to direct their own lives in accord with specific values or norms (e.g., they may require a high degree of rationality or a rejection of specific norms deemed oppressive), others are less stringent, requiring that one's autonomous decisions, preferences, or actions be formulated or taken in accord with broader content guidelines. For example, in a related account of responsibility, Benson suggests that "self-worth" is an ideal condition for evaluating standards of personal responsibility (and autonomy) that helps us make normative claims about oppressive socialization.[14] Benson usefully distinguishes between substantive theories of autonomy for which the normative content required applies to specific "preferences or values that agents can form or act upon," and those that instead focus on "normative competencies."[15] In the latter accounts, normative constraints may be applied to the agent's capacities for decision making, but not necessarily the decisions she makes.

In this book, following Benson's account above, I defend a "weak" substantive account of autonomy that attaches normative content to competencies rather than specific values. I develop this account most fully in chapter 5. The account I provide, however, diverges from other substantive accounts insofar as I stress that the "substance" of autonomy must be figured with attention to the specificity of a given context. As critics have rightly noted, substantive accounts of autonomy run the risk of being exclusionary or further marginalizing some groups; they may fail to be contextually sensitive, imposing substantive markers of autonomy that do not accurately or justly account for the nature of autonomy in a given setting.[16] In contrast, more fruitful accounts of substantive autonomy must view particular arenas—be they policy arenas, cultural arenas, political contexts, and so forth—as spaces within which the specificities of the substance of competencies associated with autonomy can be worked out. These competencies, for example, may include the relations-to-self described above (self-respect, self-esteem, and self-trust), but what form such relations-to-self take cannot be theorized in the abstract, but rather must take into account the context within which they are developed and realized. As I explain in the later chapters, this methodological approach—moving back and forth between concrete intuitions and theories that are more general—can be understood as contiguous with the value placed on "experience" in much feminist theoretical work. Ultimately, the ability to make normative claims about oppression is central to my defense of a substantive account of autonomy. Rather than generating exclusionary criteria for autonomy, a substantive account generates much-needed mechanisms for criticizing dominant social structures that constrain autonomy.

The second way I expand on the existing accounts of relational autonomy is by making use of and further developing an account of ascriptive autonomy. As I note above, I understand autonomy to be the capacity to pursue one's own ends or life plans. But there is a finer distinction to be made in specifying what it means to be autonomous. Following other theorists,[17] I view autonomy as referring not only to a capacity but also to a status. That is, one is *recognized* as autonomous; autonomy is ascribed to some individuals and not to others. It may well be the case that autonomy is ascribed to individuals who possess the capacity. But given the politically charged and conceptually muddled ways that the concept of autonomy is sometimes deployed in popular and academic contexts, the conferral of recognition and the existence of capacity may also fail to overlap. Nevertheless, the two senses of autonomy are indeed interwoven. Recognition theorists, as I discuss in greater depth in chapter 6, have noted that the psychic effect of misrecognition can often impede our sense of self, and following from this, I argue that our capacity to act autonomously can also be constrained by misrecognition.[18] On the other hand, the ascription of autonomy to one who is not necessarily fully endowed with the capacities for autonomy may in fact promote the development of these capacities: the experience of being recognized as autonomous may create certain expectations, responsibilities, and feelings of inclusion that themselves promote autonomy.[19] This interrelatedness makes attention to the dual nature of autonomy important to a fully fleshed-out theory of the autonomy-fostering state.

I use this notion of ascriptive autonomy in chapter 3 to complicate our understanding of paternalism and in chapter 6 to further elucidate the relationship between harm and autonomy. Simply by breaking autonomy down in this way, we are able to get a better handle on what it means to foster autonomy. Indeed, both autonomy understood in the ascriptive sense and in the capacity sense are relationally constituted. The ascription of autonomy is often a function of the expansiveness of our conception of the autonomous individual. In disentangling autonomy from independence, I seek to widen the possibilities for such ascription—or to theorize the institutional and social conditions under which relations of recognition are more justly configured.

An understanding of autonomy as both a capacity and status highlights the link between autonomy and citizenship. In this vein, I turn next to a brief overview of the notion of citizenship that I develop in the book. It is such a conception of citizenship that, to a great degree, motivates the concern many have with autonomy to begin with.

Citizenship

The link between relations of power and individuals' abilities to develop and exercise the capacity to act autonomously is particularly salient when we consider the relationship between autonomy and citizenship in contemporary welfare states. Much as autonomy is ascriptive, as noted above, citizenship has been theorized as referring to a "status." Autonomy, in both its capacity and status forms, I suggest, is critical to the status of citizenship and the related claims to the rights and duties associated with citizenship. The limitations placed on an individual's development and exercise of the capacity to act autonomously—by, for example, relations of dominance—directly bear on first, her attainment of recognition as a full rights-bearing citizen, and second, her capacity to exercise the rights and perform the duties associated with the status of citizenship.

T. H. Marshall most famously explored the notion of citizenship-as-status. Marshall referred to this status as one that "admitted [men] to a share in social heritage" and recognized them as "full members of the society."[20] In the nineteenth century, Marshall explains, the growing conflict between the equality claims of citizens and the inequalities between social classes created by the market system fostered increased tension between what he refers to as social rights on the one hand and civil and political rights on the other. Civil rights (and political rights, which Marshall sees as an offshoot of civil rights) are associated with the new competitive market—the equality of opportunity afforded to all (white, male, etc.) citizens—while social rights ("the right to a modicum of economic welfare and . . . to live the life of a civilized being according to the standards prevailing in the society") are associated with relatively static, predetermined rights based on *needs*.[21] Marshall suggests that the Poor Law Act of 1834 in England was particularly revealing of the effort to eliminate social rights from the status of citizenship. The poor were required to make their claims to social rights as an *alternative* to the rights afforded by citizenship, including civil rights of personal liberty and any political rights they may have possessed.[22] The status of citizenship was revoked for those who were "dependent" on the state. The protection of the state was available only in exchange for the renouncement of one's rights as a citizen.

Marshall claims that social rights encountered a revival in the twentieth century. Though he was referring to the British context, within the United States there was also a growing movement toward increased social rights, perhaps reaching its height in the form of the Great Society pursued by President Lyndon Johnson. But the status of citizenship has increasingly, since the 1970s and particularly in recent years, been regressing in the direction of the stigma and disenfranchisement that characterized the era of the Poor Law; for example, welfare reforms in Britain and the United States at the end of the twentieth century challenged entitlement-based approaches to welfare provision (to varying degrees). Moreover, though his theory has proved useful in many ways for feminist accounts of welfare, dependence, and autonomy, feminist theorists and scholars of welfare policy have criticized Marshall's account for its failure to fully account for the experience of women. For one, his chronology of the development of civil, political, and social rights, in that order, does not describe the experience of women in most of the world. Linda Gordon notes, "Throughout the world women won important social rights from the state *before* they got the vote."[23] Beyond simply perverting the chronology of the development of citizenship rights, this failure to fully consider the role of women leads Marshall to overlook various forms of dependence. While dependence on the state is, for him, mistakenly stigmatized, Marshall primarily considers dependence (in adult males) as emerging from exclusion, temporary or permanent, from the wage labor workforce. My focus on feminist conceptions of autonomy in this book draws on Marshall while pushing his analysis of dependence further, particularly by reinserting the experience of women in the development and provision of the social rights of citizenship. In turn, I move beyond a solely market-focused account of the appropriate provisions entailed in social citizenship status, taking into account the ways that social rights are implicated in the conventionally "private" realm.

While social citizenship forms a key axis along which to evaluate social service delivery and its relationship to autonomy, the legal status of citizenship—on which one's political and civil rights hinge to a great degree in the United States and elsewhere—is also a critical area of investigation. Despite what may seem to be the relatively obvious connection between legal citizenship and the social rights of citizenship (including access to welfare service provision), there is a persistent gap between immigration scholars' work on citizenship—focusing on the politics and policies of literal borders that shape nation-states—and the work of theorists who focus on nationally situated citizenship.[24] While the latter group interrogates questions surrounding the rights and duties associated with national citizenship, it often fails to connect these questions to those of legal and political boundaries. Such scholars' "disregard of the larger world frame and of the permeability of national borders serves to distort and limit any account these scholars may offer of the practices and institutions and experiences of citizenship as it is practiced *within* the nation-state."[25] Assuming necessary "completion" or "closure" with regard to the communities to which citizens belong, these studies miss important aspects of the normative questions stemming from citizenship.

One way of understanding this gap between scholarly work on immigration and work on nationally focused citizenship is to highlight the internal differentiation specific to American citizenship. That is, because the United States has historically constituted some groups of native-born citizens as "foreign," most often on racialized grounds, a great deal of nationally focused scholarship on citizenship has been oriented toward the troublesome exclusion and differentiated citizenship afforded to native-born minorities.[26] Indeed, in many parts of the book, this internal exclusion is my focus. But the issue of immigrant access to welfare benefits provides an important opportunity to bridge this gap; we cannot understand the notions of autonomy and citizenship that underlie social service delivery for immigrants without examining the statuses of "immigrant" and "citizen." In chapter 4, I flesh out the contours of the relationship between legal and social citizenship in the context of the provisions of the 1996 U.S. welfare reform bill, known as the Personal Responsibility and Work Opportunity Reconciliation Act (PRWORA), that deny many immigrants access to benefits.

Throughout the book, therefore, I explore the implications of explicitly focusing on the fostering of autonomy in theories of citizenship. In the chapter that follows, I argue for a revised notion of social citizenship, founded on a relational conception of autonomy, which highlights the necessity for autonomy-fostering service delivery as a component of the resources required for full citizenship. In the cases I explore in the remainder of the book, more inclusive notions of citizenship are always at the normative foundation of my claims regarding potentially autonomy-fostering service delivery. Accordingly, I view service delivery as a key site at which the assumptions and stigmas associated with vulnerability in our society may be challenged and the appropriate resources for developing the capacity for autonomy provided. With this in mind, I turn to the implications of and motivations for choosing service delivery as a site of importance for the autonomy-fostering state.

Service Delivery

I focus on service delivery in the book because it is a key juncture at which the relationship between state and citizen plays out. As Michael Lipsky argues in his seminal work *Street-Level Bureaucracy*, "In a sense street-level bureaucrats implicitly mediate aspects of the constitutional relationship of citizens to the state. In short, they hold the keys to a dimension of citizenship."[27] Street-level bureaucrats—the public bureaucrats by whom social welfare services are primarily delivered—play a central role in determining the access that service users have to the status of citizenship and, in turn, to autonomy. It is therefore unsurprising that the delivery of social welfare services has been a site of considerable criticism, debate, and frustration, both in the academic fields of political science and public policy and in public discourse. Nevertheless, this arena remains relatively uninvestigated by political theorists; though considerations of justice and liberty in the context of social welfare provision have been of interest to theorists, there is little theorizing of service delivery practices specifically as an arena within which citizenship—and autonomy—is constructed. I begin to fill this gap, building a theory that draws on the empirical evidence that my colleagues in the other subfields of political science provide and analyze.

The challenges of effectively delivering social services are both structural and ideological. With regard to the structural limitations that street-level bureaucracies face, Lipsky argues that there are almost insurmountable difficulties in achieving sufficient accountability within these settings, particularly where workers possess a high degree of discretion, which is indeed necessary for the jobs they do.[28] Accountability, Lipsky notes, "is the link between bureaucracy and democracy."[29] Yet, while it seems evident that we ought to work to sustain this link, attempts to impose measures of accountability within the context of social service delivery have threatened the quality of these services. For example, efforts at greater accountability, perhaps in the form of expanded or more intrusive efficiency and accuracy measures, may ultimately "erode workers' sense of responsibility for clients," leading them to carry out their duties in a more mechanistic, potentially less productive, and less empathetic manner.[30]

The reasons for this chasm in the maintenance of, on the one hand, accountability, and, on the other, flexibility or discretion, are manifold. In the United States, some of these reasons are related to the manner in which federal and state funds are distributed, bearing on the resources that specific street-level bureaucracies have available to them. Constantly pressured resources lead to overloaded workers, who, while they require discretion, may come to rely on this discretion as a way of streamlining their work and potentially acting in unfair, exclusionary ways.[31] In addition, the ideological underpinnings of social welfare service provision in general bear considerable responsibility for the problems facing street-level bureaucracies. That is, as Lipsky writes, "American street-level bureaucracies must be understood as organizational embodiments of contradictory tendencies in American society as a whole."[32] While the welfare state generates programs built to respond to the insecurity and inequality that the economic system inevitably produces, these programs—and the workers who administer them—are also designed to maintain and reproduce that economic system. In this sense, street-level bureaucrats are indeed involved in a project of social control; their job is to deliver services in such a way that they do not undermine the status quo, which often requires that they impose disciplinary constraints on clients, with the objects of this discipline ranging from the nature of clients' appearance to other aspects of their self-presentation. Yet in fulfilling the first imperative of the welfare state, to respond to *needs*, street-level bureaucrats are also often a manifestation of society's humanitarian impulses. These contravening impulses complicate our understanding of the state as an agent of social control, as I discuss in more detail below.

The form and function of social service delivery in the context I pay particular attention to here—the United States—is also a product of popular conceptions of poverty and dependence. Lipsky, whose book was published in 1980, describes Americans' "deep conviction that poor people at some level are responsible for the conditions in which they find themselves, and that receiving benefits labeled 'for the poor' is shameful."[33] Certainly, this sentiment remains prevalent and perhaps even stronger in the early twenty-first century, with the popular welfare reforms of 1996 relying heavily on such assumptions.[34] Public intellectuals and politicians emphasize the pathology of poverty—referring to an alien "underclass"—and the undeserving nature of those who, they claim, receive benefits in exchange for doing no work (i.e., participating in the wage labor economy). Lipsky also notes that social services delivered to the poor (or other marginalized groups) are seen, in general, as a cost rather than as a benefit.[35] These troubling attitudes and the consequent tensions in social service delivery that Lipsky describes manifest themselves in on-the-ground practices that directly affect the distribution of citizenship rights in the United States.

As I mentioned above, service delivery is perhaps *the* key site of state-citizen relationships. As Joe Soss writes, "Through welfare participation, individuals enter a relationship with government that may be designed in a variety of ways."[36] Lipsky, too, notes that most citizens have their sole interactions with the state (or what they think of as the state) by way of their engagement with street-level bureaucracies, be they schools, welfare offices, or police officers. The relationship that is formed, I suggest, determines the extent to which citizens will be given the opportunity to develop the capacities to act autonomously, and relatedly, but still distinctly, whether they will be recognized as autonomous. Soss argues that welfare participation teaches clients how government and bureaucracy in particular will respond to their claims, and what sorts of claims they are entitled to make on it: "It teaches citizens lessons about whether they can be effective in petitioning government and whether they have standing to act without fear of retribution."[37] The "dilemma of action," as Soss puts it, that citizens are conditioned to respond to via welfare service delivery experiences is a central component of both the exercise and development of autonomy competency. Political or social action, whether in response to the welfare system or elsewhere in the public sphere, can be a key arena for building and exercising the skills necessary for autonomous activity.

Soss's fascinating study of welfare participation as a site of political action highlights the important *political* function of making claims on the welfare state. Through interviews and participant observation, Soss finds that welfare participation can be a key site for making claims on the government that are, more so than elsewhere, effective in yielding them "tangible, immediate, and helpful actions from government." Soss argues that through the process of claiming welfare rights—which is mediated by service delivery practices—clients "can enhance their power to accomplish goals and serve as capable members of the polity."[38] Even in the context of mechanisms of social control, welfare may at some junctures afford recipients the opportunity for greater autonomy than they likely otherwise would have had. Soss's view of service delivery is thus, to an extent, more optimistic than Lipsky's. While he by no means exonerates the system of the sorts of contradictions and tensions that Lipsky finds, he acknowledges that social welfare service delivery plays an important role in clearing the way for disadvantaged, traditionally marginalized individuals to *exercise their capacity to act autonomously*.

I want to take Soss's observations one step further in proposing that, through service delivery, the welfare state can not only allow for autonomous activity, it can and should directly engage in the task of fostering autonomy. Soss's observations do not demonstrate that such activity is occurring. For the most part, delivery of public assistance in the United States has not been undertaken in a manner that serves to foster autonomy.[39] Elsewhere in the welfare state, in sometimes equally politicized and stigmatized arenas, some service delivery does seem to fulfill the goal of fostering autonomy. In the chapters that follow, I consider several examples of these programs, which I will introduce below, and extract from them some general ideas and principles that may be applicable to the delivery of public assistance as well.

It is important to note that no definitive prescription for service delivery practices emerges in the course of the book. This is the case for a number of reasons. First, as I stress throughout, contextual details are of much importance to any conception of the relational conditions that best foster autonomy. As I note above, I consider the substance of autonomy to be constituted in a manner that goes beyond abstract theoretical principles and must take account of given political and social contexts. For example, I explain one dimension of the relevance of context in chapter 3, finding that the structure of relations of power is critical to our understanding of what distinguishes autonomy-fostering practices from paternalistic practices. Moreover, as my discussion of harm reduction in chapter 6 emphasizes, service users can (and perhaps ought to) play an important role in the delivery of services and the structuring of principles according to which such delivery is organized. Given this input, it is difficult to delineate autonomy-fostering practices with great specificity unless the details of a given situation are available. Finally, as I turn to next, the "state" is not a singular entity, but rather a fragmented, diverse, and sometimes contradictory set of entities. Given this multiplicity, what constitutes fostering autonomy in one manifestation of the state may not do so in another.

The State

Some theorists view the goal of fostering autonomy as contrary to the interests of the state as a whole, while others argue that turning to the state as a tool with which to resist the oppression of marginalized groups, especially of women, is inherently misguided. The state, they claim, is either a mechanism of social control or an instrument of patriarchal power. These theorists pose an important challenge to both the normative and empirical claims in this book. Of course, most theorists recognize that the state is not a monolithic entity; rather, it is an amalgam of various institutions and practices that are not always aligned with one another's interests. But even when viewed as a complex, though abstract, entity, many theorists still question the plausibility of the state as a mechanism of "empowerment"—as the popular buzz-word might be used to describe "autonomy fostering"—arguing that the state is too fraught with gendered, racialized power dynamics that privilege the independent, white, male citizen to serve this purpose. I argue, along with a number of other feminist theorists writing over the course of the past two decades, that out of the competing and often contradictory interests and goals emerging from the network of institutions and actors that the state comprises come important opportunities for programs that can and do foster autonomy, even for the most vulnerable and traditionally marginalized members of our communities.

Throughout the book, I engage with the understanding of the state that views it as primarily a mechanism of social control and masculinist power. Frances Fox Piven and Richard Cloward present the most well-known, and perhaps most convincing, approach to the former critique.[40] Piven and Cloward's model of the welfare state pays particular attention to the social-ordering role of work, or paid employment. When the poor are working, they will think and act as required to preserve the source of their subsistence. Non-work has the opposite effect, however, especially when it is a condition endured by many people. In the absence of work as a source of order, potential unrest threatens to disrupt capitalist production and, in turn, profit making.

Without the regulating function of work, and in combination with the effects of material deprivation, people turn to various forms of protest and resistance that may, at their most extreme, "threaten to overturn existing social and economic arrangements."[41] In this model, welfare does not simply attend to the deprivation brought about by unemployment. Its primary function is to restore order. Order is restored by way of conditionality; relief depends on fulfilling certain requirements. On the other hand, the stigma associated with welfare promotes the compulsion to work under any conditions, no matter how unjust or unsatisfactory with regard to meeting basic needs or respecting fundamental rights.

Wendy Brown offers a version of the social control critique that sees the state as necessarily a masculinist entity.[42] As I discuss in chapter 5, despite the gradual diminishment of the power differential between individual men and women, Brown argues that the state has come to occupy many of the same positions of power once held by men. Moreover, the state does not deliver on its claims to neutrality, instead taking up a masculinist perspective, built on historically male-held leadership roles, masculinist institutions and modes of protection and regulation, and the reproduction of dominant notions of femininity. Therefore, Brown rejects the notion that the state can be an agent of liberation or progressive challenges to gendered forms of oppression; rather, to seek out the state as an ally in feminist aims is to turn to an agent of masculine power as a mechanism for protection from, paradoxically, masculine power. Though rationalized and bureaucratized, state power represents a continued assault on women's freedom.

Though Brown does disaggregate the state in her discussion of its different functions,[43] she maintains a relatively unnuanced view of the state's interests, even in its multiple functions: all arms of the state ultimately make use of their power for patriarchal ends, she argues. While I do not reject the claim that patriarchal power exists to a wide extent within the various divisions of the state, I challenge the notion that these various arms, even given the continued existence of patriarchy, can never act in enabling ways in the lives of women or other feminized subjects. As I will point to in greater detail in later chapters, other theorists do offer more nuanced accounts, challenging the category of "patriarchy" as an adequately cohesive way of characterizing the state. In her essay on "The New Feminist Scholarship on the Welfare State," Linda Gordon calls into question the value of the term "patriarchy" as a descriptive or analytic category for study of the welfare state. First, she notes the fuzziness of the word: "By using a word so filled with fatherly, familial, organic, fixed hier-

archical relations to describe today's male supremacy, situated in a nonfamil-
ial, inorganic, meritocratic society, we lose much of its power and nuance, and
we mask significant historical change."[44] Moreover, even if the state has come
to occupy positions of domination previously held my individual men, notes
Gordon, there is a certain imprecision in describing both individual male subordination of women *and* the gender oppression emerging from the state as
examples of patriarchy. Gordon further notes that the use of the "state patriarchy" model is inflexible because it fails to acknowledge the genuine gains that
women have made, instead representing "them as an inevitable epiphenome-
non of modernization or secularization rather than as the result of collective
political struggle, that is, of feminism."[45]

Picking up on this critique of the state patriarchy model as presenting only
a picture of the state as oppressor, Barbara Cruikshank's Foucauldian account
of the welfare state highlights the complexities of the inevitable power relations between state and citizen. Explaining the workings of state power, she
defines a "technology of citizenship" as "a method for constituting citizens out
of subjects and maximizing their political participation."[46] Such technologies
of citizenship, she suggests, do not cancel out the autonomy and independence
of citizens, but rather are modes of governance that work on and through the
capacities of citizens to act on their own.[47] Thus Cruikshank takes seriously
welfare policy that seeks to "empower" recipients; she does not simply dismiss
such policies as modes of social control. Nevertheless, she notes that the process of making citizens "self-governing" also renders them "governable."[48]
Thus, while Cruikshank's approach to the welfare state is more subtle than the
state patriarchy model, she remains suspicious of welfare programs that claim
to foster self-government in recipients, noting that such self-government often
entails the self-directed but highly conditioned assent of the recipient to align
her goals with those of, for example, individuals and groups situated in bureaucratic or therapeutic positions of power.

Throughout this book, while taking heed of the great potential for the
state to act as an agent of disempowerment, even if in the less apparent but
equally deleterious manner Cruikshank points to, I present a more optimistic account of the state—that is, of the autonomy-fostering state. While I do
not claim that such a state exists in entirety in any one place, by pointing to
the workings of particular arenas of the state's many arms, and to the interactions among these arms, I begin to offer a picture of a state that generates the
relational conditions necessary to foster autonomy.[49] There are several key
elements of the autonomy-fostering state that emerge out of my analyses of

both autonomy-hindering programs and autonomy-enabling service delivery programs:

- *Embodied recognition*: In the case of many social welfare services, the recipients of benefits lay claim to needs that are explicitly embodied; our understanding of the state must therefore consider the extent to which it accounts for such embodiment. Attention to "embodied autonomy," I argue, can be found in the autonomy-fostering state, as demonstrated by the programs I explore in chapters 5 and 6. In turn, the cases of new paternalist programs and the provisions of PRWORA affecting immigrants (discussed in chapters 3 and 4, respectively) highlight a failure to recognize both the embodied needs of some individuals and their capacities for autonomy and responsibility. These cases point to how the absence of a conception of the embodied elements of autonomy deeply affects racialized and gendered bodies in ways that perpetuate structural inequalities.

- *User involvement*: Service delivery models that involve users in the development and the *delivery* of services have profound implications for the autonomy-fostering potential of the state. When users, as in the case described in chapter 6, run their own harm reducing needle exchange program at the behest of the state, who is state and who is client? This confusion is a productive one, I argue. In a similar sense, the success of the programs for domestic violence survivors, which I discuss in chapter 5, rely in part on the checks and balances generated by the involvement of advocates who are often survivors of domestic violence themselves. The PRWORA programs I discuss that limit autonomy do not employ methods of user involvement. The absence of such elements of service delivery point to a broader implication of user involvement: by involving users in service delivery, the state *ascribes* autonomy to these users in ways that enable the *capacities* necessary for autonomy. In contrast, where pregnant teenagers and unemployed adults, for example, are seen as incompetent and immigrants as lacking responsibility (as they are in PRWORA programs), such ascription of autonomy is a long way off.

- *"Coordinated fragmentation" within the state*: At times, the conditions for autonomy-fostering service delivery arise out of the contradictory impulses of the various state arms involved in a particular type of service delivery, even if the intentionality of each arm is not itself aligned with the aim of fostering autonomy. The fragmentation of the state—the multiplicity that defines it—can be fruitful where appropriately coordinated; we see this in

my accounts of both services for domestic violence survivors and harm reduction services for drug users. This feature is related to the prior one: the
notion of the "state" is complicated when its agents—the individuals delivering the state-funded services—are service users themselves.

I return to these features throughout the book as I discuss the case studies
outlined below. These elements are relevant to varying degrees in each of the
cases, but for the sake of clarity and to allow sufficient depth, in each case I
focus on some elements more than others.

Though these features of the autonomy-fostering state are instructive, as
with service delivery, no singular theory of the state or "road map" of the
autonomy-fostering state emerges from this book. Nevertheless, the various
accounts of autonomy fostering I offer in this book usefully challenge the
social control and patriarchy models of the state (while acknowledging the
existence of these motivations at certain junctures of state power). Further,
these accounts contribute to and advance more complex accounts of the state,
like Cruikshank's, which, though nuanced, tends to focus primarily on the
constraining elements of state power, rather than the enabling ones, which
themselves are often depicted as implicitly constraining.

Plan of the Book

In chapter 2, I further develop the account of citizenship that underpins my
concern in this book with fostering autonomy. In this chapter, I focus on the
social rights of citizenship; later in the book, I take up questions of legal citizenship. I argue for a revised notion of social citizenship that has at its core a
relational conception of autonomy. The standard notion of social citizenship,
often attributed to T. H. Marshall, does indeed have autonomy at its core; it
seeks to correct the economic inequalities that compromise one's ability to act
autonomously. Because it does not account for the relational nature of autonomy, however, it occludes the reality that autonomy does not hinge solely on
the adequate provision of material conditions—that it is also fostered or constrained in the context of social relationships. Where these relationships are
well structured, autonomy is more likely to emerge. This feminist conception
of autonomy brings to light an understanding of social citizenship rights as
concerned with actively promoting autonomy by establishing and cultivating
the relational support necessary to foster this capacity. In this chapter, two

prominent critiques of the concept of social citizenship serve as an entry point to theorizing the autonomy-focused model I propose. On the one hand, some critics charge that the rhetoric of social citizenship fails to consider the mechanisms of social control that always accompany, and often overshadow, social welfare rights. On the other hand, the language of social citizenship rights is criticized for its "passive" conception of citizenship, focusing only on rights without accounting for the role of duties or obligation. By reconceiving social citizenship as a status that grants individuals not only the right to freedom from material constraints on autonomy, but also the right to access services and resources necessary to foster and develop the capacity to act autonomously, we can effectively respond to these critiques.

Chapters 3 and 4 examine aspects of the 1996 U.S. welfare reforms emerging from the passage of the Personal Responsibility and Work Opportunity Reconciliation Act. These cases present us with examples of programs and policies that *fail* to foster autonomy, as they are premised on flawed notions of the autonomous individual and her relationship to the state. From these cases, the deeply damaging effects of formulating social welfare service policy, based on misconceived notions of the self and the social relations in which it is embedded, become apparent. Along with the cases discussed in chapters 5 and 6, these chapters take up specific practices that may fulfill the requirements of social citizenship, as reconceived in chapter 2, while also developing the theoretical accounts of the state and autonomy that are at the core of the book

In chapter 3, I consider whether a theory of an autonomy-fostering state ought to be understood simply as a version of "forced to be free": Is the notion of the state "fostering autonomy" imbued with some elements of paternalism? Moreover, *can* the state force us to be free? That is, can paternalistic social service delivery ever be autonomy fostering? I approach these important questions by distinguishing autonomy fostering from paternalist practices, specifically those associated with the new paternalism, the influential theory of "supervisory" approaches to social welfare service delivery that underpins many key aspects of PRWORA, and welfare reforms in Britain and some other European countries. I consider two instances of new paternalist service delivery in the post–welfare reform United States: workfare and pregnancy-prevention programs, both directed at welfare recipients. These two programs respond to what many new paternalists claim are the two primary causes of poverty: nonwork and unwed pregnancy. A careful look at each sharpens our view of what it means for the state to foster autonomy—or to fail to do so, as is the case here. Throughout, I suggest that this incompatibility between autonomy-fostering and paternalist social policy makes most sense when founded on a notion of paternalism that highlights its implication in oppressive power relations rather than solely its association with interventionist policy. In this light, the assumption at the core of new paternalism—that of service users' incompetence—reveals the autonomy-constraining implications of such intervention, which is characterized by a lack of respect and recognition.

In chapter 4, I explore the relationship between legal citizenship, social citizenship, and individual autonomy by examining challenges to immigrant and refugee access to welfare benefits in the United States since the 1996 welfare reforms. These reforms coincided with significant immigration reforms, tightening the requirements for legal citizenship and loosening the accountability requirements for the state in its dealing with immigrants. As a result, like in the previous chapter, this policy serves to hinder rather than foster autonomy. I suggest that the reforms are founded on a claim that immigrants who seek out welfare have failed to "take responsibility" for the consequences of their autonomous choice to migrate. This claim is deeply problematic, first because it assumes an individualistic conception of autonomy, and second because it reflects a view of immigration divorced from the reality of the economic and political interdependence of nation-states throughout the world. Immigrants' decisions to migrate can be understood as autonomous, I suggest, but only when autonomy is conceived relationally. Such decisions, where taken by emigrants from impoverished nations, must be understood as relationally constituted in part by the *failure* of the United States to take responsibility for its political and economic actions, which allow American citizens to live a comparatively privileged life at the expense of citizens of other nations. In fact, if we shift the notion of *personal* responsibility at the heart of the foundational claim to one of *political* responsibility, understood as a critical expression of autonomy, we can understand many immigrants' claims to welfare rights as a way of taking political responsibility. Such claims challenge structural conditions of inequality generated by the system of "birthright citizenship," which unequally and arbitrarily distributes the benefits of citizenship status.

Chapters 5 and 6 turn the preceding autonomy-fostering failures on their head: I consider unique cases of service delivery that offer insights into state-citizen relationships that are indeed autonomy fostering. Though they fall within the category of social welfare service delivery, these cases fall outside what popular discourse tends to think of as welfare. It is partly because of this marginal status that the cases offer us the opportunity to rethink theories of the state and to revision its relationship to citizen-users.

In chapter 5, I explore a particular model of service delivery for survivors of domestic violence: "coordinated community response" programs (CCRs). This chapter is centrally focused on theorizing the state in the context of autonomy-fostering practices. I conceptualize the state as a fragmented and plural entity comprising various "loosely coupled" arms that are sometime in conflict with one another. Given this conceptualization, the notion of what I refer to as the "coordinated fragmented state" helps us to understand the dynamics that can enable the state to foster autonomy. The case helps to elucidate this notion of coordinated fragmentation: CCRs take advantage of the tensions inherent in the state in such a way that they are able to foster autonomy more effectively than conventional forms of service delivery. Moreover, the multiplicity of this model offers opportunities for a balance to be struck between care-oriented and justice-oriented elements of the autonomy-fostering state. This balance is made effective partly because of the mechanisms of self-critique extant in the coordinated fragmented state. Additionally, domestic violence services are particularly revealing as a site for considering the dynamics of an autonomy-fostering state, since questions of state intervention, power relations, and individual autonomy are at the forefront of discussions of domestic violence in a wide range of disciplines.

In chapter 6, my theoretical focus is the relationship between harm and autonomy. Although I argue that harm impedes autonomy, I resist the intuitive notion that harm and autonomy exist in a zero-sum relationship (i.e., more harm, less autonomy). This account does not sufficiently allow for the varieties of harm that exist, the multiple sites at which harm is produced and inflicted, and the plural set of actors that are affected by harm. Seeking to complicate this account, I suggest that harm reduction—a model of response to drug use and addiction that seeks to minimize the harm associated with drug use without necessarily requiring abstinence—is a unique location at which the state can foster autonomy in vulnerable citizens. Examples of such programs include needle exchanges and methadone maintenance. I explore two forms of harm. First, I suggest that successful harm reduction programs respond to the harm of *misrecognition* by enabling a space for recognition not just by the state, but by the community, too, including service users' "peers." In these spaces, a measure of ascriptive autonomy can be achieved. Second, this case demonstrates that autonomy competency requires attention to *embodied* forms of harm, where the notion of harm must be flexible and open to continual reinterpretation. In the case of harm reduction service users, the terrain of such contestation often revolves around the politics of pain and pleasure. Both forms of harm point to the fact that the notion of an autonomous addict is *not* oxymoronic, but simply an example of the confluence of a variety of harms with other potentially autonomy-enabling forces. Even in situations of extreme dependence, this case demonstrates, autonomy is, and ought to be, possible.

Finally, I conclude in chapter 7 by summarizing the elements of the autonomy fostering state and their theoretical implications. As well, I reflect upon the "empirically situated" approach to political theory I take in the book, which I argue is necessary for theorizing the inherently political substance of autonomy and service delivery.

2 TOWARD A REVISED CONCEPTION OF SOCIAL CITIZENSHIP: AN AUTONOMY-FOCUSED MODEL

Introduction

Advocates of social citizenship—the status that, as T. H. Marshall wrote, guarantees "the right to a modicum of economic welfare and . . . to live the life of a civilized being according to the standards prevailing in the society"— have seen their notion of the welfare state dissolve in the past two decades, with a growing number of Western states undertaking radical welfare reforms that impose onerous conditions and limitations on the receipt of welfare payments.[1] With this challenge to the practices of modern welfare states in the West, the conceptual terrain occupied by citizenship in general and social citizenship more specifically has become a particularly relevant and lively location for work in political theory.[2] Within the framework of this book, specifying a vision of citizenship proves particularly crucial. Implicit in the theory of the autonomy-fostering state that I put forward is a particular notion of what constitutes full citizenship in the modern state and the obligations and institutions that accompany such a notion. This chapter makes explicit this conception of citizenship, focusing on the social dimensions of citizenship. Social citizenship, in the form I elaborate in the following pages, both reflects and acts as a benchmark for the extent to which the state is able to fulfill the autonomy-fostering mandate I envision in this book.[3]

The most prevalent critiques of welfare in both the United States and western Europe come from conservatives who invoke pathologizing notions of "a culture of dependency," which often have racialized and gendered underpinnings. Though public and scholarly attention has recently focused on conservative critiques of welfare, which are the basis for dramatic policy changes on both sides of the Atlantic, social citizenship also comes under fire from voices on the opposite side of the political spectrum. In this chapter I explore two such critiques of social citizenship. First, some critics charge that the rhetoric of social citizenship fails to consider the extent to which mechanisms of social control—overwhelming disciplinary power, bureaucratic lapses in accountability, and degrading tools of surveillance—always accompany the rights associated with the welfare state. Second, the language of social citizenship rights has also been criticized for its so-called passive conception of citizenship, focused only on rights without taking into account the role of duty or obligation.

These two important critiques of social citizenship provide an entry point to theorizing a revised (or at least clarified) version of social citizenship. I argue that we need a richer notion of social citizenship, one that has at its core a relational conception of autonomy. While the standard Marshallian version of social citizenship does seem to be at bottom about autonomy—it seeks to correct the economic inequalities that compromise one's ability to act autonomously—it fails to consider autonomy as a capacity that is not only hindered by material barriers, but also fostered only in the context of well-structured social relationships. In this sense, a standard view of social citizenship is often concerned only with removing (material) barriers, and rarely with actively promoting autonomy by establishing and cultivating the relational support necessary to foster autonomy. This revised conception of social citizenship helps us to respond to the critiques mentioned above and therefore to defend a notion of social citizenship rights more generally. First, if we think of social citizenship rights as explicitly concerned with fostering autonomy, the social control critique no longer points to flaws in social citizenship as a concept, but to *incomplete realizations* of the (revised) ideal of social citizenship. Second, we can also undermine concerns about the passivity of rights-focused accounts of citizenship and the failure of social rights to emphasize duties and obligation when we shift the focus of social citizenship to an autonomy-fostering model. As I claim here, autonomy is a necessary condition for the exercise of one's capacity to fulfill duties and meet obligations. Therefore, if social citizenship actively fosters autonomy, it can hardly be thought of as promoting something that runs counter to citizens' abilities to fulfill their duties and obligations.

In advancing this conception of social citizenship, I am not making an empirical claim about the current state of social rights in the United States or elsewhere.[4] Instead, I want to articulate a conception of social citizenship that can serve both as an ideal and as a benchmark with which to evaluate social policy and programs. It is essential that we engage in this conceptual exercise if we are to advance an argument for something we call "social citizenship," and in order to provide justifications for and a defense of critical social welfare programs that have so often come under attack. My discussion of social citizenship is also not an attempt to provide a "correct" interpretation of Marshall's original conception of social citizenship. I take up "social citizenship" as it appears in the context of the critiques and subsequent defenses of the concept as articulated by other scholars, with specific attention to two critiques. What I ultimately put forth is an argument for how we ought to conceive of social citizenship if we are to hold true to the values that have motivated this concept's widespread usage in the first place—notions of inclusion, community, and participation—while also responding to the critiques that have rendered it a beleaguered concept in the context of actual policy. Moreover, this notion of social citizenship is one that takes seriously the obligations of the state to foster autonomy in its citizens. In the chapters that follow I look more concretely at examples where the goal of fostering autonomy through service delivery practices is both successful and unsuccessful, but for now an exercise in conceptual clarification will clear the way for these later analyses.

I begin, then, with two important critiques of social citizenship leveled by other theorists. The section below considers the social control critique, while the section after that turns to critiques of the rights-focused orientation of theories of social citizenship. Both critiques, though coming from different vantage points, start from a similar understanding of social citizenship and its relationship to autonomy. In these accounts, social citizenship rights are primarily focused on the provision of material resources in order to deliver the basic level of material wealth necessary to exercise individual autonomy. When viewed in light of this notion of autonomy, the critiques may indeed be warranted. But the next section then offers a revised conception of social citizenship, which, I argue, helps to resolve some of the conceptual tensions we find in the former definition. This revised conception also supports arguments for a just and equitable distribution of both material resources *and* optimally structured service delivery. At the core of this conception of social citizenship lies a feminist ("relational") conception of autonomy, which draws our attention to the structure of relationships that may either foster or hinder autonomy. The feminist conception of social citizenship that follows rejects the aspiration to overcome need and dependence, instead acknowledging their centrality to human life. In the context of this discussion, autonomy can be thought of as both a need in itself and a mechanism that allows citizens to engage in ongoing contestation over "need interpretation."[5] The following section puts this revised conception of social citizenship into action, arguing that it can help us to respond to the critiques discussed earlier in the chapter, while the final section concludes the argument.

Social Citizenship as Social Control: The Politics of Empowerment

Painting a particularly rosy picture of the early days of social citizenship rights, Marshall writes, "Social integration spread from the sphere of sentiment and patriotism into that of material enjoyment. The components of a civilized and cultured life, formerly the monopoly of the few, were brought progressively within reach of the many, who were encouraged thereby to stretch out their hands towards those that still eluded their grasp. The diminution of inequality strengthened the demand for its abolition, at least with regard to the essentials of social welfare."[6] To be sure, Marshall's treatise on citizenship and social class does not proceed only in such laudatory terms. He later notes the effects of stigma and other tensions in the social democratic state. Like Marshall, however, contemporary proponents of social citizenship are optimistic that, when fully realized, social rights will alleviate the pressures of material want and free citizens to live their lives according to their own wishes, as full members of the community. But, primarily among those advocates of social justice who are associated with the political Left, the promise of social welfare provision as a means to autonomy has been met with skepticism. These critics worry that as it provides the poor with welfare subsidies, the state also exerts excessive power over recipients. Such critics claim that social rights, especially public assistance provision (like Temporary Assistance for Needy Families payments in the United States), are a mechanism adopted by the state primarily for exerting "social control."

In his essay "Social Citizenship and Its Fetters," Eric Gorham is critical of social citizenship, arguing that the concept does not adequately describe on-the-ground practices associated with the welfare state. Further, Gorham argues that while the discourse of social citizenship highlights the increased participation and economic status of members of a community, it obscures "the increasing failure of those members to act in, and against, the modern state and market."[7] Welfare state policies associated with "social citizenship," Gorham claims, both empower and disempower citizens. The accepted notion of citizenship is therefore inadequate as a descriptive for "the modern political subject." Gorham explains, "Citizens must subject themselves to the procedures and institutions necessary to ensure that the state can continue to provide rights."[8] This notion of subjection, which I further discuss and problematize below, is fleshed out by Gorham as he describes the means by which the citizen, or "political consumer," must learn the "correct procedure" necessary to be a citizen and access the commodities that are on offer via civic, political, and social provision.[9] Though social citizenship rights may meet immediate material needs, Gorham (following Foucault) argues that the disciplinary power of the welfare state establishes "stability. . . often at the prices of individual autonomy and self-determination."[10] Though he ultimately rejects the concept, Gorham's working definition of social citizenship takes material resources as the barrier to autonomy. Ultimately, because it fails to offer autonomy even in the face of material relief, Gorham questions the conceptual and practical value of the concept.

Among the most prominent social control theorists of welfare are Francis Fox Piven and Richard Cloward.[11] Though Piven and Cloward do not lodge any conceptual complaints against social citizenship per se, their depiction of the (American) social welfare state, its failings, and its oppressive motives suggests that they, too, are skeptical of social citizenship as it has materialized over the past fifty years.[12] Though we may think of social welfare services as directed primarily at those who are unemployed, Piven and Cloward argue that "poor relief" functions to exert social control over those in the wage labor economy, too. According to Piven and Cloward, work is the primary mechanism for establishing order in modern societies.[13] They write, "So long as people are fixed in their work roles, their activities and outlooks are also fixed; they do what they must and think what they must."[14] When this fixity is disrupted—when unemployment rates rise—disorder may ensue, and the threat of such disorder remains ever present. Welfare, then, serves to restore order and is the means by which the state regains social control.

At the same time, the welfare enterprise also regulates citizens who are not current recipients of welfare. Piven and Cloward contend that in times of relative stability, the market may fail to provide incentives to work for all people; that is, some have not been socialized fully to the "ethos of the market."[15] The welfare system attempts to correct this failure. Those who remain on the welfare rolls in times of stability "have been universally degraded for lacking economic value and ordinarily relegated to the foul quarters of the workhouse, with its strict penal regimen and its starvation diet."[16] By maintaining such terrible conditions and fostering the stigmatization that renders recipients of relief pariahs, the state in effect "spur[s] people to contrive ways of supporting themselves by their own industry, *to offer themselves to any employer on any terms*."[17] In this account, then, social citizenship in the modern state determines the "shape" of its entitlements in such a way that the ideal of providing material resources as a way of protecting autonomy becomes undesirable, indeed almost intolerable.

The above discussion is just a brief sample of the variations of social control–focused critiques of social citizenship that exist in the literature. The key point is, however, that these critiques level a heavy dose of skepticism in response to the conventional account of social citizenship, which suggests that by providing the material resources necessary to elevate the individual bearer of "social rights" to an acceptable level of comfort, the state eliminates the constraints that prevent her from acting autonomously. They argue instead that the concept itself cannot stand up to scrutiny. In actuality, as it provides these resources, theorists of the social control school argue, the welfare state necessarily also exercises—sometimes subtly and not necessarily through obviously "state-initiated" entry points—an overwhelming disciplinary power over recipients of social rights–related entitlements, suppressing their autonomy as it claims to protect it.

Social Citizenship as Passive Entitlement: The Politics of Rights and Duties

Unlike the foregoing critique of social citizenship, which tends to emerge from the Left, another critique has found its greatest currency on the Right, but also holds sway in the center of the political spectrum. In their 1994 review of the growing field of citizenship-focused political philosophy, Will Kymlicka and Wayne Norman outline the New Right critique of social citizenship that weighed heavily on supporters of the postwar welfare state in both the United States and Britain. Social citizenship, they explain, "is often called 'passive' or 'private' citizenship, because of its emphasis on passive entitlements and the absence of any obligation to participate in public life."[18] Though advocates of the welfare state and its companion notion of citizenship traditionally argue that entitlements help to reconcile the inequalities created by the market, and therefore remove barriers to the exercise of political and civil citizenship rights, critics claim that the promise has not been fulfilled.

Explaining this charge, Kymlicka and Norman write, "Far from being the solution, the welfare state has itself perpetuated the problem by reducing citizens to passive dependents who are under bureaucratic tutelage."[19] From critiques of this nature emerged such popular buzzwords and phrases as "culture of dependency" and "intergenerational dependence." In turn, these phrases were liberally bandied about in the debates leading up to the mid-1990s welfare reforms in the United States and Britain.

Resisting the critiques of those who view social welfare provision as a threat to civic participation, defenders of social citizenship argue that welfare rights are indeed the basis for a more vibrant participatory democracy because they aim to curb *need*. For example, Desmond S. King and Jeremy Waldron focus on the account of the relationship between *need* and *the political* that has been prominent in what they refer to as "the tradition" of political theories of citizenship. Citing political theorists from Aristotle to Tocqueville to Arendt, King and Waldron point to the contention that people cannot participate in the polis, or cannot do so well, if a certain attention has not been paid to their material well-being.[20] That is, need undermines civic politics and renders questionable the value of an individual's contributions to the public sphere: "Desperate need is conceived to interfere with the processes of reflection and deliberation that civic politics requires."[21] While acknowledging that need is unlikely to be banished from society, King and Waldron nevertheless describe social citizenship rights as aspiring to remove need from society in order to foster adequate political debate.

But this defense of social citizenship as a tool to overcome "need," and therefore to provide the basis for civic participation, has been challenged on both theoretical and empirical grounds. If needs have been met, this critique charges, participation has not followed, and indeed, in many cases needs have not been sufficiently met. Though writing from a liberal perspective, Michael Ignatieff condemns critiques of conservative rhetoric that fail to acknowledge the genuine shortcomings of social citizenship as it has emerged in practice. The welfare state, he concedes, "did encourage the emergence of new styles of moral self-exculpation."[22] But despite claims to the contrary, "a structure of collective entitlements does not necessarily increase social solidarity," writes Ignatieff.[23] While acknowledging that the transfer of care work to the state has freed those formerly confined to caring roles (largely women) to participate in the labor market, Ignatieff also notes that such a transfer may lead to a weakened sense of familial and community obligation. As we saw in the previous section, entitlements that purport to empower citizens may be accompanied by the exertion of limiting power over citizens. To this Ignatieff adds that such entitlement has rarely brought about participation or any other form of active citizenship: "The entitled were never empowered, because empowerment would have infringed on the prerogatives of the managers of the welfare state."[24] The tensions between the interests of the welfare bureaucracy and those of the so-called empowered citizen-recipient proved too weighty to bring about any genuine empowerment, rendering references to "the enabling and facilitating state" that Ignatieff attributes to postwar social democrats contrary to empirical evidence.[25]

These critiques of the passive nature of social citizenship, then, also rely on an understanding of social citizenship as primarily focused on overcoming basic material needs in order to "enable" citizens to participate in community life and politics. The critics charge that first, dependency renders the recipient-citizens passive and therefore unlikely to participate in civil and political life; and that second, the structure of welfare receipt is so fraught with tensions that the bureaucracy itself tends to stifle the impetus and ability of recipients to participate. The latter of these critiques is related to the social control argument; if welfare acts to pacify those who are driven to protest or unrest by their wants, as Piven and Cloward argue, it also drives them away from their duties to participate in general. Despite the differences in the two critiques I have discussed, they both presuppose a similar notion of social citizenship, which they go on to find fault with.

Relational Autonomy and Social Citizenship

At the beginning of the chapter, I suggested that a revised conception of social citizenship ought to have a particular notion of autonomy at its center. In the previous two sections, I outlined two broadly conceived categories of critiques aimed at the concept of social citizenship. Both categories, I claim, are premised on a similar notion of what exactly the target of the critique—social citizenship—consists of, both in theory and in practice. Indeed, the critics may be construed as viewing social citizenship as *a status that grants individuals the rights to freedom from material constraints that may impede their ability to act autonomously and therefore to exercise the rights associated with civil and political citizenship.* Social citizenship, then, does indeed seem to turn on the concept of autonomy. But my argument is that inherent in this definition are inadequacies in both (1) the notion of autonomy at the core of this conventional definition of social citizenship and (2) the conception of the conditions under which such autonomy can be developed and exercised. In this section, I describe the "remedies" I propose to these inadequacies, and how the elaboration and discussion of such remedies can be conceived of as part of an ongoing process of contestation over what Nancy Fraser refers to as "the politics of need interpretation."[26]

The insights of theorists of relational autonomy, which, as Marilyn Friedman notes, are now relatively widely accepted even by mainstream theorists, have considerable significance for our conception of social citizenship.[27] There are two points that emerge here. First, if the capacity for autonomy is developed in the context of relationships, and if this capacity can also be disrupted, curbed, or threatened in the same context, we must consider not only the lack of material resources that may act as a constraint to the exercise of autonomy. We must also explicitly turn our attention to the *provision* of these resources and to the provision of other services, both of which will serve to constitute a set of especially pivotal relationships in the lives of recipients of the entitlements associated with social citizenship rights. Whether these relationships are appropriately structured—whether, for example, they entail relations of domination—will be crucial in determining their likelihood of fulfilling the goal of promoting autonomy. The second point follows from an argument John Christman makes: that autonomy is developed in the context of a complex mixture of resources, extending well beyond material resources (though they are certainly important). Christman, writing in defense of the closely related concept of positive freedom, explains: "Seeing freedom as more than a set of opportunities created by removing constraints from the path of thought and action . . . is to set out a view of human agency as a set of powers and abilities, ones regarding the development and expression of authentic and effective self-government. Certain political institutions and policies may well remove or minimize constraints faced by an agent but do nothing to establish or protect those powers."[28] Specifying a relational conception of autonomy as central to this conception of social citizenship, then, is critical in defining the contours of what social citizenship rights will look like. If social citizenship is concerned with ensuring the ability of individuals to act autonomously, the rights associated with it will look different depending on what we mean by autonomy.

The second point discussed above—the implications of a relational notion of autonomy for our understanding of what resources are required in order to facilitate the development of that autonomy—is closely linked to the second of the two "inadequacies" I described above. The conventional notion of social citizenship, I argue, inadequately theorizes the conditions under which autonomy is developed. Political scientists and policy analysts have devoted considerable attention to the question of service delivery. Ranging from considerations of the plausibility of a just welfare system given the vast bureaucracy of many welfare states, to more specific, empirical questions about the levels of accountability and discretion required of a successful (however it may be defined) system, these analyses place service delivery high on the list of relevant concerns for questions of social rights.[29] But political theorists examining *normative theoretical accounts* of social citizenship rarely develop a clear account of what service delivery ought to look like if it is to be consistent with the goal of fostering autonomy. This concern, I argue, must be accounted for in a theory of social citizenship.

This discussion of the role of autonomy in the conception (and practice) of social citizenship is congruent in some ways with Nancy Fraser's discussion of the politics of need interpretation. Fraser wants to shift our focus from the discussion of needs to a discussion of the "discourses of needs, from the distribution of need satisfaction to 'the politics of need interpretation.'"[30] The particular salience of "need" to this discussion in general is an important point that I will return to in greater detail in the next section, when I respond to critics in the "duties and obligations" category, as discussed above. I do, in fact, want to think of autonomy as a unique type of need, but also as a key instrument in the politics of need interpretation. But for now, I turn to Fraser's argument, which helps to generate a useful framework for further distinguishing the conventional conception of social citizenship from the revised version I propose.

Fraser divides the politics of need interpretation into "three analytically distinct but practically interrelated moments."[31] Keeping in mind the interrelation of these moments, we can identify the contours of a discussion of social citizenship within the framework of Fraser's "moments." The first moment is a struggle for validation of a need; it is the pursuit of "political" status (or some other status) for the need. In a sense, Marshall's conception of social citizenship does this with regard to autonomy; Marshall's notion highlights the importance of autonomy to both inclusion in the political community and the exercise of rights, both explicitly social (i.e., welfare), and those related to the other types of citizenship he discusses (political and civil).

The second moment Fraser describes revolves around "the struggle over the interpretation of the need, the struggle for the power to define it and, so to determine what would satisfy it."[32] It is within this moment that I want to situate both the critics of social citizenship I refer to above and my own discussion here. While I argue that there is general agreement about the centrality of autonomy to questions of social citizenship, there is not only disagreement over, but also a lack of clarity regarding, the meaning and place of "autonomy" in the context of social citizenship. Moreover, the contested nature of need interpretation that Fraser brings to our attention points to the fact that we must be clear about the meaning of autonomy, who constructs this meaning, and what interests such meanings serve. Fraser argues that analyses of needs that appeal unquestioningly to "socially authorized forms of public discourse" often "neglect the question of whether these forms of public discourse are skewed in favor of the self-interpretations and interests of dominant social groups and, so, work to the disadvantage of subordinate or oppositional groups."[33] Indeed, conceptions of autonomy that *do not* take into account its relational character often presuppose an image of the autonomous individual that is exclusionary along various axes. Even if we would not necessarily associate the critics above with such an outlook, the conventional account has infected their interpretations in a way that, intentionally or not, has exclusionary implications. Such a conception of autonomy, where it shapes the ideal of social citizenship, may arbitrarily (or even pointedly) limit the potential for policies associated with social citizenship to genuinely do the work of fostering autonomy. This "work," as it were, helps to expand the category of individuals who will be both recognized as autonomous and genuinely enabled to develop autonomy.

The implications of a more inclusive politics of need interpretation can also be linked to the ascriptive elements of autonomy introduced in chapter 1: autonomy is in part a function of being recognized as holding the status of autonomous individual. Where need-interpretation practices and procedures fail to take into account the perspectives and experience of those whose needs are at stake, this exclusion is often rooted in the assumption that those who are needy must be lacking in autonomy. This is the implication of King and Waldron's account of the clash between political agency and need described above: to be in need is to be unable to legitimately participate in deliberation in the public sphere, a practice that, in a liberal democratic polity, is often understood as contingent on an individual's capacity for autonomous action. In this account, the exclusion of groups perceived as dependent from the realm of need interpretation can be understood as the denial of the ascription of the status of autonomous individual. In contrast, where the sphere of need interpretation is expanded to include marginalized individuals whose needs are at stake, there is an implicit (or even explicit) ascription of autonomy taking place. To be called on to partake in the contestation over the meaning and appropriate response to need is to be seen as capable of acting autonomously and participating in democratic deliberations.[34] As I describe in more detail in chapter 3, the ascription of autonomy is crucially linked to the capacity for autonomy, in that being recognized as autonomous helps to foster the conditions under which one may actually develop and exercise one's capacities for autonomy. Thus, if social citizenship is reconceived in a way that takes seriously the relational conditions under which autonomy is developed, such ascriptive practices must be taken into account; just as Marshall conceives of citizenship as a status, autonomy is usefully understood as a status, too.

Responding to the Critics

The account of social citizenship developed above provides a *normative* basis for responding to the critiques of social citizenship outlined above. That is, this account in and of itself cannot remedy the practical problems of contemporary welfare states; a theoretical conception cannot serve as the antidote to the shortcomings and antipathies that exist in service delivery, political culture, and resource allocation. But as a benchmark—a way to measure whether in fact the welfare state is providing the services and resources necessary to genuinely afford all members of the community the status of social citizenship—this revised conception, I argue, can help us to evaluate and therefore work toward remedying the problems of contemporary welfare states. In this sense, both critiques leveled against the welfare state that I have discussed above can be challenged when the target of the critique is the *ideal* of social citizenship, in its reconstituted form. The critiques, then, no longer point to flaws in social citizenship as a concept, but to *incomplete realizations* of the ideal of social citizenship.

Social Control

The critique of social citizenship that expresses concern over the potential (or, some argue, necessary) coincidence of social rights and social control is on one level easily displaced by the revised notion of autonomy I have articulated. First, let us quickly rehearse the critique, where the conventional conception of social citizenship remains in place. Gorham argues that in order to attain the entitlements associated with social citizenship, recipients are subject to the disciplinary forces of the welfare state bureaucracy that coercively motivate them to conform to whatever qualities it has deemed appropriate for the subjects of social welfare benefits to embody. That is, social citizenship rights, which provide the material resources necessary to alleviate constraints on the exercise of autonomy, are accessible only to the "good" recipient—the individual who conforms and acquiesces to the demands of the disciplinary state. Thus Gorham argues that social citizenship has an inherent contradiction: in order to attain autonomy via social citizenship rights, an individual must also *sacrifice* her autonomy. He writes, "The stability that permits the exercise of liberty for the citizen"—that is, the material resources provided by the state— "also holds the subject in a network of tutelary power constituted by school, psychiatry, the military, social work, etc."[35]

When we revisit this critique wielding the revised conception of social citizenship, however, the contradiction is no longer sustainable. Social citizenship rights now refer to something well beyond the provision of material resources; these rights refer explicitly to the provision of services and resources that actively foster (relational) autonomy. Therefore, if social citizenship rights are realized only in conjunction with social control, the notion itself is incoherent. We cannot refer to a system as engaged in advancing social citizenship status if it provides a monthly check to a single mother but also dictates, for example, how she will conduct her intimate relationships and what counts as "work" for her. Such a system violates the single mother's ability to live according to her own "law"—to act autonomously.[36] Further, suppose the services—in monetary form or otherwise—are delivered in a way that reproduces relations of domination, simply with regard to the professional-client relationship established in welfare offices, or extending to other relations of power, including those organized along lines of gender, race, and sexuality. In this case, our revised model highlights the extent to which these so-called social rights fail to develop the relationships out of which the *capacity* for autonomy is always partially constituted. Instead, the relationships extant in the service delivery context are particularly *constraining* with regard to the development of autonomy. Indeed, in our society, characterized as it is by ongoing inequalities and discrimination, many individuals and families who are compelled to rely on entitlement-based programs are already subject to relations of domination in various aspects of their lives, and may therefore be particularly in need of the (relational) resources necessary to assist them in developing the capacity to act autonomously.[37] Thus the contradiction that Gorham and (to an extent) Piven and Cloward point to in their critique of social citizenship is no longer a contradiction in the concept, but rather a failure to realize the requirements of the concept itself.

While the more overt forms of social control that Gorham, Piven, and Cloward point to are relatively easily excluded from the revised conception of social citizenship, some theorists point to more subtle forms of coercion that may in fact operate by enabling citizens. Barbara Cruikshank cites Foucault's notion of bio-power in explaining the ways that welfare "is a form of government that is both voluntary and coercive."[38] That is, the simplistic view that welfare necessarily dominates and controls recipients in an entirely coercive fashion is put aside, in favor of a model that points to a much more subtle and, in some sense, insidious form of power. Cruikshank explains: "Welfare recipients are not excluded or controlled by power so much as constituted and put into action by power."[39] Foucault's bio-power helps her to elucidate this mode of working through rather than against a citizen's "agency": "Instead of excluding participation or repressing subjectivity, bio-power operates to invest the citizen with a set of goals and self-understandings, and gives the citizen-subject an investment in participating voluntarily in programs, projects, and institutions set up to 'help' them."[40]

Cruikshank's model of what she refers to as "relations of empowerment" may sound a lot like the ideal of social citizenship that I have laid out. As the scare quotes around the word "help" in the previous quotation suggest, however, she is wary about the prospects of this empowerment. While Cruikshank claims, first, that her conception of the will to empower is "*neither* clearly liberatory *nor* clearly repressive," and second, that "empowerment is a power relationship, a relationship of government; it can be used well or badly," she focuses most on the destructive possibilities that empowerment affords.[41] Claims to empowerment, she seems to suggest, may create a self-understanding of autonomy and self-sufficiency within recipients, but since empowerment is necessarily a power relationship, these "self-understandings" emerge from what she calls "technologies of citizenship." Technologies of citizenship operate based on knowledge culled by "experts" who seek to "know" the target of empowerment and construct a particular kind of subjectivity among them; such subjectivity, Cruikshank believes, is constructed to fit with a model determined by the state to be worthy of the status of citizenship. The question is, then, whether such a mode of empowerment, still so fraught with power relations and prescriptive forms of agency, can be thought of as fostering autonomy.

While Cruikshank's argument is convincing in some respects—it serves us well to recognize the always-already present power relations that must surround even projects of empowerment—it also seems to foreclose the possibility of actually fostering autonomy, and it does so without showing us any way out. Further, it in some ways reverts to an individualist model of autonomy rather than a relational one. For Cruikshank, the project of empowerment is always suspect because embedded within it are relations of power that can never simply stand by neutrally. Empowerment also means the exercise of power *over* some individual. Yet this also seems to indicate that no one can truly be empowered from without—that relationships that claim to assist us to develop our capacities for autonomy are always somehow suspect. Is it the case, then, that for an individual to be "truly" autonomous, her capacities must develop in a vacuum? The paradox, then, is that autonomy cannot be developed in isolation, and that where it is developed in the context of social relations, it is not "really" autonomous. But the latter option is also unsatisfying. In specifying a relational account of autonomy, I have already rejected a notion of autonomy as "perfect independence." But seeking to provide services that enable individuals to better or more easily choose their own life paths, even in the context of dependency, remains, I believe, a realistic and necessary pursuit, especially with regard to feminist concerns. Thus the revised conception of social citizenship that I have suggested responds to Cruikshank's concerns in that it highlights *relations* of power endemic to the delivery of welfare services, but it does so without foreclosing the possibility for autonomous agency. Rather, it helps us to distinguish configurations of relationships that hinder autonomy from those that enable autonomy.

Duties and Obligations

There are two grounds on which to address the concerns of critics of social citizenship about the effects of welfare receipt on individuals' fulfillment of obligations to the state, or more broadly, their engagement in the polity as duty-bearing members of a community. The first point of departure takes us back to the question of needs. While Ignatieff claims that need satisfaction is no guarantee of civic engagement, and in fact often renders citizens passive, King and Waldron counter that it is by virtue of the *removal* of needs that citizens become more likely and better contributors to the polity. The second point of departure more broadly addresses the relationship between autonomy and community engagement and obligations. Autonomy, I argue, is a necessary condition for the capacity to fulfill obligations and duties.

King and Waldron, following Arendt's concerns about need, argue that social citizenship, because it is able to eliminate the most desperate need through the provision of material resources, protects autonomy and therefore renders individuals more able to participate in politics. The Arendtian line, they note, is that not only does an individual's own desperate need make it difficult to call on the public spiritedness necessary for effective political participation, but it also hinders other, non-needy, individuals' abilities by invoking in them the apolitical sentiment of compassion.[42] But I do not think the aim of eliminating need from the public sphere is a desirable or plausible one. To seek out an end to need as a way of overcoming the particularity and potential irrationality of participation in civic politics obscures our constant and inevitable state of human interdependence, which must always imply some sense of need. Further, this argument has the effect of marginalizing from civic politics those who have particularly obvious or pressing needs, those who are "dependent" in ways that come to be highlighted in the context of our society, and those who care for "needy" individuals. This points back to the politics of need interpretation discussed above. Politics is largely about needs; not only welfare politics, but also much of our general political discourse hinges in some way or another on questions of needs and need interpretation. Therefore, to try to vanquish need from the political sphere is to claim that we can initiate interpretations, initiate arguments, and make decisions with regard to needs, all without acknowledging that such need is ever present in all of our lives, including in politics. Allowing those who are needy into the public debate—and such need does not have to be "desperate" and therefore impairing of our decision-making abilities—is essential to rendering the politics of need interpretation inclusively "political," rather than dominated by the voices of those who claim to transcend need. Thus need itself is a valid point from which we might fulfill our obligation to participate in politics and from which we may better be able to identify with other members of the community.

The politics of need and its relationship to duties and obligations also returns us once again to the centrality of relational autonomy to this conception of social citizenship. The wariness we may have in the face of need is related to the dominant sense in our society that *dependence* is undesirable and threatening to the "impartiality" demanded of "good" political participants. As Nancy Fraser and Linda Gordon describe it in their genealogy of the term "dependence," "In the age of democratic revolutions, the developing new concept of citizenship rested on independence; dependency was deemed anti-thetical to citizenship."[43] This sense of dependence as incompatible with citizenship remains in place today. Further, note Fraser and Gordon, dependence has been pathologized and reduced to an individualized affliction, rather than a product of social relations and a "condition" that affects almost all of us. Need is seen as putting us in a perpetual state of dependence, and therefore banishing us from civic participation. But the relational conception of autonomy is especially important in highlighting the extent to which autonomy and dependence are *not* antithetical; since autonomy develops in the context of relationships, interdependence is not only compatible with autonomy, it is a necessary condition for the development of autonomy. Since the autonomy that we now seek to cultivate via social citizenship is relational, the notion that both need and dependence compromise one's ability to act as an autonomous citizen is rendered incoherent. Moreover, given the ascriptive elements of autonomy, the importance of not only rejecting the notion that need and dependence are compromising qualities for political engagement, but also specifically recognizing the importance of the voices of those who experience need and dependence, can be understood as an essential feature of social citizenship. If social citizenship promotes the autonomy necessary for access to the other rights of citizenship, it does so in part by ascribing autonomy to those whose needs require attention and satisfaction.

It is clear at this point, then, that the aim of social citizenship both under the revised formula and the conventional one is related to autonomy; autonomy is seen as a precondition for exercising the rights associated with citizenship. But some theorists argue that a focus on rights is in itself atomizing, leading to a diminished sense of community and, indeed, a sense that other community members are primarily entities that threaten to infringe on our rights. Thus "fellow" citizens are seen not in a solidaristic sense, but rather as jeopardizing our autonomy. The relational conception of autonomy rejects the claim that social relationships in and of themselves threaten our autonomy. But what of rights? Is not the language of rights counter to the language of duties and obligations? Although I cannot launch a defense of rights here, I do want to point to an alternative way of thinking about rights as a potentially fruitful way of resisting this opposition between rights and duties. Martha Minow argues that we should think of rights as embedded in and constitutive of relationships. Thus, to briefly highlight an implication of this way of thinking, Minow writes, "By invoking rights, an individual or group claims the attention of the larger community and its authorities."[44] But, Minow explains, the rights claimant not only claims attention in an abstract sense, but also re-affirms her connection to the community. "At the same time," Minow notes, "this claim acknowledges the claimant's membership in the larger group, par-ticipation in its traditions, and observation of its forms."[45] This is especially true if we think of claims to social citizenship rights as claims to the opportu-nity or possibility to develop the capacity to act autonomously, a capacity through which one is able to become—and to become *recognized*[46] as—a full member of the community. It is *only* in making this claim that the possibility for fulfilling ones duties to the community can emerge.

Conclusion

Social citizenship rights, though under attack for several decades now, are worth defending. In order to pursue an inclusive and just society, we should seek to provide all members of the community with the social welfare services necessary to ensure that they may access and exercise full citizenship rights. But if we are to defend this notion of social citizenship rights, we must be clear about what such rights entail and what form they will take on the ground in order to fulfill their promises. The conventional conception of social citizen-ship as a status that grants individuals the rights to freedom from material constraints that may impede their ability to act autonomously, and therefore to exercise the rights associated with civil and political citizenship, leaves open the possibility of charges of incoherence and contradiction. Because this conventional conception of social citizenship presupposes a notion of auton-omy that does not take into account the social relationships from which this capacity emerges, it cannot adequately conceive of what must be present in order to foster autonomy's development. The revised conception of social citi-zenship that I propose in this chapter suggests that social citizenship rights should explicitly include the provision of services that are necessary to foster the capacity for autonomy. Because this capacity is a product of well-structured relationships, social citizenship rights must be particularly focused on enact-ing the social service *provision* that is conducive to this development; where relations of domination or other constraining relations are prevalent in service delivery situations, autonomy cannot flourish. In the following chapters I ex-plore, first, what sorts of relationships do indeed hinder autonomy in this manner, and then, what relationships that successfully foster autonomy might look like in the context of service delivery and how a state that facilitates and maintains such service delivery relationships—an autonomy-fostering state—can be theorized.

Given this revised conception of social citizenship (and given the case studies that follow), I argue that assertions that social citizenship must always masquerade as social control, or that social rights claims hinder citizens' sense of obligation and duty, are no longer salient. Though on-the-ground instances of social control and limitations on obligation may well continue to exist and even thrive at this moment in welfare state development, a revised conception of social citizenship allows us to identify these problems as failures to live up to social citizenship rather than as failures within the concept of social citizenship itself. Further, as a benchmark or ideal, this conception of social citizenship helps point the way to the strategies and solutions necessary to remedy the practical problems in today's welfare states.

3 THE NEW PATERNALISM: RETHINKING STATE INTERVENTION AND AUTONOMY

Introduction

This chapter examines the first of two case studies of models of social welfare service delivery that, I argue, fail to foster autonomy effectively. I examine the case of "new paternalist" social welfare programs, which are premised on the idea that those in need of welfare services lack certain capacities and therefore require programs with "supervisory" approaches in order to guide them toward self-sufficiency. I suggest that such programs are founded on deeply problematic misconceptions about service users' intentions and capacities. As I will explain in later chapters, autonomy-fostering service delivery is often found where the state recognizes users' needs, included those needs that are specifically *embodied* needs, while also involving users in service delivery to varying degrees. The latter element of service delivery can take the form of a more inclusive politics of need interpretation discussed in the foregoing chapter, or under more radical models it may include users in the actual delivery of services, as discussed in chapter 6. But unlike more effective and autonomy-fostering programs, such as those I discuss in chapters 5 and 6, new paternalist programs assume the incompetence of service users and therefore do not endeavor to include them in the design and delivery of services.

The failures of new paternalist programs are important not only as an instance of autonomy-hindering social welfare service delivery—of which there are many—but also as a point of entry for a broader analysis of the implications of "fostering autonomy." As I noted in chapter 1, in this book I argue that the state has an obligation to foster autonomy in its citizens, particularly its most vulnerable—those who are most at risk of being excluded or marginalized. But as I develop my argument in this chapter and those that follow, it is important to acknowledge that the notion of fostering autonomy is tricky, particularly given the tendency to conflate autonomy and independence: how can the state intervene in the lives of citizens in order to foster autonomy, without simultaneously compromising autonomy by virtue of this intervention? In what follows, I engage this quandary by using careful analyses of two examples of new paternalist programs. I argue that the tenets of an autonomy-fostering state are incompatible with new paternalism. In turn, this incompatibility makes clear that some forms of intervention by the state may compromise autonomy, but certainly not all. To arrive at this conclusion and to elucidate the contrast between fostering autonomy and acting paternalistically, I offer a nuanced and contextually situated reading of the gendered assumptions underlying conventional accounts of both autonomy and paternalism.

I begin from the premise that state "intrusion" into the lives of (vulnerable) citizens is potentially an enabling mechanism for the development and exercise of autonomy. This understanding is consistent with a relational conception of autonomy defended by feminist theorists: rejecting a notion of autonomy that conflates the concept with either independence or privacy, autonomy should be understood to emerge out of the context of social relations. The existence of autonomy does not require a "protective buffer zone" that disallows other citizens or the state from entry.[1] With this notion of autonomy in mind, I distinguish paternalist policy and autonomy-fostering policy by examining two examples of new paternalism, the theory of social welfare service delivery that can be linked to recent welfare reforms in the United States and Britain as well as some other European countries. Here, I direct my attention to new paternalist programs emerging from the U.S. welfare reforms of 1996 (under the Personal Responsibility and Work Opportunity Reconciliation Act, or PRWORA).[2]

I look specifically at two programs: workfare and pregnancy-prevention programs. These programs respond to what many new paternalists claim are the two primary causes of poverty: nonwork and unwed pregnancy. Workfare is by far the most pronounced and large-scale paternalist program in the reformed welfare states; pregnancy prevention provides a useful lens through which to examine the destructively gendered and moral (rather than solely material) implications of paternalist policy. The former case is concerned with paternalism operating in the public sphere, whereas the latter operates in the private sphere. But given the devaluation of care work that ensues in the case of workfare and the misconceptions about the opportunities that poor, young women face in the realm of paid employment, the blurring of private and public is evident. An analysis of these two programs alongside each other draws out the ways that paternalist programs intervene in public and private spheres. A number of "techniques" emerge out of new paternalist interventions; here, my focus rests on one of these, conditionality. A careful look at these programs and the techniques of conditionality they employ sharpens our view of what it means for the state to foster autonomy—or to fail to do so, as is the case here.

The incompatibility between autonomy-fostering and paternalist social policy is best understood when premised on a notion of paternalism that highlights its implication in oppressive power relations, rather than solely its association with interventionist policy.[3] The assumptions that underlie the theory of new paternalism and the techniques of conditionality, including those regarding the concept of autonomy, serve to replicate relations of power that are themselves implicated in the structural causes of poverty and inequality—the very problems that new paternalist policies claim to address. New paternalist accounts of autonomy emphasize the attainment of an individualist sense of self, bolstered neither by familial relationships nor relations of care, which are both, tellingly, feminized configurations of social relations. In such accounts, the private sphere is seen as an inadequate site for meaning making in the lives of poor women or as the site of devaluated, care-related interdependence. In both programs considered, the targets of paternalist policies are women, on whom conceptions of the ideal mother and the ideal worker are cast at once, often at odds with each other. The claim that these policies expand access to citizenship is unsettled by its reliance on, first, the idea that prevention of pregnancy will allow women to pursue other goals and prevent them from bearing ill-fated children, and second, the notion that work confers status on and generates a source of meaning for the workfare participant. These misconceived assumptions serve to narrow the boundaries of access to the autonomous agency required for citizenship.

I begin with a brief discussion of paternalism: conventional accounts of the debates surrounding it, the feminist recasting of this debate, and finally the ideas on which the new paternalism hinges. I then move on to an examination of the two programs: workfare and pregnancy prevention. I draw from these a more focused critique of the autonomy-impairing aspects of new paternalist policy, and a clearer account of the contrast between an autonomy-fostering state and a paternalist state.

Paternalism, New Paternalism, and Autonomy

Two Accounts of Paternalism

Paternalism has justifiably been a key concern for autonomy theorists. It cuts to the core of what autonomy refers to: the capacity to determine one's own life plans. Paternalistic policy programs hinge on the claim that some individuals ought not have the opportunity to exercise this capacity in given contexts, where such constraint has been deemed to be in accordance with the individuals' "own good." How, then, can such a claim be justified if autonomy is accepted as a primary value in our society? This is the question that political theorists have grappled with in their treatments of paternalism. In pursuing this problem, the question of state *intervention* into citizens' lives has often been a proxy for the question of paternalism.

What I refer to as "conventional" accounts of paternalism often begin from the work of John Stuart Mill, the great advocate of individual liberty.[4] Gerald Dworkin defines paternalism as "the interference with a person's liberty of action justified by reasons referring exclusively to the welfare, good, happiness, needs, interests, or values of the person being coerced."[5] Explaining Mill's opposition to paternalistic measures, Dworkin emphasizes that Mill views paternalism as an affront to the essence of what it means to be a human being, which is deeply tied to recognition as an autonomous agent. Dworkin writes, "It is the privilege and proper condition of a human being, arrived at the maturity of his faculties, to use and interpret experience in his own way."[6]

Autonomy, this core human characteristic as Dworkin frames it, can be understood as both an ascribed status and a capacity, the two of which are closely related but distinct.[7] It is a status insofar as being recognized as an autonomous individual has particular social and political meanings. It is a capacity because it refers to an individual's ability to determine her own ends. On both accounts, I suggest, autonomy emerges out of social relations. Our capacities are developed or restricted in the context of enabling or constraining arrangements of social relations. Our status as autonomous agents is often constituted by larger social relations that configure the distribution of recognition and respect in our society: institutional, cultural, and market relations, among others.[8] Where forms of misrecognition restrict the latter notion of autonomy, the former notion may also be impeded, since the development of the capacity for autonomy is closely tied to self-esteem or self-respect—qualities that misrecognition may quash.

The conventional critique of paternalism addresses infringements on each of these dimensions of autonomy in some respects. If autonomy is ascriptive, Dworkin and other liberal theorists' critiques of paternalistic measures suggest that these programs fail to ascribe autonomy to their targets. Dworkin's exegesis of Mill proceeds as follows: "It is because coercing a person for his own good denies [his] status as an independent entity that Mill objects to it so strongly and in such absolute terms. To be able to choose is a good that is independent of the wisdom of what is chosen."[9] The target of paternalist measures is unjustly denied her status as a "chooser," which is equivalent in these accounts to being denied her status as an autonomous individual. Moreover, in this account of the potentially deleterious effects of state intervention into citizens' lives, the opportunity to develop and exercise autonomy as a capacity is also limited. Dworkin's account demonstrates this when he refers to the most plausibly palatable forms of paternalism as couched in "a concern not just for the happiness or welfare, in some broad sense, of the individual but rather a concern for the autonomy and freedom of the person." He goes on to suggest that a potentially justifiable form of paternalism "preserves and enhances for the individual his ability to rationally carry out his own decisions."[10]

This last statement by Dworkin points to the source of criticisms of the conventional critique raised by feminist and other theorists. Dworkin suggests that it is possible for paternalism to be autonomy fostering (or at least autonomy preserving); what is noteworthy is that such a configuration of relations is still termed "paternalism." The Dworkin view, Marion Smiley writes, leads us to view "all forms of government protection as paternalistic." She explains that the accepted definitions "ignore the context of paternalistic choice-making—or in other words, the relationships of domination and inequality that exist between a paternalist and those subject to paternalistic treatment."[11] The problem with paternalism, then, is not only or entirely its infringement on individual free choice, but that it "perpetuates (or at least expresses) relationships of domination and inequality among individual members of a community."[12] With this problem acknowledged, Smiley suggests that we need not accept the assumption that all government protection is paternalistic, including that autonomy-enhancing form referred to by Dworkin above.[13] Smiley's rejection of Dworkin's version of paternalism points to one of the key insights of a relational understanding of autonomy: the necessity of distinguishing between different types of interventions in the lives of individuals (and the relationships on which such intervention hinges), rather than equating intervention with necessarily diminished autonomy.

A power differential between state and citizen in itself does not signal paternalism; it is specifically when such power is used in a coercive fashion that serves oppressive ends that paternalism can be seen. This is central to the distinction Smiley makes between paternalism and non-paternalistic "protection." Smiley emphasizes how protective legislation can challenge systems of domination and inequality, whereas paternalistic legislation perpetuates them. She notes, "Protective legislation enables individuals to organize themselves collectively against powerful actors who, because of their institutional positions of strength, are able to lead other individuals to take serious physical risks."[14] Protective legislation gives marginalized and weak citizens the collective power that they may inherently lack given their societal positioning. In contrast, the conditionality that characterizes new paternalist services, which I turn to below, compounds domination by explicitly deeming service users incompetent and ignoring contextual details that contribute to their marginalization.

Like Smiley's account of protective legislation, which stresses the importance of enabling collective action, Julie White's reconceptualization of paternalism highlights the importance of participatory politics in distinguishing it from other forms of intervention.[15] White directs us to consider the nature of the *process* of intervention. As an alternative to paternalism, "a democratic politics of care" requires "a more participatory process of defining needs, where the discussion privileges the voice of those presently 'in need' in the course of defining 'need' and determining arrangements of resources to meet those needs."[16] Thus White, too, emphasizes the value of some forms of intervention in enabling social relations that foster collective action. But for White, it is equally important that this collective action be oriented toward making demands predicated on needs that have themselves been collectively defined in a manner that foregrounds the often-silenced voices of those in need. Because new paternalists assume that welfare recipients' needs are a function of incompetence, their role in the politics of need interpretation is discredited from the outset.

Smiley's and White's accounts of paternalism usefully clarify the distinction between different forms of intervention, some of which enable subjects to challenge oppressive social structures, while others compound them. I suggest that it is useful to supplement these accounts with the dual notion of autonomy as both status and capacity, cited above. When cast in this light, the differences between the conventional notion of paternalism and the revised accounts can provide greater explanatory power. As the quotation above suggests, Dworkin claims (along with Mill) that paternalism limits autonomy as a status if autonomy is understood to be an individual's status as "an independent entity." Immediately, the conflation of independence and autonomy suggests a problem. Where paternalism is understood to be government interference in individuals' lives that perpetuates relations of domination and inequality, the status is denied not because it signifies a lack of independence, but because of the power relations that, in many cases, are tied to the assumption of incompatibility between autonomy and dependence. When the state imposes certain restrictive conditions on a woman on welfare, it acts paternalistically not simply because it fails to view her as independent (we know she is not, nor are any of us), but because *her* dependence is stigmatized. It is stigmatized in this context in such a way that it is inconceivable that her status as welfare dependent (and her racialized or gendered identity, which may connote "dependence" within given contexts) could be consistent with a status as an autonomous agent, or one who deserves to be treated as such.

The distinction between the conventional and revised understandings of paternalism can also be seen in light of an understanding of autonomy as a capacity. Again, it is useful to turn to Dworkin's potentially acceptable cases of paternalism; he suggests that an acceptable form of paternalism might allow for the enhanced ability for a citizen to carry out his own "rational decisions."[17] Putting aside the fact that we might want a more expansive notion of autonomy than one that requires rationality as a primary marker, the difference between the revised understanding of paternalism and Dworkin's is that the former situates the capacity within a given social context. Whereas some interventions by the state can be seen in Dworkin's account as examples of acceptable paternalism—to the degree that they limit the ability to act independently in order to further the aim of enhancing the capacity for autonomy overall—Smiley might suggest that such interventions resist rather than perpetuate relations of domination and equality, and therefore need not be thought of as paternalistic. In White's account, if the intervention opens up space for democratic participation rather than generating an instance of "speaking for others," we may also reject the label of "paternalistic."[18] The latter approaches to state intervention might also draw our attention to cases where the intervention is indeed paternalistic—not because it is an intervention into the lives of service users, but because it exists in a context that perpetuates relations of domination and equality. Dworkin's account might not be able to make such a distinction, since it does not highlight the contextual details that contribute to power relations in such a situation.

New Paternalism

With this revised account of paternalism in mind, I now shift to the new paternalism. New paternalism is a philosophy of social service delivery, coined as such by Lawrence Mead, that seeks to further the trend of more paternalistic social welfare policies. It is, I argue, marked by the relations of domination and inequality that characterize our revised notion of paternalism. While new paternalists acknowledge the centrality of coercion to their mode of service delivery, they suggest that these programs ultimately foster autonomy, even if they temporarily restrict it to attain this end. I contest the theoretical bases of this claim, and in doing so demonstrate this philosophy's incompatibility with a theory of an autonomy-fostering state.

According to Mead, the new paternalism involves "social policies aimed at the poor that attempt to reduce poverty and other social problems by directive and supervisory means." Such means impose penalties or restrict benefits when recipients fail to conform to certain behavioral requirements—work, mandatory attendance at various programs, abstinence from drugs, and so forth. According to Mead, "These measures assume that the people concerned need assistance but that they also need direction if they are to live constructively."[19] The relations of power involved in new paternalist measures are configured, in part, by this claim regarding the need for direction: Mead suggests that the poor are specifically lacking in some capacities, including that of autonomy. In his account, it is misguided to assume (with regard to the welfare dependent) that "behavior is consistent with intention." He argues that the poor do not have the capacity to live according to their life plans, even when they have generated these plans and express a desire to pursue them. New paternalist policy is therefore not coercive in the sense that it dictates what values individuals ought to have; rather, "the clients of paternalism commonly do accept the values being enforced. . . . However, they commonly fail to conform to these values in practice. Paternalism seeks to close that gap."[20]

Mead offers an explanation regarding why his new paternalism is indeed "new." New paternalism diverges from its forebears in several ways: first, new paternalism is not instantiated primarily by restriction of benefits through the narrowing of eligibility rules. Second, Mead notes, "today's paternalism is mostly government led."[21] A third respect, which Mead mentions briefly, is that new paternalist programs are not custodial: "The current paternalism often involves supervision within society."[22]

The first and third elements cited by Mead are true to some extent, but primarily at a rhetorical level that masks the practical effects of these policies. This is not to say that there is nothing new about new paternalism, however; it may be that this gap between the rhetoric and practice itself directs our attention to the more significant differences. Mead's claims that new paternalism is not primarily about restriction nor generally custodial can be understood as reflecting a shift to the exercise of what Foucault refers to as "bio-power." Anna Marie Smith describes this bio-power, quoting Foucault, as "largely concentrated in 'positive' functions; it mainly works to 'incite, reinforce, control, monitor, optimize, and organize the forces under it.' Instead of operating as an exclusionary and external force, it is 'a power bent on generating forces, making them grow, and ordering them, rather than one dedicated to impeding them, making them submit or destroying them.'"[23] Thus, because new paternalists aim to "optimize" poor people's behavior—aligning intention and action—such programs use paternalism not in a restrictive manner but in a manner that reforms "the self."

As it suggests that poverty ought to be seen as rooted in individual pathology, new paternalism denies its targets' status as agents capable of autonomy. The programs described by Mead and his cohorts in a collection of essays on new paternalism rely heavily on the claim that poverty can be explained only minimally by structural conditions—social, economic, or political.[24] Instead, as Sanford Schram points out in his review of the collection, the emphasis on mental health highlights the medicalization and infantilization of poverty and the poor, respectively.[25] It is may be the case that such pathologization is necessary to justify new paternalist policy. Mead acknowledges that the assumptions of paternalism can be seen as demeaning, specifically because of the lack of recognition of autonomy: "By assuming that recipients cannot be trusted to pursue their own interests, paternalism in effect treats adults like children."[26] Although he initially refers to paternalist policy as "postracial social policy," he notes that the demeaning nature of such policy "is especially egregious in the case of black Americans," ostensibly because of the historical injustices inflicted on them. Nonetheless, "the assumptions of paternalism no doubt are demeaning, but the problems the poor have with working and other civilities are far more damaging to them."[27]

As Schram notes, these claims to "reforming" the flawed individual are used rhetorically to *justify* new paternalist policies. At the level of practice, however, this justification may not reflect the actual aims of the new paternalist welfare programs.[28] While a Foucauldian analysis of the rhetoric of new paternalism would suggest that programs exercise power through therapeutic dialogue ("confessional discourses") or rehabilitative frameworks, in reality they often do not pursue such aims. Smith explains that many post-PRWORA paternalist programs have "instead contributed to a regime that prioritizes blocking needy mothers from entering the program, imposing financial sanctions upon existing recipients, pushing already working poor mothers into humiliating workfare positions, and trimming the rolls through diversions and expulsions."[29] While the rhetoric of new paternalism paints the picture of a "less offensive" form of paternalism, in fact it masks what are often more direct forms of domination, not necessarily motivated by the paternalist aim of doing what is in the best interest of the subject.

A further example of the gap between new paternalist rhetoric and practice can be found in the second element of novelty emphasized by Mead: what he characterizes as the government-led nature of new paternalism. Mead's intention is to distinguish new paternalists from those who wish to "roll back" the state; Mead suggests that even liberals should approve of this "new" aspect of paternalism. Yet, while Mead suggests that "old" paternalism (pre-1960) was initiated primarily by charities or religious groups, as early as 1935 the Aid for Dependent Children program offered federal assistance to single mothers in the United States. Such assistance was surely paternalistic as it primarily sought to shield white widows from the need to work so that they could act as full-time caregivers to their children—a goal that reflects a claim to the nature of ideal motherhood. Moreover, this account fails to acknowledge the increasingly privatized nature of new paternalist programs, which often outsource elements of service delivery to nongovernmental organizations. Sanford Schram, Richard Fording, and Joe Soss describe "the new poverty governance" as marked by a state that "has not only become more directive and supervisory in the sense described by Mead; it has also become more hollow." Devolution to lower jurisdictions and private providers, they argue, has created a governance "that is, at once more muscular in its normative enforcement and diffuse and diverse in its organization."[30]

What are we to make of these gaps between the rhetoric of new paternalism and its practice on the ground? It is perhaps these gaps that make new paternalism new, to some extent. New paternalists often claim that their preferred programs do important "work" on the self, reforming, reorienting, and remotivating the poor; but these theorists make this claim at the same time that they assume much about the nature of the self they seek to modify. Yet as my analysis below suggests, these programs often fail, primarily because of the faulty assumptions that fuel misguided programs. The relationship between the assumptions, intentions, and ensuing policies to which new paternalists lay claim may in fact reflect a level of disingenuousness. Since it is difficult to ascertain the "true" intentions of policy makers who espouse the type of rhetoric Mead uses to describe the new paternalism, my analysis of new paternalist programs focuses on the rhetoric and the intentions they imply, trying to make sense of the ideological foundations of new paternalist policies and the justifications offered to support them.

Conditionality

In order to respond to the supposed incompetence of the poor on which new paternalism is premised, many new paternalist programs employ a strategy of conditionality, making vital services conditional on conformity to behavioral requirements. The power relations that follow from the demeaning assumptions of new paternalism, in combination with this strategy of conditionality, affect not only recognition of autonomy status but also the development and exercise of the capacity itself. While conditionality on its own does not necessarily imply a violation of autonomy—under the right circumstances, it could be a sign of respect rooted in expectations that individuals can be responsible agents—because paternalist conditionality is so closely tied to a *lack* of respect, it becomes autonomy constraining.

Nevertheless, new paternalists suggest that although autonomy constraining in the immediate application, these policies ultimately enable the poor to become more autonomous. In the sense that parents may place limitations on their children's autonomy in order to enable them to become autonomous in the future, new paternalists suggest that programs like workfare make the same sacrifices in the interests of long-term gain. Mead refers to the strategy of service delivery employed under a philosophy of "help and hassle." Case managers under an entitlement system once acted "as advocates for the poor who helped them get all the benefits to which they were entitled." In contrast, paternalist case managers "do this but they are authority figures as well as helpmates."[31] But such "authority," in the context of welfare, creates relations of domination; authority in the context of parenting has fundamentally different implications, and does not necessarily constitute domination.

To make more sense of this distinction and further consider the implications of the conception of autonomy underlying paternalists' use of conditionality, we might say that it is plausible that behavioral expectations that follow from the authority expressed by these caseworkers are a marker of respect. That is, the existence of expectations indicates that the authority figure understands the service user to be an autonomous agent *capable* of conforming to these expectations; such respect, one could say, is thus autonomy fostering. Indeed, we might understand expressions of parental authority this way, too. But in the context of new paternalism, the assumption is not that the service user is an agent, but rather that she is incompetent. Instead of offering a type of enabling respect, the constraining social relations that emerge hinder the development of the capacity for autonomy. Moreover, conditionality isolates and stigmatizes service users by virtue of the regulations imposed on some, rather than all, citizens, therefore hindering recognition. While other citizens are subject to reciprocal obligations in order to access certain goods, unlike service users they have much greater latitude in negotiating and consenting to the terms of such agreements.

One example of a the way such authority is expressed in the context of new paternalism highlights why such intervention is distinct from what I refer to as "autonomy fostering." Mead quotes a caseworker in a paternalist program, John Gardner: "I'll do anything to help you [get] a job. But if you disappoint the employer—if you make me look bad—if you screw me over—you better watch out. I'm coming after you. *I'm in your face*. You'll wish you'd never been born." According to Mead, although to the sensibilities of middle-class people such a statement may seem harsh, the poor are in fact *enabled* by such an approach.[32] In such a new-paternalist account, this could be seen as an example of an attempt to enable relational autonomy: the relationship between caseworker and service user enhances the user's ability to pursue her own ends. But in fact, even in Mead's assertion about the differences between communication styles of middle-class and poor people, the lack of respect that premises such an approach is evident. Though I believe caseworkers must play an important role in a genuinely autonomy-fostering state, the required recognition and respect is absent and reinforced as such by the caseworker's language. It is hard to see how the relations of domination evident in such an approach foster autonomy, even in the long run; instead, a culture of intimidation pervades—hardly conditions that enable an individual to ultimately define her own life plans.

New Paternalism Across Spheres: Workfare and Pregnancy Prevention

In the politically charged battle to "end welfare as we know it"[33] in the mid-1990s, political actors, media, and scholars maintained the belief, embedded

in American political culture, that work—understood as labor market participation—is the conduit through which welfare rolls can be reduced and poverty ended. Through work, the poor are "cured" of the deviant qualities that
put them in poverty in the first place. In contrast to the image of the autonomous *employed* individual emerging from welfare reform rhetoric, the reproductive bodies of young, poor women (often of color) present an image that is
anything but autonomous; unchecked, these bodies threaten the "cure" offered by welfare and exacerbate the ills of dependence it seeks to dislodge.
Pregnancy and childbearing is intimately tied to work in the context of welfare reform: it affects women's ability to work outside the home, it is the foundation of social reproduction, it is an embodied manifestation of the differing
effects of working conditions on women versus men, and so forth. Yet this
interconnectedness is deeply distorted in the rhetoric and philosophies that
accompany workfare and pregnancy-prevention programs.

Workfare is the most developed and known example of new paternalist
policy. Spun as the ultimate rehabilitative program for the often-pathologized
poor, work is now not simply strongly encouraged but required as a condition
for receiving aid from the state.[34] Underlying misconceptions about the intentionality and competence of service users and about the values associated with
work of various kinds undermine arguments made in favor of this theory of
welfare provision. Pregnancy-prevention programs, too, are rooted in misconceptions about intentionality and vulnerable young women's relational
needs. Conventional rhetoric tells us that the "private" sphere is where relationality is most suitably situated. Yet there, relational conditions are conceived of through the lens of middle-class perceptions of the sources of
meaning in women's lives, a lens that paradoxically both privileges "independence" and idealizes self-sacrificing motherhood. The privileging of independence follows from assumptions regarding work that emerge in the case of
workfare, including the devaluation of activities that take place in the private
sphere. Where poor young women revaluate these activities, pointing to the
resources motherhood provides *them* with, they are at once seen as rejecting
the ideal of the selfless mother and the notion of the self-respecting worker.

Mistaken Assumptions I: Incompetence or Incoherence?

New paternalist workfare policy and pregnancy-prevention policies are premised on two types of assumptions: first, assumptions about the competence
of the service user, and second, assumptions about the value of paid employ-

ment and care work. Women who become pregnant at a young age or while living in poverty are seen to do so because of incompetence, not autonomous decision making. In a similar vein, the primary reason for nonwork is assumed to be incompetence—not lack of opportunity, not the market, and not discrimination. These claims follow in part from new paternalist assumptions about values. In keeping with widely held beliefs in the United States, "work" is valorized as a good in itself, one that is somehow constitutive of our identities as citizens and human beings. Moreover, the boundaries of what is considered work are relatively narrow and inflexible. Work refers to paid labor outside the conventionally understood private sphere. In turn, since the value—at least in terms of meaning making or "fulfillment"—of work is primary, child rearing or other domestic care work is seen as both less desirable and less legitimate as a life choice. Delaying childbirth and focusing on work as a source of dignity and full citizenship status is presented as an obviously superior life plan. Below, I look at the assumptions of incompetence framing pregnancy prevention and workfare policy. In the section following, I return to the set of assumptions around values.

Teenage pregnancy, and multiple fertility in poor, unwed women more generally, has long been a focus for poverty researchers, who worry about not only the material implications of additional mouths to feed, but also the effects on a variety of other outcomes typically measured in children. Moreover, they warn of the possibility of a generational cycle of unwed pregnancy and welfare dependence. New paternalist thinkers have turned their attention to these issues, too, citing teenage pregnancy in particular as a classic example of the rift between values and actions of poor people. Rebecca Maynard claims, "As a group, those who unintentionally get pregnant and begin parenthood at a young age signal their inability to make decisions that are in their own best interests, the best interests of their children, and the best interests of society."[35]

The unemployed also signal their incompetence by failing to act in accordance with their own interests. According to new paternalists, nonwork is a problem not of lack of opportunity or structural constraints, but rather of competence on the part of the job seeker. Deterred by previous experiences of failure, preoccupied with other concerns, or simply lacking in motivation, the poor fail to find work because, without the coercive force of the state, they cannot organize themselves to do so. Mead presents a psychosocial explanation for this failure. The poor share with the rest of society the value placed on work; indeed, "not working . . . causes shame and discouragement, since they are not living by their own values." But the "gap between intention and behavior makes work enforcement necessary." This enforcement is facilitated by the fragmented yet existing "work ethic" that already exists among the poor: "Mandatory work programs do not ask most people to do something alien to them. . . . They now *have* to do what they always wanted to do." Despite these shared values, Mead argues, the poor are "different" psychologically from more successful members of society: "Better-off people generally behave according to their own intentions. If they do not do something, it is because they do not want to. They will resist anyone telling them to do otherwise. Middle-class analysts too readily assume poor people are equally consistent."[36] In our blurry middle-class analysis, we mistakenly believe that those who do not work choose not to, according to Mead.

Mead emphasizes an individualized explanation for nonwork. Though some explanations of joblessness refer to what William Julius Wilson calls "spatial mismatch"—"a growing mismatch between the suburban location of employment and minorities' residence in the inner city"—Mead rejects such structural explanations of poverty.[37] Although he acknowledges the mismatch between skills and jobs that resulted from deindustrialization in major U.S. cities, Mead dismisses this as relatively insignificant. A study conducted in Chicago by Wilson, he notes, "found . . . that low-skilled immigrants worked at high levels in the same ghetto areas where poor blacks and Puerto Ricans worked at low levels."[38] Therefore, if some groups are able to find work while others are not, the problem is with the intention-behavior relationship and not the system.

But other research suggests that Mead's analysis is overly simplistic and fails to take into account complexities that deeply affect employment possibilities. One important factor is the structure of social relationships that shape the ways that individuals both view and participate in the job search process. Some research suggests that because of chronic conditions of racism and poverty, black job seekers may adopt an approach to searching that is particularly individualistic, failing to seek out the support (and when sought, to successfully receive this support) necessary to secure employment. Sandra Smith describes a phenomenon of "defensive individualism."[39] Defensive individualists do not reach out to the community for fear of failing to live up to the expectations of those around them; they justify this behavior in individualistic terms. Smith explains: "Within the context of poverty, friends, relatives, acquaintances, and institutions in their social milieu blamed the black poor and jobless for their persistent joblessness, deploying discourses of joblessness that privileged individuals' moral shortcomings and stressed personal responsibility and self-sufficiency as a panacea."[40] Defensive individualism is a reaction to the experience of being viewed in this manner. The individualizing message of new paternalism exacerbates this phenomenon of defensive individualism; the discourses that Smith refers to may stem in part from the internalization of the messages espoused by privileged actors who deploy such strategies as workfare to respond to supposed incompetence. This argument calls into question Mead's claims about the availability of jobs based on the success of some groups over others in finding employment.

While Smith's arguments seem to counter some earlier studies of poor black communities, wherein the importance of connectedness through kinship relations in particular is stressed, she notes that the individualistic reaction to joblessness does not necessarily prevail in all arenas, particularly in the "private sphere."[41] Given the individualism—motivated by distrust—that may characterize some arenas of poor black women's lives, it might make sense to suggest that seeking relational support in other arenas—for example, through childbearing—follows logically. This points to the flaws in logic underpinning pregnancy-prevention programs, too.

Pregnancy-prevention policy puts in place "directive" programs to respond to the supposed failure of young, poor women (largely of color) to implement family planning strategies that are in their interest. But as with the case of work above, ethnographic data demonstrate a much more complex picture of the intentionality of poor, young women who become pregnant than do those presented by Maynard. Pregnancy in poor women and teenagers may have much greater personal and symbolic implications than the explanations provided by Maynard suggest; these implications are directly tied to the conditions of injustice and oppression that many of these women face. Even Maynard's own ethnographic data seem to suggest that the assumption of incompetence is misleadingly straightforward. Maynard quotes teenage mothers who signal their ambiguous intentionality. Says one mother, "I didn't plan it, and then again, I kind of knew that it was going to happen because I wasn't really taking the pills like I was supposed to. I couldn't remember every day to take the pill. And, I still don't."[42] Although the pregnancy was not planned per se, it is also unclear that the interviewee specifically believed that she should avoid pregnancy.

Going beyond this ambiguous intentionality, other research more explicitly sheds light on alternative explanations of teenage pregnancy. In a study of motherhood and marriage among low-income women, Kathryn Edin and Maria Kefalas highlight the central role a child can play in a context where relational support is limited and the ability to define oneself is constrained by material and relational conditions.[43] Like Smith, they point to the "relational poverty" that emerges from "the social isolation that is the common experience of those who live in poverty [which] is heightened for adolescents, whose relationships with parents are strained by the developmental need to forge an independent identity." These limitations of relational support "can create a compelling desire to give and receive love."[44] The question of intentionality in teen pregnancy, then, is in part colored by the real, and arguably logical, reasons why these women may be motivated to become pregnant, or at least to not actively prevent pregnancy. "Pregnancy offers the promise of relational intimacy at a time [when] few other emotional resources are available," the study suggests.[45]

In this light, pregnancy and child rearing can be seen as signaling the *competence* of the young women who make such choices in order to further their interests. This is not to say that it is ideal to live in a society where one's *primary* (or only) chance for relational support is to be found in care work, with few other options available. Yet given the circumstances that exist on the ground, it is hardly incompetence that leads to such a conclusion. Maynard's assumption that the young women she studies could not have "competently" chosen to be become pregnant parallels the narrow nature of the scholarship offered by advocates of workfare: when they claim that nonwork reflects a disjuncture between a value system that favors work and actions that help to access work, they refer only to work as defined by paid employment. As many feminists have pointed out, this overlooks the unremunerated caretaking labor that many women are engaged in and may rely on for important sources of relational support.[46]

Women engaged in such care work are counted as "able but unwilling to work," and therefore as undeserving. Their domestic work, the narrow definition of work ultimately implies, does not "earn" them any benefits. Mead argues that one of the demands of citizenship is the civility of work. But Carole Pateman points out that such a view ignores another important role of social reproduction, which refers not only to motherhood but also to "the maintenance and future of the public or common weal and the care of citizens."[47] If work is a condition of citizenship because it is something "owed" by one citizen to another, social reproduction, too, ought to be included in this notion of obligation. Although welfare reform rhetoric links dependency to a "failure to perform a duty owed to fellow citizens," it does so only by ignoring the other duties citizens perform outside paid employment.

Mead rejects feminists' claims that care work ought to be acknowledged as falling under the umbrella of status-granting "work." Instead, he suggests that "civic labor" must fulfill certain conditions: it needs to be accountable to society, and it needs to be done "well enough to serve a public interest." With regard to the first condition, Mead suggests that the "self-chosen" character of bearing children renders caregiving an inappropriate means of fulfilling the conditions of accountable work; paid employment in public or private sectors is assigned by others, and is therefore legitimate. To claim support for raising one's child, he suggests, is equivalent to making a claim to societal support for "writing this essay." Caring for someone else's child or a sick relative, since these tasks are externally assigned or not chosen, may be seen as legitimate.[48] Yet it is ironic that Mead attributes agency to poor women who have children and make welfare claims. As I have suggested, the premise of new paternalism is the incompetence of the welfare recipient, her inability to link intention and action. It is convenient, then, that when evaluated in terms of what counts as work, childbearing becomes intentional. This contradiction aside, even if poor women intend to bear children, it is unclear why "self-chosen" tasks ought to count as less legitimate means of meeting the requirements of civic labor. In fact, social, political, and economic privilege grants increased levels of occupational autonomy, and such autonomy is supported not only by private means but also by public funds (e.g., education funding, tax benefits).

Though Mead cites studies regarding the poor outcomes of children whose mothers are on welfare, the disadvantages that he points to emerge within the context of a system that fails to provide the material and social supports necessary to enable poor women to best care for their children. Under different circumstances, these women may indeed be better able to "serve" societal interests. If poor women were such incapable caregivers, the suggestion that caring for other people's children would be a more legitimate form of civic labor is perplexing. Moreover, the lack of checks in place on mothers' performance is hardly unique to this form of work, as opposed to the forms of work Mead claims meet the requirements of civic labor. Further, wealthy women who rely, by virtue of privilege rather than desert, on private sources of support (e.g., spouses, extended family) in order to care for their children are not seen as failing to contribute to society when they choose caregiving as their primary activity. As I discuss in the following section, this class-based valuation of women's caregiving is evident not only with regard to civic contribution but also on a more individualized level, with regard to the expected meaning women can derive from this activity versus paid labor market participation. The devaluation of poor women's ability to mother is evident in extant policies in some states that actively encourage welfare recipients to give their children up for adoption.[49]

Ultimately, Mead claims, "what counts as civic labor is . . . a political question."[50] That is, what matters is that American society does not *recognize* caregiving as an activity comparable to work. This claim, however, fails to account for the fact that not only does politics influence policies, but the reverse is also true. Policies that reject caregiving as a form of civic labor, discourage poor women from having children, and encourage poor women to give up their children surely have an effect on the politics of civic labor.

Not only do the accounts of Mead and other new paternalists overlook the societal value of care work, they also overlook the personal fulfillment derived from care work—a point that complicates the picture painted by paternalists of paid employment as the sole route to dignity and fulfillment, as described below.

Mistaken Assumptions II: Whose Values?

The second set of assumptions underlying new paternalist policy hinges on the notion that work, as opposed to nonwork or care work, is a primary source of value in the vast majority of citizens' lives, and is therefore a conduit to fulfillment and meaning making in all of our lives. New paternalists claim that, for most able-bodied individuals, work is a marker of citizenship and a gateway to the rights that citizenship bestows on us.[51] Paralleling this claim is the one highlighted in Maynard's work: young unwed mothers, she argues, appear to share in the mainstream value system that suggests waiting until one is older to bear children. (This claim, of course, serves to justify the claims regarding incompetence discussed above.) Given the value assigned to paid work, it makes sense to seek out work before bearing children. Maynard's claims about pregnancy represent a larger ideology found in dominant discourse and new paternalist thought, which presumes an individualistic view of the ideal self. This is accompanied by an overarching devaluation of relationality and interdependence that is, paradoxically, accompanied by an unrealistic view of the ideal, altruistic mother. As the discussion above regarding the potential for relational support via childbearing indicates, this view obviates the importance of a range of other values associated with childbearing in young, poor women.[52]

Edin and Kefalas's work underlines the ways that not only masculinist conceptions of the self but also many appropriations of feminism are at odds with the positioning of childbearing as a primary source of meaning making. They note that "the idea of a woman viewing her offspring as a resource violates powerful social norms about how a mother should behave. Altruism, not need, ought to govern her relationship to her children."[53] Though feminists have long endeavored to destabilize it, the ideal of the mother as self-sacrificing and entirely devoted to others remains strong in our society. Yet, despite the feminist critique of this self-sacrificing ideal of motherhood, a typical feminist alternative conception of motherhood still does not fit comfortably with the empirical evidence that Edin and Kefalas offer. Even if we reject the notion of motherhood as necessarily *only* altruistic, the idea of women deriving meaning *primarily* from their role as child bearers might be seen as constraining from the vantage point of white, middle-class feminism. Are these women simply falling victim to normative conceptions of the sexual division of labor or idealized notions of "maternal yearning"?

Consider Aliya and Pamela, two of the women Edin and Kefalas interview. Aliya, says, "Some people may say it was for the wrong reasons, but it was like too much around me going on. . . . I guess that was my way out of all these situations. [But] I wanted a child because it was *mine*. It was [for] love." Pamela, in turn, contends, "I just *knew*, growing up, 'Oh, you're gonna have your kids. . . . The kids are gonna love you. They're *yours*.'"[54] Although Aliya and Pamela express different sentiments here, it is noteworthy that for both women motherhood is not only or even mostly about the needs of the child, but also about the fundamental needs of the mother for love, affirmation, and support. Moreover, as Edin and Kefalas note, "the stronger preference for children among the poor can be seen in the propensity of the women we interviewed to put children, rather than marriage, education, or career, at the center of their meaning-making activity."[55]

I interpret the comments of Edin and Kefalas's interviewees in two ways. First, whereas some women may fall prey to the dominant ideal of white, middle-class motherhood, poor women who see their children as providing them with much-needed self-affirmation *subvert* the dominant paradigm, and within this resistance we find a kernel of autonomy. Second, viewing childbearing as the primary source of women's meaning making seems antiquated, a result of the oppressive socialization attributed, for example, to the "self-abnegating mother."[56] The women's movement has struggled to open up a far greater range of opportunities that can contribute to a fulfilling life; these women, in this interpretation, are limited in their autonomy if they fail to access or take advantage of such expanded opportunities. In reality, however, their assessment of the opportunities available to them is accurate, thereby complicating the oppressive socialization explanation.

In the first account, consideration of the contextual variables at play suggests that situating childbearing as an avenue to the types of self-affirmation and support described by the interviewees can be seen as resistant, and thus, perhaps, as autonomous. Kaplan's theory of the poverty of relationships helps to explain why viewing childbearing as a relational resource makes sense and may be considered to be a marker of autonomous agency. The poor, black, young women she interviews "describe being disconnected from primary family relations, abandoned by their schools and by the men in their lives, and isolated from relations with other teenagers at the time of adolescence, when it is most important that they experience positive relationships."[57] Motherhood is a *strategy* used to cope with the conditions under which these young women are operating.[58] This does not mean that childbearing at a young age is an *ideal* autonomous choice under the given conditions. In fact, that it is not ideal is exactly the point; to question paternalist pregnancy-prevention strategies is not to endorse teenage pregnancy or multiple pregnancies of poor women per se. It suggests instead something about what types of interventions are necessary, shifting the terms of both the "diagnosis" and the "cure" (to use the paternalist language of pathology).

In the second interpretation, the structural conditions that affect these women suggest instead that poor women are not necessarily succumbing to sexist norms or values that limit women's opportunities. Instead, they are making a fairly accurate assessment of the limitations that exist on their potential resources for fulfillment. As Edin and Kefalas write, while middle-class women face significant opportunity costs when they have children at an earlier age, the same cannot be said for poor women.[59] Rather, "disadvantaged girls who bear children have about the same long-term earnings trajectories as similarly disadvantaged youth who wait until their mid or late twenties to have a child."[60] Early childbearing has similarly minimal effects on other outcomes as well. Situating childbearing as a primary source of meaning not only disrupts the assumptions made by new paternalists about the centrality of work as a meaning-making device, it also draws our attention to the lack of opportunities that exist for poor women.[61]

Conditionality in New Paternalism: A Failure of Reciprocity

If child rearing is a greater—and more legitimate—source of meaning making in citizens' lives than new paternalists makes it out to be, the value of the sort of work associated with workfare is in fact a much *lesser* source of meaning making than this theory suggests. I do not wish to dismiss the possibility that work is indeed an important source of meaning in people's lives and, in the context of our social and economic systems, a primary means of gaining recognition. Nevertheless, most workfare jobs, and those jobs that welfare recipients who leave the rolls take, are low-wage, low-flexibility positions that tend to be associated with low levels of personal fulfillment. This is not to say that these jobs are necessarily burdensome and never enabling, but rather that the conditions are not ideal.[62]

Advocates of workfare lay claim to the technique of conditionality as an important key to enhancing recognition of service users as citizens, or as potentially autonomous agents. Mead and Christopher Beem claim that moving welfare recipients into the workplace renders their dependency acceptable and allows them to integrate into broader society.[63] Even though income may not increase greatly for these recipients, Mead argues that "gains to equal citizenship, however, were significant."[64] Though they are dependent on the state, like social security recipients,[65] welfare recipients who work are accepted because, "in citizenship terms, fulfilling the demand to function is far more important than minimizing one's demands on the society."[66] Work serves to "rebuild ties between the poor and the rest of society."[67]

Mead suggests that the public's acceptance of the radical changes made under PRWORA is evidence that average citizens now regard welfare recipients engaged in "work activities" as full citizens.[68] But *if* participation in the labor market actually garners recognition that was once denied to dependents in our society, the conditional nature of benefits that is the hallmark of workfare programs undermines this recognition by flagging service users as lacking the qualities the dominant culture ascribes to citizens. While I do not think conditionality is necessarily unjust, in the context of our current social and political conditions it fails to foster autonomy, which I regard as one element of a just welfare policy. In this context, as Desmond King charges, conditionality in the form of "workfare might well produce a deepening sense of alienation and exclusion among those it claims to help."[69] Mead either neglects or minimizes the deleterious effects of the assumptions that underlie the policy, and the stigma that follows from the singling out certain individuals to be the targets of coercive policies. King argues that "participants in workfare are treated differently, and not in a positive sense, from participants in other state-administered benefit programs."[70]

In fact, post–welfare reform research indicates that Mead's predictions regarding the eroding stigma of welfare recipients thanks to workfare have not panned out. Soss and Schram evaluate the policy feedback mechanisms at work in the case of the 1996 welfare reforms, considering the claim that "new policies create a new politics."[71] Do work requirements minimize public opposition to welfare assistance and, as Mead argues, shift politics to the left and reduce racism?[72] According to Soss and Schram, though the public views work requirements and time limits in a positive light, these changes "did not generate more positive images of poor people, welfare recipients, or welfare itself."[73] Supporting Soss and Schram's findings, Dyck and Hussey have shown that following welfare reform, most Americans continue to associate welfare with negative perceptions of African Americans' work ethic.[74]

These findings may suggest that the stigma associated with being compelled to work under workfare inevitably shapes citizens' perceptions of workfare participants. Contrary to the claim that work will enhance citizens' views of welfare claimants, King argues, "we may instead view them as incompetent, hence lacking the qualities need for membership in the polity as equal citizens."[75] Mapped onto the racialized nature of welfare stigma, workfare only further differentiates recipients from their fellow citizens. Indeed, the risk of viewing workfare participants as incompetent is high given that incompetence is the foundation of paternalist policy. Consider James Q. Wilson's claims about paternalism. He suggests that government should extend paternalism to people "who have by their behavior indicated that they do not display the minimal level of self-control expected of decent citizens."[76] Those lacking self-control include "the homeless, criminals, drug addicts, deadbeat dads, unmarried teenage mothers, and single mothers claiming welfare benefits."[77] There is a difference between viewing an individual as reciprocating for the benefits she receives and viewing her as duty bound to obey because she is personally flawed. Moreover, the flaws that are attributed to welfare recipients, as Wilson's argument suggests, are specifically those that cast the recipient as an individual *incapable* of autonomy; therefore, whatever recognition labor market participation may have garnered is ultimately obscured by the underlying reasons for the coercive conditions under which they work.

Nevertheless, as Stuart White notes, the argument for *reciprocity* in the realm of welfare benefits is not easily dismissed. White argues that conditionality in social welfare benefits is not necessarily unjust; under some conditions, the imposition of conditional welfare benefits may be acceptable and indeed necessary to uphold our egalitarian institutions. That is, "free-riding, or accepting benefits without social contribution, generates a clear risk that the egalitarian institutions in question will provoke feelings of alienation and resentment and so undercut the very spirit of solidarity on which they depend." The obligation to reciprocity, he writes, can only be enforceable under certain required background conditions for distribution; "to assert otherwise is to assert that significantly disadvantaged individuals in a highly inegalitarian society may have an enforceable moral obligation to cooperate in their own exploitation." Instead, he suggests four intuitive conditions that must be in place for fair reciprocity to be enforceable: guarantee of a decent share of the social product for those meeting minimum participation standards; decent opportunities for productive participation; equitable treatment of different forms of participation; and universal enforcement of the minimum standard of participation.[78] Indeed, such requirements make conditionality appear more palatable when compared to paternalist arguments hinging on incompetence claims. In practice, however, stigma and material circumstances in our current social and political context make the fulfillment of such requirements unlikely.

When examined within the actual structural context in which it is enacted, the conditionality applied in the realm of pregnancy prevention suggests a deep misunderstanding of the problems that advocates of this strategy claim to address. One paternalistic approach to pregnancy prevention makes benefits conditional on teenage parents (under eighteen) residing with their own parents. If they do not, they will receive less income support from the state. Another program described in Maynard's piece offers young women "clear" moral messages discouraging further pregnancy; again, benefits are conditional on participation. The perversity of such programs is vast. Given the explanations proffered by the women Edin, Kefalas, and Kaplan have interviewed, we see that parents often *fail* to provide the support that girls and young women need. This is partly the motivation for bearing children. We can see that a failure to grapple with the intentions of pregnant teenagers leads to faulty policy prescriptions. If teenage pregnancy were truly the result of incompetence alone, then perhaps parental supervision would help to rein in such behavior. Yet since it seems this is not the case, an autonomy-fostering state would seek to provide options for alternative sources of meaning making and relational connections. This requirement and the program of moral indoctrination referenced above individualize the behavior of teenage parents, failing to recognize the ways that teen pregnancy can be understood as a response to institutional oppression, wherein childbearing appears as a reasonable and viable *strategy*.[79]

The strategies of conditionality employed in both the pregnancy-prevention and workfare instantiations of paternalist policy point us back to the distinction made earlier in this chapter between paternalist and interventionist policy. Paternalism is best understood as referring to forms of intervention that serve to perpetuate oppressive social relations by way of their coercive and stigmatizing tactics. As Kaplan notes, the ways that a lack of relational support contributes to teen pregnancy suggest that service delivery personnel ought to be "retrained to see themselves as supporters, to be empathetic, to offer real job training, and to seek economic and emotional support for the entire family unit."[80] How this is enacted depends on context and further research, but what is important is that such intervention need not be paternalistic; rather, it can foster autonomy when the faulty exercise of unequal power relations entailed by new paternalist policy is curbed.

The value of such a revisioning of social service delivery extends to our democratic commitments as well. As Julie White's account of paternalism highlights, non-paternalist interventions must be premised in some way on the service user's involvement in the definition of her needs and the determination of how these needs are to be met. Social service delivery that is founded on such a participatory model, rather than marked by "speaking for others in the process of defining their needs," moves us toward affording service users equal citizenship rights.[81] As Mead suggests, the question of what constitutes civic labor is a political one; an autonomy-fostering model of service delivery would, unlike new paternalist models, respect the points of view of service users and afford them opportunities to participate in the definition of, among other things, needs and social requirements. Because paternalist policy intervenes in marginalized citizens' lives because of a form of misrecognition—the misattribution of incompetence—it ultimately restricts the possibilities for autonomous agency and undermines democratic participation.

Conclusion

New paternalists challenge an economistic notion of the individual as a rational self-maximizer. Feminists, too, wish to complicate this view of the self, arguing against rationality *alone* as a marker of autonomous agency. Yet new paternalism does not actually do away with the *ideal* of rationality as a prerequisite for autonomy; instead, it challenges the *extension* of the ideal to all individuals. Mead argues that "understanding dysfunction requires positing a more complex psychology, where people fail to do what they themselves desire and thus fail to exhaust the potential of their environment."[82] Pathologizing the poor and dependent, Mead reinforces what, from a feminist perspective, the critique of conventional notions of autonomy wishes to overcome. Instead, I argue, we need a notion of autonomy that takes into account affective needs and relational ties, one that makes room for a wider range of values, while also providing the tools for the development of capacities related to autonomy. Fostering autonomy requires not a narrow view of autonomy toward which we must coercively instruct citizens to strive, but rather a relational account of autonomy that responds both to the limitations of the structural conditions under which individuals exist and to the complex ways in which autonomy can be expressed—thereby enhancing access to autonomy, understood in both recognition- and capacity-related terms.

As both the workfare and the pregnancy-prevention examples show, paternalist policy is founded on flawed assumptions about incompetence and intentionality. Rather than fostering autonomy, new paternalism replicates the relations of power that have contributed to the need for these services in the first place. An autonomy-fostering state, in contrast, would seek out interventions that correct or respond to these unjust power relations. Moreover, the revised notion of paternalism discussed above, which distinguishes paternalism from interventionist policy in general, is an important lens through which to understand the contrast between the two approaches to service delivery. Finally, these two cases bring to light the ways that relationality comes to be either marginalized or misconstrued, in part because of its association with the feminized private sphere. This insight is noteworthy for the development of autonomy-fostering programs, which must revalue the activities of the private sphere—in particular caregiving activities—while challenging the constructed line that separates private and public.

4 TAKING RESPONSIBILITY: PRWORA'S LIMITS TO IMMIGRANT ACCESS

Introduction

In the previous chapter, I argued that the assumptions underlying new paternalist programs—a genre of welfare service delivery programs central to
PRWORA, the legislation that brought about the 1996 U.S. welfare reforms—
serve to narrow the boundaries of access to the autonomous agency required
for full citizenship. These assumptions included the belief that work is the
primary, perhaps only, conduit to individual autonomy; that such work includes only participation in the paid labor force and not care work; and that
the failure to engage in such work is the result of individual incompetence
rather than economic, political, or social factors. New paternalist programs, I
have argued, are founded on faulty claims that have dire consequences for
recipients' equal access to the rights and status of citizenship. In this chapter,
I turn to another aspect of PRWORA that also reshapes the boundaries of access to autonomous agency: the changes enacted by the act with regard to
immigrant eligibility requirements for social services.

As a whole, PRWORA limits provision of benefits that are critical to full
membership in society, which I argue includes the capacities to develop, exercise, and be recognized as an autonomous individual. So far, I have linked
these provisions to the notion of social citizenship, or the right to the resources
necessary to exercise one's political and civil rights of citizenship.[1] Melding
the notion of social citizenship with feminist relational conceptions of autonomy, I have suggested that these "resources" should be understood as specifically including configurations of social relations that foster autonomy; like the
important material resources that are conventionally associated with social

citizenship, enabling social relations are necessary for the exercise of full citizenship. Autonomy, then, is a precondition for full citizenship; in turn, just conditions require that the social rights of citizenship foster this autonomy. But while social citizenship is central to issues of welfare provision, particularly those that interest political theorists, in this chapter I suggest that we must also carefully consider the second and third of Marshall's three tiers of citizenship: civil and political citizenship, or collectively, the legal status of citizenship. Though social citizenship mediates an individual's ability to exercise his or her political and civil rights of citizenship, questions regarding who is to be designated a legal citizen, and the implications of this designation, are also deeply relevant sites of inquiry for scholars of social welfare services and individual autonomy. As Lynn Fujiwara notes, "Citizenship-as-legal-status—that is, as membership in a particular community—and citizenship-as-desirable-activity, where the extent and quality of one's citizenship is a function of one's participation in that community, converge when societies struggle to position cultural newcomers outside social entitlements."[2]

Located at this site of convergence, PRWORA limits immigrants' autonomy. This is, to my mind, relatively uncontroversial; as I understand it, the debate in the field is focused not on whether such limitations exist, but on whether they are warranted and just. In this chapter, I argue that they are not. My argument takes the following form. First, I suggest that the drive to limit immigrants' autonomy through welfare reform is founded on a claim that immigrants who seek out welfare have failed to "take responsibility" for the consequences of their autonomous choices to migrate. I argue that this foundational claim is deeply problematic, first because it assumes an individualist conception of autonomy, and second because it reflects a view of immigration divorced from the reality of the economic and political interdependence of nation-states throughout the world. Immigrants' decisions to migrate can be understood as autonomous, I suggest, but only when autonomy is conceived relationally. Such autonomous decisions, where taken by emigrants from impoverished nations, must be understood as relationally constituted in part by the *failure* of the United States to take responsibility for its political and economic actions, which allow American citizens to live a comparatively privileged life at the expense of citizens of other nations. In this sense, the call for immigrants to take responsibility for their plight upon their arrival is unreasonable in the wake of the failure of the U.S. government to take similar responsibility. But if we shift the notion of *personal* responsibility at the heart of the foundational claim away from responsibility as the equivalent to being called to account for one's self-sufficiency and instead focus on acts of *political responsibility* as critical expressions of autonomy, we can understand many immigrants' claims to welfare rights *as* forms of taking political responsibility. Toward this end, I suggest that an analysis of immigrant welfare rights is most convincing when founded on a notion of political responsibility as making shared claims to enact structural change.

Drawing on Iris Young's notion of political responsibility, I interpret immigrant acts of welfare claims making as acts of shared responsibility that seek to remedy the injustices of what Ayelet Shachar calls "birthright citizenship."[3] This stunted notion of citizenship, Shachar argues, is similar to an entail form of untaxed, inherited property because it arbitrarily distributes privilege associated with citizenship in prosperous nations, without in any way remedying the inequities that follow from such a model of distribution. Yet, unlike the case of this form of inherited property, which Shachar notes is "deeply discredited: it is banned in most jurisdictions and, indeed, is largely associated with a bygone feudal system," the presumption of birthright citizenship goes largely uninterrogated by political and legal theorists.[4] In Young's account, to take political responsibility is to act in a forward-looking manner that seeks to remedy structural injustices, bringing into question "background conditions" taken to be normal—including, I suggest, birthright citizenship. Young argues that those who are the victims of structural injustices "can be called to a responsibility they share with others in the structures to engage in actions directed at transforming the structures."[5] One way of understanding immigrants' claims to welfare rights is to understand them as taking up this call to responsibility by attempting to subvert the system that sustains the unequally and arbitrarily distributed benefits of birthright citizenship. Laying claim to welfare benefits is a move that seeks to bring about redistribution and therefore "take responsibility." Thus, by *denying* welfare to many immigrants, the state ironically prevents them from both exercising autonomy and taking responsibility—the very values that welfare reform advocates argue PRWORA is meant to enhance.

To elucidate the skewed notions of autonomy and responsibility that follow from PRWORA's eligibility criteria for immigrants, I draw on two ethnographic accounts of groups affected by the reforms: Latina immigrants in Southern California and Southeast Asian refugees in the San Francisco Bay Area.[6] These studies situate immigrants' decisions to migrate and to seek out social assistance within a global context, bringing into sharp contrast both the attempts of poor immigrants to take responsibility for remedying the global injustices to which they have been subject, and the failure of the American state to accept shared political responsibility for its role in generating these injustices. While welfare policy could be a site at which to begin to compensate for the injustices of birthright citizenship, PRWORA instead exacerbates the injustice of this form of inherited property by presuming that access to potentially autonomy-enhancing benefits undermines the individual responsibility of those born without such a birthright who have chosen to emigrate. The distinction between citizens and immigrants/asylees written into PRWORA has the effect of corrupting a potentially fruitful site for fostering autonomy and claiming political responsibility.

This chapter proceeds as follows. First, I outline the provisions in PRWORA regarding immigrant and refugee eligibility for welfare benefits. I then provide an account of migration decisions as autonomous, where autonomy is rightly conceived. Following that, I suggest that the account of migration underlying PRWORA relies on an individualistic notion of autonomy, possible only when the interdependence of nation-states and the global forces that structure migration decisions are obscured from vision. When we take up a more realistic conception of the global forces at work in such decisions, the failure to provide welfare benefits to immigrants can be exposed as a failure to take shared political responsibility for the global injustices in which the American state is implicated. Finally, I develop an argument for conceiving of immigrant welfare claims as acts of *claiming* political responsibility, rather than shirking personal responsibility.

PRWORA's Immigrant Eligibility Provisions

Noncitizens residing in the United States were some of the hardest hit by the 1996 welfare reforms. Although the most commonly stated aim of welfare reform was to end the "cycle of dependence" created by the now-extinct Aid to Families with Dependent Children program and send welfare recipients "from welfare to work," another aim of welfare reform was targeted at both existing and potential immigrants. By including strict bars to immigrant access to many welfare programs, welfare reform advocates hoped to discourage immigration by those who would depend on benefits, and to reduce the expense created by existing immigrants who claimed benefits. Half the savings attributed to PRWORA were the result of the original immigrant eligibility provisions under the legislation.[7] The reforms were passed at the same time as two other pieces of legislation that affected immigrants in the United States: the Illegal Immigration Reform and Immigrant Responsibility Act (IIRIRA), which brought about more severe penalties for unauthorized immigrants, and the Antiterrorism and Effective Death Penalty Act (AEDPA). These acts tightened restrictions on immigrants, both explicitly through legal constraints and implicitly by virtue of the heightened fear of deportation or other legal troubles they aroused. Emerging around the same time as the IIRIRA and the AEDPA, some scholars see PRWORA, ostensibly a social welfare policy and not an immigration bill, as a "back door" to immigration reform. In this vein, Marchevsky and Theoharis argue that welfare reform "widened the gap between citizens and legal immigrants, created immigrant categories entirely new to U.S. law, and opened up new channels of surveillance and information-sharing between social service agencies and the Immigration and Naturalization Service."[8] Without explicitly billing itself as a component of immigration policy, PRWORA brought about fundamental changes to the meaning and structure of legal citizenship in the United States.

The immigrant-focused aspects of PRWORA constitute a complex and often-confusing web of eligibility categories that deem some immigrants eligible for limited benefits and bar others from accessing the vast majority of benefits. Despite the division of immigrants into the categories of "qualified" and "nonqualified," PRWORA renders the vast majority of even "qualified" immigrants ineligible for many benefits. Nonqualified immigrants include the undocumented, asylum applicants, and those on temporary visas. Qualified immigrants include legal permanent residents and refugees.[9] Nonqualified immigrants were barred from most federal benefits aside from emergency medical care. For qualified immigrants, PRWORA distinguishes those entering the United States before the 1996 welfare reforms from "post-enactment" migrants; the former group retains eligibility for Temporary Assistance for Needy Families (TANF), the primary source of income support for welfare recipients, though states have the option of barring these immigrants from receiving benefits. Those entering after the passage of PRWORA are barred from receiving benefits for their first five years in the country, after which they still face stringent eligibility rules, which, Fujiwara argues, render "eligibility nearly impossible."[10] Again, states had an option to provide benefits for post-enactment immigrants during the five-year waiting period using their own funds

As with other aspects of PRWORA, policies oriented toward immigrants were marked by the devolution of many aspects of public benefits dispensation (and discretion thereof) to the states: states determine whether to provide supplementary benefits for legal immigrants who have been cut off from federal benefits, while also determining whether those eligible for benefits will be placed in workfare programs or in training programs (including English language instruction). The incentive structure set up by the federal legislation heavily favors states that forgo provision of education and training to recipients, since these programs do not count toward the minimum level of work participation required by states in order to receive federal funding.[11] The politics of individual states, including attitudes toward immigrants, shape state decisions regarding the eligibility and generosity of state-provided benefits, thereby creating disparity between states.[12] For example, while many states do provide some income assistance during the five-year waiting period, Texas provides no such assistance to noncitizens. Alabama is the only state that excludes even those who entered before enactment.

There are some exceptions to the limits on TANF provisions placed on qualified immigrants: refugees/asylees, active-duty service members, veterans, individuals granted withholding of deportation, and those who can prove ten years of employment can claim assistance. Refugee and asylees are not subject to the waiting period, but they are eligible for TANF only for the first five years of their residence in the United States and for Supplemental Security Income for the first seven years. As Fujiwara notes, these exceptions "reflected ideas of belonging and membership in the nation."[13] Military service signals patriotism and loyalty, while wage earning (which was often difficult to prove) "superseded legal citizenship as a form of duty," in keeping with the highly privileged status of paid employment in American political culture (discussed in the previous chapter).

As this description of the provisions of PRWORA for immigrants suggests, the eligibility rules are *highly* complex, rendering it difficult for both immigrants and caseworkers to discern eligibility in many cases. While many immigrants lost eligibility for benefits, studies have found that there has also been a steep decline in welfare claims by *eligible* immigrants.[14] Some scholars view this "chilling" effect on welfare claims as exacerbating the attack on immigrants, creating fear and reluctance to seek aid. Marchevsky and Theoharis argue, as I discuss below, that in Long Beach, California, the chilling effect was accompanied by "systematic denial of applications from eligible immigrants, and widespread removal of existing immigrant recipients from the welfare rolls."[15] Taken together, the "diversion" practices aiming to steer potential recipients off the rolls (using varying degrees of coercion) and the confusing nature of the regulations concerning eligibility work together to limit noncitizens' access to crucial benefits—and indeed, this was the goal of the reforms where immigrants are concerned.

Choosing Immigration

In a report on the effects of welfare reform on immigrants' welfare use, the immigration scholar and critic George Borjas explains that "by setting up a five-year waiting period before newly arrived immigrants qualify for many types of assistance, the legislation presumably discourages the immigration of potential public charges. By tightening the eligibility requirements for immigrants already living in the United States, the legislation [PRWORA] presumably increases the incentive for some immigrants to return to their home countries."[16] Elsewhere, Borjas and his coauthor Lynette Hilton suggest that more generous benefits prove a "magnet" for immigration.[17] Immigrants, supporters of this theory suggest, perform the equivalent of a cost-benefit analysis when they leave their home countries; in this equation, the increased benefits of welfare weigh heavily in favor of migration. But like similar theories about the effects of differing levels of benefits on migration between states *within* the United States, the vast majority of welfare scholars reject the "welfare magnet" theory as it applies to immigration across national borders.[18] Despite the fact that magnet theories have been largely discredited, they are nonetheless used as justifications for the immigration provisions in the welfare legislation. Such theories highlight the assumption that immigrants make an autonomous choice when they migrate to the United States. Indeed, as I explain below, when autonomy is understood as a relationally constituted capacity (or set of capacities) that one can access even under situations of duress or dependence, many migrants' decisions to emigrate from their home countries can be seen as autonomous. Yet this is not the conception of autonomy at the heart of the assumptions underlying PRWORA and magnet theories; rather, embedded in those assumptions is a highly individualistic notion of autonomy that is basically identical to independence—the conception that I and other feminist theorists argue is both flawed and exclusionary.

By casting the decision to migrate as an independent one, critics of immigration are able to elide the relational context within which this decision is made. In turn, critics assign individual responsibility to immigrants for their decision to immigrate and their status once they have done so, shirking shared political responsibility for the plight of immigrants who make the choice to leave their native lands. The link between individual autonomy and personal responsibility that hinges on these faulty assumptions vastly oversimplifies the complex processes of migration, attributing agency to immigrants while suggesting that receiving communities—both national and local—are merely the passive targets of the rational calculations carried out by benefit-seeking migrants.[19] Such an explanation has the effect of demonizing immigrant welfare recipients while erasing the historical and political contexts of the countries from which they are emigrating and their relationship to the United States. Moreover, explanations emphasizing the magnet theory attribute the movement of human beings to the erosion of borders created by the vague and unaccountable entity of "globalization," thereby relieving receiving countries of any responsibility for the economic and political structures that are central to the inequalities and injustices that shape migration patterns.[20]

An anecdote in the opening pages of Shachar's book *The Birthright Lottery* highlights the ambiguities found when we consider the relationships among migration, autonomy, and responsibility, suggesting that the straightforward attribution of independent choice to immigrants is considerably lacking in nuance. Shachar tells the story of five Dominican men who hid themselves on a ship bound for the United States. As with many stowaway situations, what follows is a story of the dangerous conditions they endured to make this hidden journey, which ends with another vessel finding two of these men's "shark-eaten bodies." The five men who began this journey, which a Texas court later interpreted as founded on a belief that it "represented their only hope to fulfill the American dream," surely knew that they were embarking on a dangerous and potentially life threatening voyage.[21] This "American dream" ostensibly implies the belief that in the United States a better life is attainable through hard work and persistence, which in their home country would not yield the same results. Moreover, if for them the risk of death outweighed the costs of remaining in one's homeland, the implication is that the homeland presents risks of a fate worse than death. With these conditions in mind, then, did the Dominican men make an autonomous choice to pursue the "dream" in a way that included the prospect of a bloody death at sea? And if so, to what extent are they *responsible* for the outcomes of that decision?

Autonomy is not a capacity enjoyed only by those who are fully independent and unencumbered. Indeed, as the notion of relational autonomy I offer in this book highlights, the status of autonomous individual cannot exist in the absence of social context. Thus, to argue that the Dominicans' lacked autonomy because their decisions were not "entirely their own" would be to mis-construe the contexts within which autonomy is possible. In fact, if we assume that, on a most basic level, the reason for the men's decision to board the ship was to avoid the fate of losing their lives (or worse), then in many accounts of relational autonomy their decision would fulfill a wide range of conditions for determining whether a decision is autonomous. In procedural accounts of au-tonomy—which are concerned not with the substance of one's actions or deci-sions, but with how one arrives at those decisions or actions—the criteria for determining whether one's decisions or actions are autonomous includes such requirements as the accord of one's first-order desires with her second-order desires; the integration of "different levels of self"; the ability to endorse one's actions upon critical reflection; and the use of a variety of skills and capacities consonant with autonomy. Substantive accounts may require that the decision or action be taken in a context that is not limited by the impairments of op-pressive socialization or by forms of coercion.[22] Although the men's decision to flee their home country may have been made in the context of oppression, the decision seems to be an appropriate response to the existing (and likely future) constraints on the men's autonomy.

All this is to say that we can interpret many decisions to emigrate from a country that is marked by economic, social, or political limitations or unrest to be autonomous. Yet the implications of this ascription of autonomy to im-migrants depend, in part, on the notion of autonomy to which one adheres. If the autonomous decision to migrate is conceived as emerging from social rela-tions (broadly understood), the ensuing notion of responsibility to which one might hold the autonomous is different from that which follows from an indi-vidualist notion of autonomy.

From Autonomy to Responsibility

As Paul Benson explains, feminist theorists have tended to be wary of the no-tion of responsibility because it frequently reflects the view that "the respon-sible person is the self-governing, self-constituting, and self-sufficient agent whose natural freedom and moral identity do not essentially depend on so-cially elaborated powers, roles, and relationships."[23] Such a conception of re-sponsibility in the case of migration would indeed be problematic: while I have suggested that many decisions to immigrate may be autonomous, I have rejected this claim where autonomy is understood to indicate self-sufficiency or independence. On such grounds, individuals who are leaving their home countries because they are deeply constrained in these contexts would not fulfill the conditions of such a notion of individual responsibility. As Benson explains, "Being responsible is itself a matter of occupying a certain social position, having *the status of an eligible participant in a community of moral dialogue*."[24] If the community of moral dialogue is the global economy, which structures many decisions to migrate, citizens of impoverished nations can hardly be understood as having such a status. Yet American immigration and welfare policies often fail to take account of the context of social, economic, and political exclusion in which many immigrants make their decision to leave their home countries.

In a 1989 article, Saskia Sassen warned that "U.S. immigration policy will continue to be counterproductive as long as it places the responsibility for the formation of international migrations exclusively on the shoulders of the immigrants themselves."[25] Yet both the explicit reforms to immigration policy that took place in the 1990s and the indirect immigration reforms that followed from the passage of PRWORA take just that approach. As Fujiwara explains, "National immigration policies are increasingly shaped by an understanding of immigration as the consequence of the individual action of emigrants; the receiving country is taken as a passive agent."[26] Where welfare policy is concerned, if the provisions of PRWORA either completely deny access to welfare for some immigrants or impose significant limitations on benefits, the implicit message is: it is your choice to immigrate, and it is therefore your responsibility to find the means to survive in this country. This foundational assumption is rooted in an understanding of migration that fails to "recognize the larger global processes that have led to particular collective circumstances."[27] Such global processes shape not only the decision to migrate, but also the ability of citizens of some countries to emigrate and the conditions that immigrants to the United States face once they arrive.[28]

With "responsibility" firmly situated in the name of the legislation responsible for these reforms, the 1996 welfare laws ascribe responsibility for poverty not only to immigrants, but also, to some extent, to citizens as well. As I argued in the previous chapter, however, the assumption of incompetence underlying new paternalist programs suggests that while responsibility is ascribed to citizen welfare recipients, those who fail to *take up* this responsibility can at least be "rehabilitated" in order to fix the disordered sense of self that leads to such failure. For the many immigrants who have no access at all to welfare rights, even such demeaning notions of incompetence do not provide a pathway to assistance. The immigration provisions of PRWORA exacerbate the already problematic assumptions of individual responsibility that shape policies for citizen recipients, making the rhetorical claim to "the end of entitlement" much closer to the substantive truth where immigrants are concerned.

Sassen's warning rests on her argument that "by focusing narrowly on immigrants and on the immigration process itself, U.S. policymakers have ignored the broader international forces, many of them generated or at least encouraged by the United States, that have helped give rise to migration flows."[29] Sassen suggests that U.S. foreign direct investment changes the traditional economic structures of other nations, while also shifting the occupational structure within the United States to increase low-wage jobs (which promotes immigration). More than two decades after Sassen's article was published, the interdependent structure of the global economy has only increased and expanded; her claim above is perhaps more true than ever. Another aspect of Sassen's argument also holds true: though poverty drives immigration to the United States, other factors are important, too. She writes, "The establishment of political, military, and economic linkages with the United States seems to have been instrumental in creating conditions that allowed the emergence of large-scale emigration."[30] Not only do such linkages allow for massive migration flows, they also shape the terms on which immigrants' lives are structured upon arrival in the United States.

In this regard, Marchevsky and Theoharis's reference to a statement by Bill Clinton in their account of Latina immigrant workers in the Long Beach area is telling: "We must not—and we will not—surrender our borders to those who wish to exploit our history of compassion and justice."[31] In the context of a society that increasingly relies on the exploitation of noncitizens' labor, Clinton's use of the language of exploitation is troublingly ironic. According to Marchevsky and Theoharis, although anti-immigration rhetoric suggests a goal of keeping out the resource-draining immigrant population, immigration control is less about constructing rigid boundaries between nation-states than about dictating the terms on which foreigners may enter the country. Immigration control, they write, "aims not to keep immigrants out, but rather to regulate and relegate them into a class of flexible workers that sits outside the boundaries of full membership in U.S. society."[32] Making space for the labor of noncitizens—by way of relaxed regulation or complete lack thereof—the United States makes no such "accommodation" for the needs of these workers. Instead, what emerges is a distorted and entirely unsatisfactory system of exchange: the federal government "actively facilitates the flexibility of capital by forcing millions of workers into a deregulated labor market, while it erects higher barriers to full citizenship in the national community."[33] The juxtaposition of the increased regulation of social welfare benefits that follows from PRWORA and the increased demand for flexible—often insecure, devoid of benefits, and exploitative—immigrant labor highlights the failure to connect U.S. responsibility for labor conditions to immigrants' supposed "individual" responsibility to live self-sufficiently (i.e., without government aid).[34]

Finally, exacerbating the already-precarious conditions that immigrants living in the United States must endure, cultural discrimination and marginalization serve to legitimize unjust treatment of foreign-born workers. On the one hand, exploitation of immigrant labor is justified either with naturalized accounts of the "hard-working immigrant" or by claims regarding the curative function of paid employment for a host of ills that are seen to plague the character of some groups of immigrants. Marchevsky and Theoharis note in particular that immigrant women, conceived of as necessarily oppressed by their "cultures," are called on "to liberate themselves from their culturally defined gender roles, [which] however, conveniently correspond[s] to the nation's growing demand for immigrant domestic labor."[35] On the other hand, immigrants are seen as either compromising the social safety net by drawing on the state's resources, ordinarily reserved for "deserving" citizens, or depriving natives of access to jobs. "Cultural racism," as Jonathan Inda describes it, classifies the immigrant as the "other," who "poses a threat to the nation and is therefore relegated to the margins of society, often blamed for all the social and economic ills that befall the nation."[36]

Keeping in mind the global economic forces that shape decisions to migrate, neoliberal policies that structure the nature of immigrants' labor once in the United States, and domestic antipathy toward foreigners, we can now more effectively evaluate the implications of the charges against immigrants who are seen as failing to take "responsibility."

Shared Responsibility and the Failures of PRWORA

While "responsibility" is the buzzword of welfare reform, the term is used almost exclusively to refer to the *individual*. Political theorists contending with questions of global justice have, however, grappled with the question of how and to what extent *shared* responsibility should be assigned for the conditions of the globalized world. As the previous section suggests, to look at the plight of immigrants outside the context of global economic and social forces is to miss much of the picture of immigration decision making and experience. Once we do take into account this global context for migration, the question of whether immigrants from impoverished nations ought to be responsible for their decision to migrate, and hence their ability to support themselves upon arrival, seems to lack sufficient nuance to attend to the realities of their diverse situations. If, as Benson's argument cited at the beginning of the previous section suggests, one must have some semblance of equal footing—of equal ability to participate in "a common dialogue"—in order to be held responsible, we might assume that immigrants escaping economically or politically dire situations should not be held responsible for their inability to support themselves immediately. In this account, the underlying premise of PRWORA's immigration restrictions—that immigrants ought to be responsible for the consequences of their own decisions to migrate, and therefore are not entitled to state support—could be rejected as unjust on the grounds that it places responsibility where it ought not.

In the next section, I suggest that upon reconceiving the notion of responsibility as *political* responsibility, we need not (and should not) see immigrants as exempt from "responsibility." But before I make this argument, another apparent void of responsibility must be addressed. With Benson's framework for understanding responsibility as a starting point, questions of responsibility in the context of welfare lead us to focus on the affluent countries that rely on the poverty of other nations to sustain this affluence. It is these countries that have the status of participants in the "moral dialogue" that is the global economy. By moral dialogue, I do not mean a dialogue that meets some criteria for moral justice, but rather the dialogue in which those who make moral decisions participate. Affluent countries participate in such a dialogue both with regard to their decisions regarding economic policies, which have far-reaching implications for human beings across the globe, and insofar as they determine the policies that distinguish the rights of citizens from the rights of aliens. As such, we must see such affluent countries—in the context of this book, my focus is primarily the United States—as having a great deal of responsibility to the immigrants who enter the confines of their borders. By withdrawing social assistance from immigrants, these countries do not adequately take up such responsibility. Indeed, they reinforce and reproduce the conditions for which such responsibility ought to have been taken to begin with.

Can we really assign blame to the United States—and, in turn, citizens of the United States—for something as diffuse as the effects of globalization on impoverished nations? According to Iris Young's notion of shared political responsibility, there are profound ways in which we must accept responsibility for the conditions of strangers whose lives are affected by our actions. While many theorists suggest that we owe a special obligation or have a particular responsibility to those who are citizens of the same polity to which we belong—those with shared national citizenship status—Young suggests that this reasoning is flawed.[37] Instead, our political responsibilities "derive from the social and economic structures in which [we] act and mutually affect one another"—a much wider range of connections than a model based on connections with a single polity would allow for.[38] Such responsibilities are not, as Young points out, to be understood as the same in form to those emerging from a "liability model" of responsibility, wherein blame is assigned to a specific individual or group and punitive or monetary compensation is sought. Instead, political responsibility is forward-looking, focusing on the structural changes that must be made to avoid future injustices. In the case of sweatshop abuses, which Young focuses on in her article, political responsibility serves the function of allowing "us to call on one another to take responsibility *together* for the fact that our actions collectively assume and contribute to the complex structural processes that enable the working conditions we deplore and make them difficult for any single agent to change."[39] While differential access to power may shape our respective abilities to take such action, it is still a shared action. (I return to the implications of such power differentials in the following section.)

What is more, according to Young, "political institutions are an important means of . . . discharging [our political] responsibilities" to those to whom we are socially and economically connected.[40] Social welfare programs are clear instances of a way that we can use political institutions to "discharge" our responsibilities to those who have suffered because of the privilege we enjoy as citizens of affluent countries. To some extent, we view social welfare programs as serving such a function for fellow citizens, even in a post–welfare reform era. From the relatively optimistic Marshallian point of view, we seek to overcome some—though certainly not all—of the negative effects of a capitalist system through the expansion of social rights.[41] (Of course, such rights may also make possible the maintenance of other status distinctions, but the intent is still a redistributive one.) If we take Young's argument that our obligations ought to be understood as applying not simply to members of the *same* political institutions, but as also extending to those who populate our increasingly broad sphere of social and economic relations, the responsibility of the state to provide social welfare services to immigrants is clear. To fail to do so is to shirk an important responsibility and to lose an opportunity to minimally redress the injustice perpetrated in the interests of Western comforts.

In some sense, there are already important instances in which citizens of the United States and the state as a whole take shared responsibility for those who are not official members of the community (i.e., those who are "aliens"). Such instances are telling in that they highlight the contradictions that allow for such responsibility to be seen as legitimate in one circumstance but not another. Linda Bosniak's discussion of the case of undocumented immigrant children sheds light on the assumptions that underlie citizen/alien distinctions and our sense of political responsibility to each.[42] Bosniak interprets the decision in *Plyler v. Doe*, wherein the state of Texas argued that undocumented alien children could not rely on the equal protection clause of the U.S. Constitution to challenge the denial of state-provided public education.[43] Finding that the children could, as "persons," invoke the Fourteenth Amendment, the Supreme Court also evaluated whether the state of Texas had violated the children's rights by denying them education. Here, too, it found that the state had not shown any compelling interest for the denial of education to these children, rejecting the claim that the state's concern with fiscal integrity met the standard that would allow for such a denial of rights. Despite the fact that the finding seems friendly to immigrants—here, undocumented ones—Bosniak notes that "the Court structured much of its opinion around an opposition between the 'innocent children' and their culpable parents, attributing sharply contrasting degrees of deservingness to each." The key to this distinction, Bosniak explains, is that "undocumented status should be treated as substantially irrelevant here because the undocumented status of these children was acquired involuntarily, and its consequences cannot, therefore, fairly be visited upon them."[44]

If the involuntary nature of children's status is what grants them legitimacy with regard to the state's willingness to take responsibility, a closer examination of the implied voluntarism of adult immigrant actions calls into question whether the Court's arguments (and widely held societal views) regarding innocence and culpability in such cases are coherent. What is it about this involuntary quality that makes us more sympathetic? It is a sense that, through no fault of their own, such *powerless* children have been forced to participate in extreme acts—illegal acts, even—that place them in a vulnerable situation for which we do not think they ought to be blamed. Though I have argued above that we *can* see immigration, even for those leaving behind dire circumstances, as founded on relatively autonomous choices where autonomy is understood relationally, does this autonomy negate the relative powerlessness and deep levels of constraint that shape such autonomous decisions? What really compels our sympathy for children in cases like *Plyler v. Doe* is not so much a lack of autonomy but a sense of powerlessness and vulnerability.

The parents of these children, however, are seen as culpable, because their "status was acquired through purposeful action."[45] Yet, even with this claim shaping the distinction between children and adults in the *Plyler* case, Bosniak notes that there is a tension within Justice Brennan's decision. Along similar lines as Marchevsky and Theoharis's critique of the contradictory implications of state policies that limit provisions for immigrants while promoting these individuals' availability as sources of cheap and flexible labor, Brennan questions the structure that allows for not only children's vulnerability and powerless but also for their parents' predicament. Citing "sheer incapability or lax enforcement of laws," Brennan writes, "This situation raises the specter of a permanent caste of undocumented resident aliens, encouraged by some to remain here as sources of cheap labor, but nevertheless denied the benefits that our society makes available to citizens and lawful permanent residents."[46] In fact, almost three decades later, the latter group referred to in Brennan's claim above—lawful permanent residents—no longer has access to many of the same benefits as the former. My focus is on documented rather than undocumented immigrants, but the same mixed messages exist for the documented immigrant with regard to encouraging cheap labor but denying adequate protections and benefits.

It is not only the contradictory incentives that Brennan and Bosniak refer to that should make us question acceptance of responsibility only in cases of childlike, complete dependence. The structure of citizenship in most countries raises the specter of a whole other level of "involuntariness" where such status is concerned. Shachar's notion of birthright citizenship makes this clear. By birthright citizenship, Shachar means the almost universal system of assigning citizenship according to birth, based on either land (*jus soli*) or blood (*jus sanguinis*). Both systems allocate citizenship based on a "birthright transfer of entitlement" due to parentage or place of birth. What is critical to this system is that "both criteria for attributing membership at birth are arbitrary: one is based on the accident of birth within particular geographical borders while the other is based on the sheer luck of descent." Since this system is used almost universally in national citizenship systems, we are all subject to such arbitrariness, though the effects on some are dramatically different than on others: to be "accidentally" born within or luckily descended from citizens of an affluent country shapes one's life chances in profoundly different ways than were one born within or descended from those of an impoverished nation. Yet, says Shachar, we take these systems to be "natural" or "apolitical."[47]

Although we rarely question the validity of this naturalized form of allocating citizenship rights, political theorists and philosophers have long called into question a similar system—that which applies to "entailed property." Inherited property (which goes untaxed) has, Shachar notes, widely been deemed the basis for an unjust and intractable system of privilege. The similarities between such a system and the system of birthright citizenship are striking when one considers the complex ways that theorists have come to understand property. Drawing on Charles Reich's analysis of property, Shachar notes that "like other property regimes," birthright attribution rules "define access to certain resources, benefits, protections, decision-making processes, and opportunity-enhancing institutions which are reserved primarily to those defined as right-holders." Both property and citizenship also have positive functions, granting us access to rights and the ability to exercise those rights. Where citizenship is concerned, a positive conception "entails the obligation to mitigate inequalities among social actors," and conceives of participation in the polity as hinging on an "expectation of generosity by those citizens with greater authority and wealth toward those without it." Such a conception of citizenship, Shachar acknowledges, is largely unrealized by even the wealthiest societies today. Nonetheless, it "serves as a normative yard stick against which we can measure how countries fare in their enabling commitment."[48]

When both the positive and negative aspects of citizenship—its protective and enabling features—are taken into account, the fact that citizenship is, according to this model of birthright allocation, arbitrarily conferred makes the distinction between the citizen of an impoverished or insecure nation appear to be not so different from that of a child whose situation is involuntary, and who therefore falls within the purview of a wealthier state's responsibility. The wealthy state's security and affluence depends to a great extent on a collection of arbitrarily allocated goods; that these goods are allocated in such a manner hinges on the fact that the birthright citizenship model *requires* that many people be arbitrarily excluded from access to those goods. As Shachar writes, "Ours is a world of scarcity; when an affluent community systemically delimits access to membership and its derivative benefits on the basis of a strict heredity system that effectively resembles an entail structure of preserving privilege and advantage in the hands of the few, those who are excluded have reason to complain."[49] The legitimacy of such "complaint," I want to suggest, implies the shared responsibility that affluent states ought to bear for the results of this system of inequality and injustice that is so entrenched in our notions of citizenship.

Shachar's alternative to the birthright models of jus soli and jus sanguinis is a model based on "genuine connection": *jus nexi*, which emphasizes the importance of societal participation and the relationships that follow from it. That is, what is important is "a tie between citizenship and the *social fact of membership* rather than blind reliance upon the accident of birth."[50] This model of allocating citizenship is meant to emphasize that "real and genuine ties fostered on the ground deserve some form of legal recognition."[51] What constitutes such ties? In Shachar's account and those of the scholars she draws on, genuine connection develops through residence, community, economic involvement, political participation, and so on. While many immigrants may develop such sites of connection over time, such an approach suggests a relatively narrow notion of connection. In contrast, Young's notion of political responsibility requires us to take into account "a complex set of structural relations across the globe which condition the material circumstances and possibilities for action of most of the world's people."[52] While the extent of such connections may seem unending, if we leave intact the immigration policies of the United States, there is a finite number of noncitizens in need of welfare assistance for whom such responsibilities can be fulfilled.[53] This is not to say that to provide social welfare services to a select group of immigrants is to discharge all responsibilities we may have as arbitrarily privileged possessors of birthright citizenship in a wealthy nation. It begins to move, however, in the direction of correcting the structural inequalities of birthright citizenship.

Arguably, providing immigrants with basic social rights, as welfare services are meant to do, enables them to act autonomously—to resist injustice and to contribute to facilitating the collective action necessary to move in the direction of transforming the institutions and practices that create this injustice. In this vein, in the following section I argue that where welfare is available to immigrants—where the state begins to fulfill its responsibility to immigrants—the act of claiming welfare becomes itself a form of political responsibility.

Welfare Claims as Political Responsibility

Young's account of political responsibility suggests that although responsibility may be greater or more accessible for those occupying positions of power or those enjoying access to privilege, we need not think of oppression or relative powerlessness as antithetical to taking responsibility. Rather, Young explains, "those who can properly be argued as victims of structural injustice can be called to a responsibility they share with others in the structures to engage in actions directed at transforming the structures."[54] In this model, it is possible for immigrants living in the United States to take responsibility, in some form, for resisting the injustices they face as those on the losing end of systems of birthright citizenship. Paradoxically, the act of taking such responsibility may come in the form of just what anti-immigrant proponents of PRWORA suggest defines a failure of personal responsibility: laying claim to welfare rights. In this regard, Lynn Fujiwara's account of the effects of welfare reform on Southeast Asian refugees living in the Bay Area proves particularly instructive. First, because these migrants are subject to a failure on the part of the United States and its citizens to fulfill their shared responsibility to these individuals, the women and men in Fujiwara's ethnography do not readily fit with the model of "personal responsibility" embedded in the assumptions underlying PRWORA. Second, through their claims to welfare, their resistance to the cuts made under PRWORA, and their juxtaposition of welfare receipt against the threat of perceived *failures* in familial responsibility, these immigrants demonstrate an alternative formulation of political responsibility that challenges our assumptions regarding autonomy, dependence, and responsibility.

Before the reforms of the 1990s, refugee policy in the United States could be seen as one instance of American acknowledgment of collective responsibility for the plight of migrants. In *Mothers Without Citizenship*, Fujiwara explains the relationship between refugee policy and American actions in Vietnam, Cambodia, and Laos. In Laos, American military forces organized mercenary armies of Hmong tribesmen, who were then imperiled when those troops left the area and the tribesman and their families were identified as allies of the United States. After the airlifting of some Hmong to Thailand, more than 10,000 individuals remained on the ground, vulnerable to retaliation by the Laotian government. Ultimately, Fujiwara writes, the United States admitted 130,400 refugees from Southeast Asia, beginning in 1975.[55] A subsequent "wave" of refugees arrived from Southeast Asia in the 1980s and later, some for purposes of family reunification.

At first, Southeast Asian refugees arriving in the United States in the 1970s were seen as "freedom fighters" who had escaped the evils of communism and therefore warranted "calculated kindness" from the American government.[56] This sentiment, however, did not last. The evolution of American governmental and popular attitudes toward these refugees shows us that, upon closer examination, the actual rationale for the structure of refugee policy in the United States is less rooted in a sense of collective responsibility for U.S. actions abroad than it is something of a reward or gratuity given to foreigners who have directly furthered U.S. interests.[57] Moreover, the *erosion* of this sense of responsibility over time, culminating in the 1996 reforms, reflects the highly situational and particular nature of this relationship, which therefore cannot be understood as lasting recognition of interdependence.

Fujiwara points to the high levels of poverty and social assistance among Southeast Asians who migrated to the United States. High unemployment rates and limitations on health, language, and job skills contribute to this phenomenon. With the pressures emerging from the recession of the 1980s, the freedom fighter characterization was lost, and instead public resentment regarding welfare dependence was aimed at Southeast Asian refugees, drawing on the same themes that shape antiwelfare rhetoric in the United States more broadly, such as "'learned dependency,' 'freeloading laziness,' and 'irresponsibility.'"[58] Such sentiments brought public support to the immigrant provisions of the 1996 welfare reforms. Constrained by the factors above and high rates of posttraumatic stress disorder, the loss of benefits that followed from PRWORA posed a grave threat to Southeast Asian refugees, some of whom were left in a desperate situation.

The story of Chia Yang, retold by Fujiwara in *Mothers without Citizenship*, highlights the disturbing and distorted ways that notions of *personal* responsibility and individualistic accounts of autonomy are deployed in welfare reform rhetoric. Faced with the loss of her benefits, Yang, a fifty-four-year-old Hmong woman, became increasingly distraught when she first received warning that she would lose her Supplemental Security Income benefits and then that her food stamp allocation would be cut in half. Ultimately Yang committed suicide, leaving behind a note that expressed her feelings of despair and loss, directly tied to the loss of her livelihood and its effect on her family. Another Hmong immigrant, Ye Vang, also took her life in response to what she experienced as a threat to her survival. These tragic stories speak to the devastation caused by PRWORA's immigration provisions, but they also make an important point about the notion of responsibility at work within the community of Southeast Asian refugees that Fujiwara's study describes. According to Fujiwara, "In each suicide resulting from welfare reform, the distraught person perceived the burden she or he might become on the family to be more taxing and detrimental than the curse caused by suicide."[59]

With this explanation of the sentiments behind such a drastic response to welfare reform—a response that, though not widespread, reflected a concern that *was* indeed widely held—an interesting notion of responsibility arises. The U.S. government withdrew its earlier sense of duty to those who had fought on its behalf or aided in its military efforts in some way, now demanding "personal responsibility" from these refugees who had "chosen" to take up residence in the country. Yet it was government support—welfare—that had in fact enabled Southeast Asian refugees to access the autonomy necessary to have a sense of responsibility, rather than rendering their children and families responsible for them. But such a logical construction of the relationships at hand makes sense only when autonomy is understood relationally and as potentially consistent with dependence. Had such an understanding been employed in the policies and politics that led to PRWORA, relationally conceived notions of autonomy and responsibility would turn the rhetoric of welfare reform on its head. Dependence on the state can actually foster autonomy, and in turn, laying claim to this assistance can be seen as a form of taking responsibility for oneself *within the context* that these refugees faced—one marked by the physical and mental effects of participation in U.S.-led military campaigns and shaped by the lack of job and language skills necessary to live independently in this foreign land. The relationship between welfare dependence, autonomy, and responsibility can be seen as one not of contradiction but of interdependence.

But it is not just by rearticulating immigrants' welfare dependence as an expression of personal responsibility that we can challenge the underlying assumptions of PRWORA. By drawing on Young's notion of political responsibility, it is possible to conceive of immigrants, disadvantaged by their birthright citizenship and seeking to remedy that disadvantage through migration, as taking political responsibility *by claiming welfare*. Such claims can be understood as acts that challenge structural inequalities, foster redistributive policies that force affluent states to take responsibility for their actions, and bring to public debate the typically unquestioned assumptions held about the appropriate *desert* of citizens and noncitizens.

In the wake of these suicides, Fujiwara's ethnography reports, Southeast Asian immigrants in the Bay Area mobilized, fighting back against the cuts that threatened to deny them benefits that they had long relied on—a denial that was seen as a significant betrayal on the part of the U.S. government. Having once cooperated with the CIA and other American agencies, Southeast Asian refugees voiced their discontent publicly. According to Fujiwara, "Elderly Southeast Asian refugee women and veterans held signs that said REMEMBER US? WE ARE THE CIA, AND WE WANT OUR FOOD STAMPS."[60] Further demonstrations and public testimony drew media attention across the country. The disturbing discrepancy between promises made by the U.S. government at the time and the present denial of the rights associated with those promises began to raise public ire. In 1998, President Clinton signed into law the Agriculture Research, Extension, and Education Reform Act. The bill provided a remedy that restored food stamps to Hmong and Laotian veterans and their families. Though not all benefits were restored and Hmong and Laotian veterans were not given official veteran status, Fujiwara writes that "the extraordinary efforts by Southeast Asian veterans to publicly state their grievances, as rightfully deserving the public assistance from which they were cut, challenged the racial and gendered emasculation that denied them their veteran status."[61] More broadly, I would add, these immigrants' resistance to the PRWORA cuts and their subsequent use of the semi-restored benefits amounts to "taking political responsibility." Challenging not only the gendered notions of veteran status and desert, the men and women who fought back against these cuts challenged the larger structure of unjust allocations of birthright citizenship. This unjust structure puts aliens in a constant state of vulnerability. As Bosniak notes, by definition "an alien is a person who is present in a state's territory only conditionally."[62] Moreover, the tendency of popular anti-immigrant stances to shift the "political tides" and threaten immigrants' survival heightens this vulnerability further.[63] By both resisting benefit-loss and laying claim to these benefits, immigrants can be seen as claiming political responsibility.

It may seem that the case of Southeast Asian refugees is not necessarily representative of the context within which all immigrants make welfare benefit claims: their refugee status, the particularly military history within which they were embroiled, and the specifically collective actions that fostered their claims to political responsibility are distinct from other examples of immigrant welfare claims. Though not all immigrant welfare claims are unambiguously "political," the case Fujiwara describes is not an isolated example of such political consciousness, even if this consciousness is often mediated by factors shaping the context within which welfare claims are made. In their study of

Latina immigrants in Long Beach, California, Marchevsky and Theoharis suggest that rather than being "just 'subjects of experience,'" the women they interviewed "develop their own analyses of the structure of the labor market, the ways that race and gender position them within it, as well as a sharp critique of how others benefit from these structural arrangements." For example, one of their interviewees points to American reliance on cheap Latino labor. She says, "It's Latinos that are sustaining the United States. . . . And for us Latinos, they [employers] see that we are desperate and that we will work for whatever they pay us." Other interviewees offered critiques of the exploitative nature of workfare programs; as one woman suggests, "With the new changes in welfare . . . they're forcing people to take jobs where they don't pay them well and where they are being exploited." Another woman interviewed by Marchevsky and Theoharis challenges exclusionary American attitudes toward Latinas by highlighting the historical annexation of Mexican land by the U.S. government.[64]

These examples from Marchevsky and Theoharis's *Not Working* provide instances of welfare claims made in a context of collective resistance to perceived structural injustice. But within the same study, and in other scholars' research findings, a seemingly contrary trend has emerged: even among immigrant women who are still eligible for welfare benefits (like the women mentioned above), there has been a decline in welfare claims. Such declines are not accompanied by rising income levels among the immigrant population.[65] Explaining this phenomenon, Marchevsky and Theoharis describe widespread misconceptions of eligibility rules for welfare among Latina women in their study, resulting in many eligible women failing to claim needed and *legally* available benefits. Caseworkers, themselves subject to increasingly constraining surveillance, sometimes directly fostered the dispersion of such misinformation. The "systematic denial of applications from eligible immigrants, and widespread removal of existing immigrant recipients from the welfare rolls," consolidated the "chilling effect" of welfare reform on legally entitled immigrant women and their children.[66] In the study described above, those who did seek out benefits were often subject to work conditions that were falsely presented as legally required.

In addition to this chilling effect, a number of the women Marchevsky and Theoharis interviewed embraced the ideology of personal responsibility. Even where their decisions whether to claim welfare seemed to be shaped by heavily coercive elements of the social welfare delivery system, they framed their actions in the context of individual choice.[67]

The existence of the chilling phenomenon and the acceptance of the ideology of personal responsibility that Marchevsky and Theoharis find speak to the conditions necessary for eligible immigrants to engage in welfare claims making as a form of taking political responsibility. An important factor in the ability of the "victim" to take political responsibility must be the degree to which those with comparatively more social, political, and economic power do the same.[68] In the current immigrant-hostile context of the United States, such support is hardly ubiquitous. In the case of the Southeast Asian refugees, the convergence of a number of factors, particularly the link between military service, patriotism, and citizenship, made such support more likely.[69] In the context of the nativist discourses that were gaining strength at the time that Marchevsky and Theoharis were conducting their study, and particularly in the context of the anti-Latino sentiments in Southern California (and elsewhere), the lack of supporting claims to political responsibility by those with greater power sheds light on why the frame of political responsibility may at times fit awkwardly with immigrant welfare claims (or lack thereof).

Despite the fact that it would be misleading to conceive of all immigrant welfare claims making as acts of taking political responsibility, where supportive shared responsibility is taken by those with greater resources and power, such a reframing usefully challenges the assumptions underlying PRWORA's immigrant provisions. Moreover, it reminds us of the political nature of welfare claims, and thus of the potential for such claims to be understood as forms of resistance. Like many citizens, as discussed in chapter 1, noncitizens may interact with the state most often through street-level bureaucracies, including welfare offices.[70] At these sites, Joe Soss writes of citizens, welfare claims making becomes an act of "survival politics": "It emerges out of interpersonal processes of mobilization and takes root in informal community networks that provide individuals with resources needed for survival."[71] In a similar vein, Marchevsky and Theoharis describe immigrant women's "most concrete and regular experience with the state" as taking place in welfare offices, which "become a stage for daily struggles over entitlement, citizenship, and rights."[72] Where those around them, particularly those who are privileged by birthright citizenship, take shared political responsibility, so, too, can immigrants claim welfare as an act of political responsibility that seeks to challenge the unjust social structures that hinder them. While immigrant welfare claims do not rectify the injustices created by the system of birthright citizenship—such a shift would require much greater changes in both citizenship policies and global economic and political power structures—they do provide a means of resisting the effects of this system, perhaps motivating more significant, long-term change down the line.

Conclusion

Like the new paternalist programs emerging from PRWORA, the restrictions on immigrants that are a part of this legislation limit the capacities for autonomy for welfare recipients (and those now unable to become welfare recipients). Whereas new paternalist programs are founded on faulty assumptions regarding the relationship between paid work and women's autonomy, PRWORA's immigration restrictions are rooted in a problematic notion of personal responsibility that is itself founded on an individualistic, atomistic notion of autonomy. For both of these facets of PRWORA, the foundations of the programs at hand serve to exclude members of a community from access to the relational and material resources necessary to exercise autonomy. In the case of restrictions on immigrant access to welfare, the failure of the state to acknowledge and enact its shared political responsibility further undermines the assertion that immigrants who seek out welfare upon arrival in the United States are exhibiting a failure of responsibility.

In this chapter, I have argued that the personal responsibility foundation of PRWORA's immigration restrictions can be discredited by drawing attention to the global context within which immigration decisions are made and the ensuing shared responsibility that affluent countries must take for the factors that shape these decisions. Further, I have argued that more than just acknowledging the distorted nature of calls for personal responsibility without acceptance of shared responsibility, we can reframe immigrants' welfare claims themselves as *acts of taking political responsibility*. This reframing brings to the fore the ways that claiming assistance from the United States, given its location within the global economy and its role in global politics, serves to challenge the existing structure of birthright citizenship—which perpetuates the arbitrary allocation of citizenship without any means of compensating those unduly harmed in the process. Resisting their relegation to the margins of society based on their alien status, immigrants who claim welfare also make a claim for inclusion based on genuine connection, which I have suggested extends far beyond those in our national community.

Although some immigrant restrictions have been removed from PRWORA since its enactment in 1996, for those who still lack access to welfare benefits, this legislation signifies both a woeful failure of the state to take shared political responsibility and an ironic limitation on immigrants' ability to claim responsibility—albeit a different sort of responsibility than that most commonly referred to by advocates of welfare reform.

5 "COORDINATED FRAGMENTATION" AND DOMESTIC VIOLENCE SERVICES

Introduction

Together, two important strands of recent work in feminist political theory point to the need to reconsider the structure of the relationship between the state and the (gendered) citizen. First, as I explore throughout the book, feminists have challenged individualistic notions of autonomy that ignore the constitutive role played by social relationships in its development and exercise. Second, an increasing appreciation of the complexities of the state has emerged in feminist work, with monolithic interpretations of the state increasingly falling out of favor.[1] Insofar as the relationship between state and citizen is one of those constitutive relationships highlighted by the feminist relational account of autonomy, the now more-nuanced feminist accounts of the state should consider the possibilities for autonomy-enabling relationships to emerge. We need an alternative theory of the state in order to integrate the relational account of autonomy with the various other complexities now highlighted in feminist accounts. As the previous two chapters have demonstrated, a flawed notion of the autonomous self has grave implications for the ability of the state to deliver social services in an autonomy-fostering manner. In the case of new paternalist programs, assumptions about preconditions for autonomy that exclude relations of care and, in particular, familial relations from the realm of potentially enabling factors lead to programs that achieve neither their own goals nor the goal of fostering autonomy more broadly. In the case of PRWORA's restrictions on immigrants, the assumption that welfare dependence and autonomy—and, in turn, responsibility—are incompatible leads to harmful limitations that actually prevent both individuals and society from "taking responsibility." By "reading" service delivery models that successfully engage in an enabling form of service delivery, in this chapter and the next I show how integrating what I have argued is a more inclusive and realistic notion of autonomy into a complex theory of the state offers us alternatives to the problematic models discussed thus far in the book.

In the pages that follow, I conceptualize the state as a fragmented and plural entity comprising various loosely coupled[2] arms that are sometimes in conflict with one another. Given this conceptualization, the notion of a "coordinated fragmented" state helps us to understand the dynamics that may, or may not, enable the state to foster autonomy, where autonomy refers to an individual's capacity to determine his or her own life plans. I come to this understanding of the state by examining a particular mode of service delivery for survivors of domestic violence, "coordinated community response" (CCR) programs. CCRs, I argue, take advantage of the tensions inherent in the state in a way that allows them to foster autonomy more effectively than conventional forms of service delivery. In articulating this vision of the state through an analysis of how CCRs can effectively harness its multiple and contradictory aims, I also describe the larger notion of the "autonomy-fostering state," a conception of the state as a set of fragmented but coordinated arms that may work together to foster autonomy in our most vulnerable citizens. In the context of such a state, as the CCR model shows, feminist commitments to particularity and partiality have the potential for realization. Moreover, within the multiplicity that defines CCRs, a balance is struck between the care-oriented aspects of the state[3] and those more committed to notions of "impartial" reason. This balance is made effective partly because of the mechanisms of self-critique extant in the fragmented coordinated state—mechanisms that can be responsive to feminist critiques of impartiality and universalism.

Though many feminist accounts of the state reject the view that sees it as purely a constraining means of social control, Wendy Brown is skeptical of feminist projects that call on the state to support their emancipatory aims.[4] Even as the distribution of power and resources has shifted to alter the relationship between individual men and women in our society, Brown suggests, the state has come to wield great (masculinist) power over women's lives, rendering "male" power as potent as ever. Yet, by framing the state as necessarily threatening to women's autonomy, views like Brown's all but rule out the possibility of an autonomy-enabling relationship between state and citizen, and they lose sight of the intricacies revealed by a relational approach. The notion of the coordinated fragmented state is not only conversant with theorists who recognize the complexities of the state, but also provides one of the tools necessary to take on the challenge presented by theorists like Brown.

The issue of domestic violence is a particularly appropriate location at which to theorize this revised notion of the state and service delivery. For many years, feminists struggled to move the issue of domestic violence from the "private" sphere to the "public" sphere. Though this struggle has proved successful—the state recognizes domestic violence as a serious public offense and pursues and punishes offenders—the appropriate role of the state in the lives of women survivors is still a contentious issue. The fear that increasing women's dependence on the state for protection may imperil women's autonomy is widespread in both academic work and within the movement against domestic violence. I offer an approach to theorizing the state that helps us to reconcile state intervention and relational autonomy without forgoing the important aim of publicizing domestic violence.

CCRs encompass "a system of networks, agreements, processes, and applied principles created by the local shelter movement, criminal justice agencies, and human service programs."[5] This system is built around a community approach to domestic violence that draws on multiple resources, including police, legal practitioners, housing services, financial and employment services, advocacy services, and mental and physical health services. Advocates of this model suggest that without such coordination, "batterers will take advantage of the fragmentation, misunderstanding, and bias of the criminal justice system to avoid prosecution and subsequent consequences for their acts of violence, often further isolating, manipulating, and controlling their victims in order to do so."[6] In contrast, CCRs acknowledge and respond to the systems of power relations in which service users are embedded, and which may compromise their autonomy.

In order to elucidate the nature of this distinctive mode of service delivery and the notion of fragmented coordination, I will proceed as follows. First I lay the groundwork for the rest of the chapter as I build on the relational account of autonomy that underpins the arguments in this book more generally, presenting a broad account of the coordinated fragmented state. I then describe coordinated community response programs. The following section recapitulates the debates over one particularly controversial aspect of CCRs: mandatory arrest and prosecution policies, which require that all cases with sufficient evidence proceed through the criminal justice system. These debates highlight the perceived conflict between publicity and autonomy in the context of service delivery. Moreover, they bring to the fore the distinction between a

substantive and procedural account of autonomy. Whereas procedural accounts of autonomy usually require only certain processes of self-reflection or
higher-order endorsement of preferences, substantive accounts of autonomy
require that autonomous action be consistent with certain normative conditions (e.g., those that are consistent with the *value* of autonomy itself). Finally,
focusing in particular on the balance that emerges between ethics of care and
justice under this model, I explain how CCRs put the notion of fragmented
coordination into practice, and therefore effectively foster autonomy.

Complicating Autonomy and the State

In order to conceptualize the autonomy-fostering state, we must rethink conventional notions of not only the state but also autonomy. Moreover, it is not
only dominant narratives of the atomistic, unencumbered individual located
within a supposedly neutral, universalizing state that must be called into question, but also some of the more severe feminist critiques of the state and their
implicit notions of autonomy.

Questions regarding domestic violence services bring debates over the relationship between intervention, nonintervention, and autonomy to the fore—
debates that lie at the center of my concerns with a relational conception of
autonomy in this book. Some writers suggest that the publicization of domestic violence and the ensuing intervention of the state severely limit women's
autonomy. For some, such a loss is a price that must be paid for the now-*public*
treatment domestic violence receives, while for others it is intolerable. But
such an analysis mistakenly equates autonomy with privacy; the erection of
boundaries around the individual is seen as a viable means to achieving autonomy.[7] Whereas autonomy is best understood as developed in the context of
relations to others, this boundary-focused notion of autonomy reproduces an
untenable and unrealistic notion of atomistic man. In addition to obscuring
the fundamentally interdependent nature of human beings, it also suggests
the desirability of what can plainly be seen as both impossible and *un*desirable: existence in a vacuum that somehow entirely restricts incursions into
any and all aspects of the individual's life.

In contrast to this unrealistic notion of autonomy, the contextual and relational conception of autonomy that emerges from the feminist critique is the
basis for Marilyn Friedman's understanding of an autonomous person as "one
who has these capacities [for autonomy] and exercises them at least occasion-

ally." For example, the experience of being a survivor of domestic violence or of finding oneself compelled to conform to certain regulations established by the state (even contrary to one's will) does not exclude the possibility of an autonomous life, "one lived by someone who has the capacities for autonomy and is able to exercise them frequently over a substantial stretch of time."[8] Indeed, in the case of the state's regulations, this instance of coercion may ultimately make the autonomous life more feasible.

What kind of state can actively foster such a relational notion of autonomy? For an important aspect of such a revisioned state, I turn to the sociologist Lynne Haney. She takes up a concept used by the criminologist John Hagan: the state as a loosely coupled system. Trying to make sense of the conflicts, tensions, and even contradictions of the modern state, she argues that feminists can use this notion to "make sense of the diversity of gender regimes within particular state apparatuses." This helps us to see the state as a series of different arenas linked to one another (in varying degrees). Haney's objective is to urge feminists to theorize "the nature of the links within state subsystems," complicating feminist state analysis beyond those oriented, for example, wholly toward a "social control" model of Brown's masculinist state.[9] I argue that in some cases it is the "looseness" of the linkages, visible by way of conflicting perspectives in a given mode of service delivery, that serves to foster autonomy more effectively than is possible within more tightly bound systems. The latter systems may not have the mechanisms to mediate the types of tensions that are particularly relevant for questions of autonomy.

Using Haney's concept of loose coupling alongside my analysis of the workings of the linkages that constitute these couplings, we can begin to configure a feminist theory of the (autonomy-fostering) state. This theory runs contrary to the model of the state as primarily or solely an agent of social control and male dominance, a model that has made some feminists reluctant to view the state as an ally in feminist struggles. Though individual power relations between men and women have shifted, social control theorists like Brown claim that the effects of male power have hardly been neutralized. Brown writes, "[The state] mediates or deploys almost all the powers shaping women's lives— physical, economic, sexual, reproductive, and political—powers wielded in previous epochs directly by men." The state's various arms, she writes, are collectively involved in a "politics of protection," an exclusionary system of regulation that hinges on the claim that women require the protection of men. This protection, she charges, provides women with a choice between the arbitrary force of violence, harassment, discrimination, deprivation, and a host of other typically gender-based forms of oppression on the one hand—not the least of which is domestic violence against women—and what she refers to as "rationalized, procedural unfreedom" on the other hand. Given these circumscribed options, Brown argues that to turn to the state to foster the autonomy of (vulnerable) women is inherently misguided, for it "involves seeking protection *against* men *from* masculinist institutions, a move more in keeping with the politics of feudalism than freedom."[10]

In Brown's account, the nature of the domination exerted by the masculinist state is equally, if not more, constraining than the oppression women have long faced at the hands of individual men. She argues that despite its appearance of neutrality and its intangible vastness, the state is a highly masculinized set of practices, institutions, and discourses. Explaining what she interprets as the essentially masculinist nature of the state, Brown writes, "The state can be masculinist without intentionally or overtly pursuing the 'interests' of men precisely because the multiple dimensions of socially constructed masculinity have historically shaped the multiple modes of power circulating through the domain called the state—this is what it means to talk about masculinist power rather than the power of men." The oppressive power of the masculinist state as conceptualized by Brown is exacerbated by the dependence of (American) women, who are, she notes, now dependent on the state for their survival in unprecedented numbers.[11]

Brown's exposition of protection as the exploitation and misappropriation of power held over the vulnerable is deeply pessimistic, as it almost entirely closes the door to state-centered solutions to women's subordination. Rather than abandoning the state as a source of protection, I argue that we might instead reconsider which practices we include as "protection," especially since protection can be read in relation to the explicit enabling of the capacity for autonomy. Despite the ways that "protection" has so far manifested itself in the masculinist arms of the state, elsewhere in the complicated and plural state we *can* find instances of alternative manifestations of protection. Domestic violence emerges as a poignant example of where the need for protection is evident, and where the possibilities—especially when we examine the model of the CCR—for autonomy fostering, even in the context of dependence, can be realized. Although Brown acknowledges that the state is complex and has multiple functions, she does not provide a comprehensive analysis of the effect of this multiplicity on such appeals to the state for protection. I argue that the tensions and even contradictions between the various arms of the state, which

CCRs acknowledge and harness, may prove *useful* for feminist aims when they are exploited effectively.[12]

Pointing to the importance of conceptualizing the multiplicity of the state, and the configuration of this multiplicity at given points in time, Haney suggests that it is "fruitful to conceive of the state as fragmented and layered, with various sites of control and resistance."[13] With this *fragmentation* a productive balance emerges. Whereas some arms of the state pursue care-based forms of service delivery, others attend to more traditional justice-based forms, and hybrids of these forms emerge in still other arms. But this variety alone does not establish the autonomy-fostering state; rather, it is a *coordinated* fragmentation that brings about such a possibility. The role of coordination in the fragmented state is extremely important. Fragmentation of the state can undermine accountability, yield a lack of coherent agendas in various policy realms, and ultimately lead to failures in serving citizens.[14] In the case I discuss in this chapter, it is in fact the nature and location of the coordinating body that makes fragmentation beneficial rather than detrimental to service users.

The emphasis on coordination flags two important aspects of this model of the state. First, despite their different and contradictory aims, various arms of the state may adapt, evolve, or shift their modes of service delivery in response to the other arms of the state with which they are connected via a coordinating body, the nature of which will depend on the particular service to be delivered. In this sense, fragmentation allows for a plurality of approaches to service delivery, each potentially structuring their relationships to the service user in different autonomy-enabling configurations; coordination, in turn, links these different arms together in such a way that they offset one another's (often) otherwise-unitary understandings of the ideal approach to service delivery. Second, and of particular importance, the conflicts that the fragmentation of the state inevitably leads to are important "checks" on potentially paternalistic and confining modes of service delivery that may crop up within some arms. But such conflicts become "checks" only in the context of some mode of coordination that institutionalizes processes of evaluation and resolution. With this mechanism in place, the coordinated fragmented state is endowed with something like a mode of immanent self-critique. Combining accommodation to a plurality of approaches to service delivery, which inevitably shape one another, and the mode of immanent self-critique fostered by the unavoidable conflict of the fragmented state, a theory of the coordinated fragmented state complicates feminist understandings of the state, particularly in its service-delivery role.

While abstract in the foregoing pages, the example of CCRs developed below fleshes out the contours of one version of a service delivery system that, in theory, effectively coordinates the fragmented state. In doing so, it begins to approximate the ideal of the autonomy-fostering state.

Coordinated Community Responses: From "Bad" Victims to Multifaceted System

After a decades-long struggle to bring the issue of domestic violence to the attention of the community, removing it from the shadows of the so-called "private sphere" and into the domain of the state (in particular, the criminal justice system), the women's movement succeeded in fundamentally changing public response to this gendered form of violence. By the 1980s, Melanie Shepard and Ellen Pence write, the movement had successfully argued that the state has an obligation to intervene in "personal" relationships and "private" homes, protect women from batterers, and arrest and prosecute such perpetrators.[15] Yet, despite these victories, advocates of battered women were frustrated by the lack of implementation of the state's expanded powers. In addition to state actors who failed to take seriously the issue of domestic violence and held otherwise sexist beliefs, even those committed to taking domestic violence against women seriously were often disillusioned by their limited ability to prosecute such cases effectively. Survivors of domestic violence frequently refused to testify against their batterers, and substantial evidence against the batterer was often hard to produce and defend. Although increased criminal justice intervention still represented significant progress, advocates were finding that the strategy often failed.

Explaining this failure, Pence and Shepard point to the structural disjuncture between domestic violence as a gendered phenomenon of power and control and the criminal justice system as an incident- and individual-focused mechanism for achieving justice. Because of this mismatch, survivors of domestic violence were often seen as "bad victims" because "domestic assault needs to be understood in terms of ongoing patterns of behavior rather than as a single criminal act or incident."[16] The *contextual* variables out of which specific incidents arise are often more telling than any particular incident. This coheres with an understanding of domestic violence as a systemic issue that reflects gender oppression in society as a whole but is instantiated in particular and concrete acts of violence experienced by actual women. For many survivors, such violence drastically constrains autonomy via their relationships to their abusers *and* by the failing criminal justice system. Cognizant that a different approach was required in order both to resist the social conditions that make domestic violence possible in our society and to foster autonomy in survivors of domestic violence, advocates formulated an alternative approach: the CCR. Organized by a coordinating institutional body, CCRs attempt to overcome the aspects of the criminal justice system that are conceptually and practically ill suited to respond to domestic violence, where it is understood as an ongoing attempt to gain power and control over individual women within the context of unequal power relations, stratified across gendered lines.

Pence and McMahon describe the fragmentation of agencies and individuals involved in domestic violence cases as a key motivating factor for the development of the CCR model. This fragmentation can often depersonalize and distance the case from the actual survivor's experience—the woman becomes a "case"—while reproducing unequal power relations not only between the batterer and the survivor, but also between the survivor and the bureaucratic system with which she is now engaged. Pence and McMahon write, "Individual women's experiences of violence become translated into and 'absorbed' by bureaucratically sanctioned, objectifying accounts, designed for 'case management' and the control of those people who are part of 'the case.'" During this process, they explain, "officially sanctioned 'knowledge' is expressed in terms of management-relevant categories and becomes part of the way power works in the reproduction of gender inequality." Coordination of services—orchestrated by often explicitly feminist organizations, such as the Domestic Abuse Intervention Programs (DAIP) in Duluth—aims to overcome the relations of domination exacerbated by the bureaucracy's orientation toward expertise. Instead, the focus is shifted back to the survivors' own experiences, in particular their safety. They explain that "the DAIP reduces the consequences of bureaucratic fragmentation by promoting the coordination of the activities of the different agencies around the practical goal of victim safety."[17]

Coordinated community response programs are often mistakenly associated *solely* with mandatory arrest and no-drop prosecution policies. These policies were developed in response to the limited success the criminal justice system found in arresting and prosecuting batterers, often due to the perceived lack of cooperation of survivors in the process. Seeing this problem as a result of the coercive behavior of batterers, most states have passed laws that mandate battered women's participation in prosecution and that require police to arrest when they see evidence of assault. I describe this controversial aspect of CCRs in detail in the next section. It is important to keep in mind, however, that mandatory procedures are *not* synonymous with CCRs in their entirety, as is sometimes suggested. Instead, as explained by Pence and Sheppard, successful CCRs include a strong base of services for battered women.[18] These include shelter and housing services, employment services, primary health care services, children's programs, counseling, and individual, legal, and institutional advocacy. These aspects of the CCR are administered by a variety of partners in the system, extending well beyond the criminal justice system, yet still acting on behalf of the state.

Public Gains, Private Losses? Autonomy and Mandatory Policies

As suggested above, the nature of domestic violence has often made effective criminal justice intervention difficult. Many supporters understand mandatory policies as both a further manifestation of the shifting understanding of domestic violence as public rather than private, and a response to the shortcomings of conventional methods used by police and prosecutors. In this section, after briefly laying out the dynamics of public and private that have shaped the movement against domestic violence, I describe how this analysis is linked to the advent of mandatory policies. I consider both critiques and defenses of mandatory policies. The former are often founded in claims regarding affronts to women's autonomy as a result of the increased role of the state, especially police, in women's lives, while the latter are often founded on the claim that publicity in such cases *warrants* some sacrifice of autonomy. I criticize the equation of privacy and autonomy that seems to frame both sides' arguments. I further suggest that attention to the difference between substantive and procedural autonomy, as well as to the *political* nature of individual autonomy, is important to clarifying this debate.

In the context of the feminist argument that the public/private division renders domestic violence private, individual, and episodic, feminists have lobbied for greater intervention by the criminal justice system. Supporters of mandatory policies suggest that they are necessary in order to uphold the state's responsibility to respond to these *public* wrongs enacted against the community and to ensure the eventual elimination of domestic violence.[19] On the other hand, some feminists have worried about mandatory arrest policies increasing state control of women's lives. This latter concern is part of a broader claim suggesting that these policies undermine and fail to recognize women's autonomy. Critics charge that, in assuming that the state is best able to make choices and determine "life plans" for survivors of domestic violence, these policies are paternalistic and reproduce the relations of domination already extant in the abusive relationship. Such policies assume that women's choices to stay with their batterers are "wrong" and often nonautonomous. Critics note, however, that women are often correct in predicting increased violence if they leave, that they may face a lack of access to material resources, and that they may incur problems with child custody.[20] Donna Coker argues that "[a] woman who opposes prosecution is taking a calculated risk, as is the woman who pursues prosecution."[21] A decision to stay or a desire to avoid prosecution can reflect autonomy, on Coker's terms. Even where norms of adherence to ideals of self-sacrifice and a desire to "save" one's partner motivate staying, survivors of domestic violence may be acting autonomously; that is, for Marilyn Friedman, they may be "living their lives in accord with norms that are evidently very important to them."[22]

On the other side of the debate, many feminists argue that policies mandating victim participation *do* protect women, individually and as a group, from subsequent acts of domestic violence. Though they may acknowledge that these policies compromise autonomy, they see women's interests and liberation as ultimately advanced by them. Cheryl Hanna's argument in favor of strong mandatory policies is framed around the significance of retaining the public understanding of domestic violence that such policies have reinforced.[23] While recognizing the tensions arising when state intervention is increased and individual women's choices removed, Hanna defends mandatory policies primarily on two grounds: First, mandatory policies, because they both remove the *responsibility* for action from the survivor and deny her the opportunity to choose a course of action, highlight state accountability for domestic violence, rejecting the notion that, as a private issue, individual women must deal with the problem themselves.[24] Second, publicity shifts the focus from the individual to the community by seeking to protect not only the woman in a given case, but also other women who may face abusers in the future. With regard to the loss of autonomy, Hanna claims, "such an infringement on her liberty is necessary to protect women overall."[25] If this process of publicization compromises autonomy, Hanna argues, it is worth the sacrifice.

Like Hanna, Friedman argues that "going public" is worth the sacrifice in autonomy. In the context of the social changes that advocates of battered women have sought to make (and continue to pursue), Friedman claims that "gaining respect for our autonomous—and our nonautonomous—preferences about how our abusers are to be treated ceases to be an overriding concern."[26] Instead, the publicity attained by introducing such measures *in itself* enhances women's access to citizenship. That is, "Citizenship transforms violence to oneself into an injury to the community of which one is a member."[27] Thus, Friedman concludes, "the deterrent and citizenship benefits to women [as a whole]" are worth the loss of autonomy such policies entail.

Disentangling Privacy and Autonomy: Reframing the Debate

Based on empirical evidence, it is difficult to resolve the debate over the utility, or peril, of state intervention in the form of mandated arrest and prosecution.[28] I return to the question of state intervention in the next section, where I argue that *in the context of CCRs*, state intervention, including mandatory policies, can be seen as autonomy fostering rather than as disempowering. But the debate over mandatory policies on their own highlights a problem with the frame of reference that many scholars use to ask and respond to questions regarding autonomy, the private/public distinction, and state "interference." In this section, I do not aim to resolve the debate over mandatory procedures, the contours of which have been extensively traversed, in particular in the law reviews. Instead, because my aim is to theorize a feminist conception of both autonomy and the autonomy-fostering state, I use this controversy to set up the conception of the state I develop in the next section. By paying attention to the distortion of the privacy-autonomy relationship that exists even in the feminist literature, we can reconceptualize the state in the more nuanced manner toward which feminist thinkers have already made great strides.

Arguments that equate the loss of privacy with the loss of autonomy perpetuate a problematic notion of autonomy. Indeed, in the case of domestic violence, the irony is that such a lack of intervention has been deeply constraining to our ability to protect and develop autonomy. With police historically treating battering as "noncriminal" and, when they did respond, rarely arresting the assailant, the pervading notion was that "women's bodies were the province of others, and women's bodily integrity within marriage was fictitious."[29] Women living under this system see their autonomy compromised in order to sustain their partner's autonomy. Privacy, here, is not equivalent to autonomy for battered women; indeed, the rejection of privacy as a shielding mechanism for the brutality of such acts against women has been a founding principle of the movement against domestic violence. Yet some feminist arguments have weakened the power of such publicity by equating it with the (necessary, they concede) loss of autonomy. This argument relies primarily on a procedural view of autonomy.[30] I argue that we can more usefully understand such interventions as mechanisms by which various arms of the state are engaged in the task of fostering *substantive* autonomy.

Substantive views of autonomy require that autonomy be consistent with certain conditions that go beyond the procedural requirements of, for example, self-reflection.[31] While some strong substantive theories require that autonomous individuals have the capacity to direct their own lives in accordance with specific values or norms, others are less stringent, requiring that one's autonomous decisions, preferences, or actions be formulated or taken in accord with broader content guidelines. For example, in a related account of responsibility, Benson suggests that "self-worth" is an ideal condition for evaluating standards of autonomy, especially in the context of oppressive socialization.[32] While self-worth may well be an appropriate substantive marker for discerning autonomous agency in many cases, I argue that the substance of autonomy is always constituted within a given political and social context. In this sense, establishing a specific substantive marker for autonomy may not be appropriately figured within a broad theory of the autonomy-fostering state. I want to endorse an alternative methodological approach to theorizing autonomy, emphasizing that the content of autonomy must necessarily be established with attention to the details of a given context. This is especially important given the risks of a substantive approach, which, figured wrongly (for a particular context), might be too restrictive or potentially marginalizing for certain individuals. Indeed, this account of a particular policy arena suggests one "space" within which the specificities of the substance of autonomy can be worked out. Such a methodological approach can be understood to follow a similar trajectory—moving back and forth between concrete intuitions and more general theories—to that which has been taken up by feminist theorists in their emphasis on the relevance of "experience."[33]

The importance of a substantive account, then, is vast, especially if our approach to it is rooted not in abstract values but in empirical realities. A substantive account of autonomy gives us the tools to criticize dominant social structures—including the misogynistic pursuit of power and control that characterizes domestic violence—that constrain the exercise of and limit the development of autonomy within a given political context. With the focus shifted from a politics of nonintervention to one of relationality, the substance of autonomy comes into view within a given context, allowing us to discern between contexts that appear to grant "free choice"[34] but maintain relations of domination and exclusion, and those that are genuinely supportive of autonomy.

The need for such scrutiny is evident in the case of domestic violence. Although it is uncontroversial to claim that women in battering relationships face added and intensified constraints on their autonomy, this does not mean that they are not or cannot be autonomous. Similarly, whereas the state's mandatory policies are coercive in many cases, their application does not imply that battered women who are subject to these policies are not autonomous. In each case, instances of coercion, domination, or limitation of available options compromise women's autonomy at a given moment. Yet neither negates the possibility of autonomy as a capacity developed *over* time that one exercises to varying degrees over the course of her life, nor does either case suggest that women cannot resist the constraints and oppression they may face.

In the case of domestic violence, some of the reasons why survivors may object to the arrest and prosecution of their violent partners are a function of gender socialization that runs counter to the value of autonomy. Whether these survivors believe that their abuse is warranted, that they will be bad mothers if they leave their abusive partners, or that they have a duty to help their partners overcome their "problem," we can reasonably assume that the pervasive gender norms that exist in our society are in some significant way responsible for generating such potentially self-injurious commitments. It is here that bringing the "substance" of autonomy into view allows us to make alternative normative claims.[35] That is, the reasons for staying reflect commitments that, in addition to being largely inconsistent with future autonomy, fail to reflect a number of values we see as reflecting a lack of autonomy (self-respect or self-preservation are two possible candidates among many). As Marina Oshana argues, referring to a case similar to that of the domestic violence survivor, "[Her] lack of autonomy is due to her social relations with others and to the social institutions of her society."[36] For Oshana, these social relations and institutions trump the expressed desire of an individual to stay in an oppressive situation. Her lack of autonomy reflects not her endorsement (or lack thereof) of her way of life, but rather her capacities to make decisions that shape the direction of her life.

An examination of the context within which women might endorse a decision to live in an abusive situation leads us to the intuition that such decisions are not made "freely," and that they are decisions that impose constraints in the present but that imply future access to autonomy. This *does not* mean that women who subscribe to such normative commitments are to blame for their continued abuse or that they are guilty, incompetent mothers, or lesser citizens. On the contrary, this reflects a deep acknowledgment of the insidious nature of domestic violence as a reflection of the oppressive gender norms that exist in our society.

I want to emphasize again that the substance of autonomy should be understood as contextual, contested, and political. That we can refer to the existence of oppressive gender norms as a means for ascertaining whether a decision is consistent with values of self-respect or self-preservation reflects the social and political context within which we formulate the substance of autonomy. This is not an argument for a relativistic account of the substance of autonomy; instead, it is meant to draw attention to the fact that this substance is socially constructed in given contexts and is therefore fluid and political. Insofar as a contextual notion of substantive autonomy highlights this socially constructed basis for evaluating what "counts" as autonomous, it should make us more reflexive about the potential pitfalls usually associated with substantive accounts of autonomy—for example, the claim that such accounts "say that we are autonomous only if related in certain idealized ways."[37] That there are ways we may be related that are most conducive to autonomy is inevitable; that certain among these are *idealized* is a function of the political and social context within which we exist, which points to their contested nature. But a notion of autonomy that exists in empirical and not just theoretical contexts will always be attached to some idealized relational contexts. Rendering these idealized relations conducive to a more just society rather than one that replicates unjust power dynamics is central to the practice of politics.

In addition to those circumstances where women may remain in abusive situations due to oppressive gender norms, it is important to note that women's reasons for resisting their partners' arrests and prosecutions are also based on *material* circumstances. The loss of the batterer's income and childcare support may be a threat to the family's livelihood, as may be the fear of retaliation by the batterer or the concern for the well-being of their children, whom these women view as better off with their fathers in their lives rather than in jail.[38] In these cases, neither the choice to remain in the relationship nor the choice to leave, or have the batterer extricated, is wholly consistent with future (substantive) autonomy; *both* options are potentially threatening to autonomy.

Despite the admittedly difficult dilemma that such an array of options poses for the survivor of domestic violence, it is still arguable that remaining in the battering relationship is most often a *greater* threat to autonomy than is facing the alternative material or familial barriers, considerable as they are in many cases. Domestic violence poses a real and persistent threat to women's lives. Research convincingly shows that such violence typically escalates as time passes. Approximately 30 percent of female homicide victims in the United States are killed by their current or former intimate partners.[39] To fail to acknowledge the threat to survival that domestic violence poses is to underestimate the seriousness of this crime perpetrated against women. Thus, although the reasons for staying in a battering relationship may reflect autonomy if they are concerned with preserving future autonomy, an autonomous decision in the final determination should reflect a choice that is *most* consistent with future autonomy and with the maximal possible realization of values associated with autonomy, such as self-respect or self-worth. It is useful to think of autonomy as existing on a continuum.[40] My account of autonomy does not deny these acts of autonomous agency; instead, it highlights the potentially greater autonomy possible where the batterer is removed.[41]

The forgoing analysis, then, suggests that the argument in defense of mandatory policies is more helpfully framed around a defense of autonomy. But such a defense makes sense only when we understand autonomy in the substantive sense. A procedural account will not provide us with the tools to distinguish between the options that are based on oppressive socialization and those that are not, or between those that are either more or less autonomy fostering in the long run. Rather than equating privacy and autonomy—a move that threatens to reproduce both individualistic notions of autonomy and idealized notions of privacy, both of which have historically *excluded* women—a focus on substantive autonomy as a *benefit* of publicization reframes the debate in a more helpful manner. Moreover, it is important to keep in mind that the substance of autonomy is itself negotiated and contested within a (political) context.

This reframing by no means resolves the dilemma posed by mandatory policies. Although I suggest that in most cases the negative outcomes of arrest—material and familial—are outweighed by the positive, there may be some instances where this is not the case. In some circumstances, the hardships associated with the batterer's arrest and with the state's intervention into women's lives may indeed turn out to be extremely destructive—even life threatening. Such cases indicate that the state's response is severely inadequate, and they highlight the fact that, on their own, mandatory policies do not solve the problems associated with domestic violence. The next section puts mandatory policies back into the context of coordinated community response programs. These programs can contribute the resources, material and relational, that are much more likely to make mandatory policies tolerable, and indeed to swing the balance in their favor with regard to concerns about autonomy.

Navigating the State: The Fragmented-Coordinated State in Practice

Commentators on domestic violence services have noted the importance of situating criminal justice responses to domestic violence within a framework of community care. Following these commentators, I argue that the tensions associated with mandatory arrest and prosecution in our current social and political context, while not resolved, are much more readily mediated when they emerge in the context of the diverse set of services of effective CCRs.[42] Though they note this possibility with some optimism, few provide an extensive analysis of why exactly this structure is promising: why does state service delivery in this form promote autonomy while other modes of state intervention pose serious threats to women's autonomy? I have argued above that the potentially autonomy-fostering state can be realized where the fragmented state is coordinated effectively. Here, I flesh out this claim by arguing that CCRs are effective because, via coordination, they "exploit" the fragmentation of the state. Although the CCR philosophy emphasizes coordination, the system still represents a fragmented patchwork of programs and institutions rather than a unitary "state" delivering services. By bringing together these programs and institutions, CCRs manage to effect a balance between justice and care, as well as between commitments to both impartiality and partiality. Moreover, the structure of this mode of service delivery reflects and acknowledges the political nature of service delivery. This politicization is critical to averting the threat of relations of domination often arising in service delivery contexts.

Fragmentation Meets Coordination: CCRs and the Loosely Coupled State

As my analysis of mandatory policies above suggests, it is only in the context of the other services offered (or not offered) by the state that we can judge the value of state intervention in the lives of survivors of domestic violence. In this case, where CCRs are administered adequately, the various arms of the state, which are sometimes in conflict with one another, may work to create an over-all *system* that has autonomy-fostering potential.

Above, I briefly described some of the key tenets and institutions of the CCR; let us now consider a brief sketch of their typical daily workings:[43]

- Jennifer and John's neighbors telephone the police to report a domestic dispute. The police dispatch officers to the specified location. At the scene, the police review evidence and interview the victim and assailant; they record evidence in a specific manner and ask particular questions, in keeping with the protocols that have been negotiated among law enforcement, advocates, community members, and others. For example, they ask about previous instances of abuse in order to document a pattern, and they note the presence of factors—for example, John's suicide threats or aggressive behavior toward household pets—that have been identified by domestic violence experts as evidence of "lethality" or particularly grave danger. In keeping with mandatory arrest policies, the police arrest John because there is evidence to suggest that a domestic assault has taken place: Jennifer has red marks on her face and there is broken glass on the floor. Her story about his attack is credible and supported by this evidence.

- Once the arrest has been made, the police contact advocates from a local organization and pass on information about the situation. The advocates record this information and then make contact with the survivor. At the survivor's home, the advocates ask her about the incident and the history of John's abuse. They allow her to relate her experience without imposing any particular framework or narrative on it. When she expresses her reluctance to leave the situation because of the welfare of her children, the advocates affirm the difficulty of the situation, while still noting that neither she nor her children deserve the abuse. The advocates provide her with some basic information about domestic violence and specific information about the services available in her community. Jennifer indicates that she is interested in a personal protection order; the advocates make note of this and a legal advocate from the organization contacts Jennifer to assist her with this process the next day. In the course of their discussions, Jennifer notes that when the police arrived at her home, one officer was particularly sarcastic, commenting on the fact that she had called them on other occasions and yet had allowed her husband to return home. This upset Jennifer and she suggests that it made her weary of telephoning the police. When John is released from jail on bail the next day, the police first call Jennifer to inform her (as agreed on by the members of the CCR), then they contact the advocates, who contact Jennifer to check in and help her with possible safety planning.

- In days following, a coordinator reads the advocates' report on this situation, and at a meeting of members of the CCR she raises the issue of ongoing reports of inappropriate police behavior. The police representative at the meeting pledges to address the issue among her staff. At the same meeting, a government representative solicits members of the coordinating body to participate in consultations regarding new sentencing recommendations for domestic violence offenses.

CCRs still involve arms of the state that may create exclusionary conditions through problematic conceptions of impartiality, and which may be paternalistic. As I suggest above, however, the coordinated fragmented state manages to overcome some of the perennial feminist critiques of service delivery by (1) accommodating a plurality of modes of service delivery that influence one another and (2) providing mechanisms that institute a mode of self-critique within the system. Concretely, the CCR model responds to feminist critiques of impartiality in two ways. First, in accordance with the potential influence of participating and coordinating organizations within the system, services under the umbrella of CCRs sometimes self-consciously act partially even *within* those institutions that conventionally understand themselves as impartial decision makers. Second, in capitalizing on the fragmented nature of the state, CCRs support the perpetual questioning of "impartial" decisions and procedures undertaken by the criminal justice and legal system via a system of institutionalized self-critique initiated by those arms of the state that are *outside* the impartiality-oriented "ethic of justice." In this sense, a critique of the impartiality-oriented aspects of the state is immanent within this mode of service delivery. Thus CCRs also respond to a key concern for those who are critical of the notion of a blindly neutral or impartial state: the seeming elimination of the need for democratic decision-making practices or politics itself. Rather, CCRs have "politics" embedded within their framework insofar as they embody the negotiation and compromise that define politics.

Nevertheless, on the surface, the criminal justice aspect of CCRs—the arena of mandatory policies—seems to be committed to notions of impartiality, applying one standard to all perpetrators of domestic violence, and hence to their victims. It is plausible, then, that such a framework might be seen as an instance of Wendy Brown's "rationalized, procedural unfreedom."[44] But other agencies involved in CCRs more closely approximate an ethic of care in their approach to service delivery, taking up an explicitly partial agenda. These institutions ideally seek to foster the relationships necessary to reintegrate women into their communities, once it is safe to do so. Perhaps most distinctive among the various care-based services offered within the framework of CCRs is the role of "advocacy" in this model of service delivery. Individual advocates offer support and guidance to survivors as they navigate the social institutions from which they require resources and protection to avoid further abuse.[45] Systems advocacy is aimed at institutional responses to battered women. On both fronts, advocates working with and on behalf of individual survivors provide the relational support that helps survivors to make decisions regarding their course of action following a reported incident of domestic violence. An important contrast emerges here: whereas the criminal justice system does not permit the survivor to guide the direction of its intervention, advocates may endorse a contrasting, and perhaps even conflicting, form of support that is directed by the wishes and needs of the survivor herself. That is, although the survivor does not have the option to prevent arrest (at least where the letter of the law is followed), there are other decisions to be made—whether to get a personal protection order, whether to leave the home and enter a shelter, whether to seek out legal assistance for possible separation or divorce proceedings, how to handle issues relating to children—that advocates can support in a noncoercive way, promoting women's autonomy.

How ought we understand the apparent conflict between the mode of service delivery that advocates subscribe to, and that of the criminal justice system, especially when these two may be closely linked within the structure of the CCR? For example, in the CCR responsible for Washtenaw County, Michigan, following police notification advocates intervene, providing support without directing the survivor toward any particular course of action. The training manual for advocates working in the Washtenaw program emphasizes that "[the survivor] is responsible for her own life decisions and the advocate's role is to help her tap her own strengths and abilities and to recognize and experience her potential as a woman."[46] There seems to be significant tension between this approach to noncoercive "empowerment" and the approach of the police, which applies the mandatory policy.

Yet, when we look more closely at the criminal justice arm of CCRs, the picture of mandatory arrest as an impartial policy embodying the values of justice is not entirely accurate. Rather, recall the plural yet mutually influencing nature of the coordinated fragmented state. In fact, there is a fair amount of (partial) attention to the particularity and lived experience of battered women even by the criminal justice system in this context, as it refocuses agents to recognize the power imbalances inherent in domestic violence cases. Although still reflecting many of the standard philosophical stances of the criminal justice state, we should not ignore the extent to which, by its very participation in the CCR, this arm of the state has acknowledged the unique power dynamic—the gendered pursuit of power and control—that characterizes domestic violence.

Moreover, the function of impartiality in the context of such attention to particularity may be different than a standard critique reveals. In the case of mandatory arrest, the impartiality of arrest and prosecution decisions—the mandate to proceed in all instances of domestic violence—actually protects the interests of the less powerful (namely, women) by putting the weight of the state behind her (instead of rendering her individually responsible for ending her abuse). Here, though initially assumed to embody aspirations to impartiality, given the feminist origins of these policies and the ongoing interaction between the criminal justice system and feminist advocates and agencies, mandatory policies may not be as rigidly committed to norms of impartiality as they appear.

Another way that CCRs complicate our notion of the power relations endemic to service delivery can be seen in the mechanisms of systems-level or institutional advocacy, mentioned briefly above. Here, a particularly clear picture of the dynamics of self-critique emerges. Thelen describes systems advocacy as "an effort to reform institutional responses to battered women, collectively, so that the totality of their experience is taken into account, leading to greater safety for victims and greater accountability for batterers."[47] Systems advocacy, now an important part of CCRs, has also helped to forge the structure of CCRs themselves; mandatory arrest, the coordination of various services in the community, and the overall shift of domestic violence from private to public can be understood as *results* of systems advocacy. Systems advocacy has shaped CCRs since their initiation, and it continues to be a critical part of ensuring that changes made in the legal and social service systems actually result in increased safety for survivors.

Beyond the work of ensuring that survivors are able to access the services that enhance their safety, the structure of CCRs institutionalizes sources of criticism and demands for change from the system as a whole. In doing so, it also preserves a baseline of participatory decision making in the system, "institutionaliz[ing] ongoing feedback from advocates on the effect of any reform on the victim." Advocates, as the term "advocate" implies, are explicitly partial; as Thelen writes, their "primary allegiance is to the victim."[48] Advocates may not be employed directly by the state, and even where the funding for organizations that train and employ advocates comes from the state, they are generally independent agencies. Hence, from the position of their institutionalized role in the CCR system, advocates act on behalf of the interests of the diverse set of women they encounter in their individual advocacy and other work with survivors.

In the pioneering DAIP CCR, Thelen's research suggests, "the voice of battered women [via their advocates] at the table provides a valuable perspective which leads to solutions that do not pathologize her behavior but rather take the totality of her experience into account."[49] For example, advocates shed light on the reluctance of women to participate in the criminal justice system's response to domestic violence, highlighting the system failures that work to make her participation an apparent or genuine risk to her safety and communal ties. In the Washtenaw County CCR, legal advocates participate in systems advocacy by monitoring the legal process and "deal[ing] directly with the errant individual" in the system, or where this is unsuccessful, consulting with supervisors and taking public action to remedy injustices in the system.[50] Through specific instances of interagency communication (designated "coordinating counsels"), one-to-one transmission of knowledge, and public action, CCRs are effective in part because they have mechanisms within them to criticize the system, often from different perspectives.

This mode of self-critique points to a larger point about this mode of service delivery: its political nature. Mary Asmus and Denise Gamache suggest that "victim safety" should be the primary commitment of coordinating counsels.[51] But, they note, this does not necessarily mean that the counsel (the body that "coordinates" the CCR) must have a "common goal." Instead, with safety in mind, these goals are negotiated and modified over time using feedback from advocates, survivors, and agents of the legal system. Because of the fragmentation, albeit coordinated fragmentation, that characterizes this mode of service delivery, an explicitly political vision of both the state and service delivery emerges. The state is not a uniform entity that imposes social control on service users, nor is the mode of service delivery an already-manifested structure that limits autonomy. Instead, both the contours of the state and the particular service delivery mode in operation are continually negotiated by a variety of actors. Because some of these actors, feminist activists among them, reject dominant commitments to impartial reason, their interactions with survivors may disrupt the hegemonic, rational-legal legitimacy of, for example, the criminal justice system.[52] Thus, by virtue of its political nature, this mode of service delivery overcomes concerns about the anti-participatory tendencies of impartial decision making by promoting system-wide contestation.

Threats and Obstacles to the CCR Model

While I have argued above that the innovative structure of CCRs effectively responds to some critiques of the impartial state lodged by feminists and others while forging a unique, autonomy-fostering relationship between the ethics of justice and care, it is important to note that there are numerous threats to the effectiveness of this model. First, the self-critique aspect of the system relies heavily on the presence of diversely populated institutions within the care-oriented arms of the state. Donna Coker highlights the importance and often-limited existence of diverse advocacy. She writes, "Law and policy that is based on the experiences of poor women, and especially of poor women of color, is likely to result in reforms that benefit all battered women."[53] It is important to acknowledge, as well, that the self-critique function of the CCR I have described will be ineffective if the legal system and the advocacy system are administered from the perspective of the white, middle-class survivor. That is, though advocacy may mediate the impartiality of criminal justice for white women with material resources as far as it is "partial" to them, it may fail to do so for other women already disadvantaged in our society.[54]

Professionalization poses a threat to the potentially radical effects of the "loose coupling" of state arenas described above. Haney notes that "at historical junctures, when the political environment makes proactive demands on [a particular] state sphere, there is often a 'tightening' of the links among subsystems." That is, "the system's boundaries tend to tighten in an attempt to maximize desired outcomes . . . [or to] direct public attention to certain political goals."[55] Increased professionalization of advocates and other system actors may also result in such a tightening, which *reduces* the partiality that is crucial to the ongoing self-critique of the system.[56] When the perspectives or orientations of service delivery personnel working within "care-oriented" arms of the state become increasingly close to the orientations of those arms of the state that tend toward an ethos of universality and impartiality, the advantages of fragmentation, as such, are lost. Professionalization may also be accompanied by a de-radicalization of domestic violence services and an ensuing depoliticization of the movement.[57] The political nature of CCRs, I have argued, is crucial to their success.

Finally, as Coker and others note, there are too few CCRs and often a lack of funding for the services and programs within CCRs that enable them to provide genuine options to survivors of domestic violence. As I have argued, mandatory policies on their own *do not* constitute CCRs; the autonomy-fostering benefits accrued by CCRs are not found in locales where mandatory policies exist outside the context of a community response plan.

Conclusion

Many feminists agree that significant gains have been made in modifying both societal and state responses to domestic violence over the past few decades. Yet, as with many other areas of state service delivery, there remain controversies about how and whether the state should be seen as an ally to which we ought to turn, both as theorists and activists, in furthering feminist aims of equality, inclusion, self-determination, and freedom. But, as Frances Fox Piven writes, it is not just a naive belief in the state's emancipatory potential that is problematic, "it is an undiscriminating antipathy to the state." That is, the constructed polarity between autonomy on the one hand and dependence on the state on the other is misguided. "All social relations involve elements of social control," Piven writes, "and yet there is no possibility for power except in social relationships."[58]

The model of service delivery found in coordinated community response programs suggests a novel way of understanding how such power can be manipulated in order to serve feminist ends, even when it must be garnered in the presence of state arenas that are often understood as excluding women and other oppressed peoples through social control or other mechanisms. I have argued that when viewed through the lens of a (substantive) relational conception of autonomy, a perspective which I defend, CCRs suggest a model of service delivery that responds both to critiques of loss of autonomy in the face of publicization of what was once private, and to critiques of the claims to impartial reason made by some arms of the liberal state. Considering the most controversial aspect of CCRs—mandatory policies—I have argued that both critiques and defenses of mandatory policies often misguidedly suggest that in shifting domestic violence from the private to public sphere, feminists have sacrificed women's autonomy. I suggest that we ought to frame the debate in terms of the state's ability to *enhance* substantive autonomy via publicization and intervention. In making this claim, I acknowledge the hardships that the arrest and prosecution of batterers may cause for survivors, yet I find that in most cases, these hardships are ultimately a lesser threat to autonomy than is the failure to hold the batterer accountable.

As I have shown, CCRs—and possibly other similar practices—can lessen the hardships. The varied elements of CCRs politically and ideologically mediate the conceptual tensions (for feminists) inherent in state service delivery. In particular, such services as individual and systems-level advocacy are delivered from a perspective that embraces a sometimes particularistic and partial approach. In the context of CCRs, however, even the criminal justice system self-consciously embraces partiality in some aspects of its work, while upholding its (aspirational) claims to impartial application of the law. The combination of the two ethics in the different aspects of service delivery under the umbrella of CCRs demonstrates how the loose coupling of state arenas can work to create mechanisms of self-critique that undermine potentially anti-participatory and exclusionary aspects of some purportedly neutral or impartial state policies. The system of service delivery found in CCRs is potentially successful in fostering autonomy in our most vulnerable citizens, I suggest, *because of* the coordinated fragmentation of the state.

6 EMBODIED RECOGNITION, ASCRIPTIVE AUTONOMY, AND HARM REDUCTION

Introduction

The possibilities for an autonomy-fostering state rest, as we have seen, on a conception of autonomy as developed in the context of social relations, which may foster or constrain its development and exercise. In chapters 3 and 4, I explored the ways that service delivery practices are critical to the success (and in these cases failure) of the autonomy-fostering state. In order to comprehend further the complexities of an autonomy-fostering state, we must also consider the factors and relationships that impair autonomy *before* service delivery—and the remedies administered *through* service delivery that these constraints on autonomy make necessary. Chapter 5 offered an account of a model of service delivery for domestic violence survivors that highlights the potentially fruitful implications of a coordinated fragmented state, wherein the fragmentation of the various arms of the state can be exploited to effect a balance between alternative ethics (care and justice) and to implement mechanisms of self-critique in the system. That account emphasizes in particular the importance of conceiving of the state as multiple and plural, and directs our attention to the spaces where autonomy-fostering relations emerge, disrupting monolithic, social control notions of the state. While elements of coordinated fragmentation can be seen in the case I discuss in this chapter, I offer a corrective to another conceptual relationship that may hinder our ability to theorize those spaces in the state that are potentially autonomy fostering: the relationship between harm and autonomy.

Intuitively, we might initially suggest that things that *harm* us necessarily impede our autonomy. In such an account, we might suggest that autonomy and harm are connected in a zero-sum relationship: more harm, less autonomy, and vice versa. But a closer look reveals that this evaluation is not so straightforward; complications follow when we ask, for example, what counts as harm or who determines what counts as harm? In what ways is harm socially constructed? Who or what gives meaning to things we understand as harm? Moreover, what is the status of self-inflicted harm? In order to understand the relationship between harm and autonomy, it is necessary to look carefully at not only the social relations that constitute autonomy—as I have been doing throughout—but also those that constitute harm.

In order to better grapple with what now emerges as a complex conceptual relationship, I want to turn to a set of polices and practices that fall under the umbrella of "harm reduction." Harm reduction is a model of response to drug use and addiction that seeks to minimize the harm associated with drug use without necessarily requiring abstinence. With the rise of HIV/AIDS and the prevalence of other blood-borne infections, such as hepatitis B and C, policy makers and advocates around the world have championed harm reduction interventions as potentially more effective than abstinence-based or criminalizing models of "treatment." This particular service delivery model is fruitful for our consideration of harm and autonomy because it explicitly and actively targets something going under the name of "harm." Further, users of harm reduction services—people who use drugs—are typically cast as nonautonomous. A closer look at harm reduction philosophy, and the harm-autonomy relationship that is central to the theoretical foundations of this philosophy, complicates and adds important nuance to our understanding of autonomy, challenging the often-held assumption that dependence and autonomy are incommensurable. Below, I provide two divergent glimpses of each of the programs I will examine in this chapter; the tensions and paradoxes that emerge in these excerpts provide a window into both the difficulties and possibilities this case presents for theorizing the autonomy-fostering state.

Steve

In the documentary *Methadonia*, the narrator interviews Steve, who is attempting to stop using methadone.[1] Charismatic and effervescent in earlier scenes, now there are tears running down Steve's face as he experiences the withdrawal effects of methadone cessation:

> I feel real bad. It's like destroying my whole life. Methadone is the worst thing you can get on . . . 'cause they treat you like fucking shit once

they . . . once they get you hooked. You're nothing but a junkie. Come get your fix in the morning. And I want to be a normal citizen. Now I'm on sixty [milliliters] today. Today is when they hit me with sixty . . . and I feel like shit. I'm being honest with you: I'm very suicidal right now. Because if I don't have something to make me happy, to make me worth living for, and I'm in a lot of pain . . . this methadone . . . what, they want me to come back to beg and plead, "Oh no I can't take it, put me back on." Yes, they want me to do that so they can have me back! Back in their clinches . . . *liquid handcuffs*. But I would rather drop dead with this shit on me than ever go back.

Lisa

Lisa Torres is a middle-aged lawyer and methadone advocate. In an extra feature on the *Methadonia* DVD, titled "Methadone 101," she explains that she has been on methadone since she was sixteen and addicted to heroin. At first, she resented methadone, attributing various physical ailments to her use of it and believing it to be a "crutch": "It was a real badge of shame. I remember I didn't tell many people."

Despite this initial reticence, Lisa describes the evolution of her attitude toward the treatment drug:

> There was no controlling my addiction . . . but methadone allowed me to have some consistency. . . . [On methadone] you can have your life back. I mean, you can literally do just about anything. And I remember going back to law school, allowing myself first of all to get on an effective dose. And the effective dose for me was a lot higher than I would have allowed myself to go before; I never wanted to go too high because I was just a "visitor" in methadone clinics. I was going to get off eventually and I didn't want to go too high because I didn't need it and all this stuff . . . but my effective dose was a dose at which I acquired blockade and I stopped getting cravings.

VANDU's Needle Exchange Program

In Vancouver, Canada, the Vancouver Area Network for Drug Users (VANDU), an organization consisting primarily of heroin and cocaine users, began operating an unsanctioned needle exchange program (NEP) in September 2001 to respond to a serious limitation of extant NEPs—their early closing time (8:00 p.m.). VANDU, which is funded primarily by provincial government funds, opened its unsanctioned after-hours NEP, dispensing an average of 1,200 syringes per night. The site, which, like VANDU, is almost entirely user-run, later gained government sanction. The experience of user involvement is captured by one user's description of VANDU:

> It brings together a collective experience and wisdom, but also you begin to get a different feeling about yourself. To become a part of something for who I am and not for who I am not. For who I am as an addict, I'm poor, I've got hep C, I lived in wretched housing and all this, and then someone says, "Yeah, that all makes you a really valuable person. You have a lot to contribute to try to help people and to save other lives, and your experience can do that." Then I get a different feeling about myself.[2]

Operation 24/7

At the same time that VANDU began to operate its unsanctioned but well-used NEP, Vancouver police mounted an intensified effort to alleviate the city's illicit drug use problem. In accordance with the renewed police effort, known as Operation 24/7, "a plan to place a constant and highly visible police presence on the street corner in front of the VANDU NEP" was launched.[3] A study by Evan Wood and colleagues found that the presence of police near the table where clean needles were being provided produced a dramatic (26.7 percent) reduction in the distribution of sterile syringes.[4] The police ultimately shut down the VANDU site in 2002, alleging that criminal activities were taking place there. Though the police chief later apologized and the NEP was reopened, this incident prompted considerable outcry among both local people who use drugs and their advocates, also commanding the attention of the group Human Rights Watch, which issued a report condemning the city and in particular the police force for its actions.[5]

Reconciling Harm Reduction and Autonomy

In the foregoing examples, methadone is at once a paralyzing substance that allows the state[6] to hold clients hostage, by imposing "liquid handcuffs," and an enabling, even freeing mechanism that provides opiate addicts with a chance to live normal lives and pursue their goals. Needle exchange programs are a state-supported but user-run way of reducing harm to injection drug users while also providing a space for user mobilization and self-realization. But they are also a target of the policing functions of the state, which view the programs as challenging or violating the state's prohibition-oriented narcotic control objectives. Even the users of harm reduction services, it seems, have divergent views of what constitutes harm, and what constitutes the appropriate remedies to harm. How, then, can we begin to understand harm, and in particular harm in the context of the "difficult case" (for autonomy theorists) of addiction?

In this chapter, I embark on an investigation of harm that proceeds from three questions: *What or who* harms? *Who* experiences harm? *How* do they harm or experience harm? And if we accept conventional academic and popular views of addiction, the answers to these questions are relatively straightforward: drugs cause harm and, since this harm is "self-inflicted," drug users, too, cause harm; drug users experience the harm of drugs; and harm is caused by physiological effects of drugs. Yet as the examples above already suggest, this narrative fails to capture the multiple dimensions of harm. Harm, I will argue, comes in a number of forms, with their implications for autonomy varying accordingly. While harm can be physical, it can also be a result of misrecognition—of needs, of identity, of rights to citizenship and participation, and so forth. Moreover, even the physical aspects of harm, as the cases below demonstrate, are not as clear-cut as they may seem; ideological forces always shape our conceptions of pain and pleasure. Although in this chapter I will argue that harm indeed impedes autonomy, I resist the idea of a zero-sum relationship between the two. Instead, I suggest that some forms of what we typically understand as harm can coexist with autonomy given the appropriate context—for example, one that "reduces" the harm to a tolerable level, as harm reduction services aim to do. In turn, I argue that the notion of an autonomous addict is not oxymoronic, but rather an example of the confluence of a variety of harms with other potentially autonomy-enabling forces, particularly autonomy-fostering service delivery. Even in situations of extreme dependence, autonomy is, and ought to be, possible.

Harm reduction programs, I argue, are a unique location at which the state can foster autonomy in some of its most vulnerable citizens. The central features of this model of service delivery are elucidated when we understand both harm and autonomy as emerging out of relationships—personal and institutional—that are structured in various ways and manifest themselves in the form of various state practices. In this chapter, I focus on two relationally constituted forms of harm. First, this case demonstrates that autonomy competency requires attention to *embodied* forms of harm. While such attention may take on straightforward material forms, this type of harm is also developed in a context marked by interpretation and contestation of existing discourses of harm. In the case of harm reduction service users, the terrain of such contestation and interpretation revolves around the politics of pain and pleasure. Second, I suggest that autonomy-fostering harm reduction programs respond to the harm of *misrecognition* by enabling a space for recognition not just by the state, but by the community, too—especially "peers." It is only within these spaces of multifaceted recognition that a measure of "ascriptive autonomy" can be achieved in a meaningful sense.[7] As they facilitate recognition, or ascription of autonomy, to service users, harm reduction programs also provide the mechanisms for the development of the *capacity* for autonomy—a capacity that may well be underdeveloped in the context of the stigma and material constraints of addiction.

I develop this account of harm and autonomy through an analysis of two types of harm reduction programs: methadone maintenance treatment (MMT) programs and needle exchange programs. Before delving into the analyses of these programs, I provide an overview of the philosophy and practice of harm reduction. I then turn to the cases themselves. Each example fleshes out certain elements of the embodied and inclusive politics of harm reduction that I suggest is required in the autonomy-fostering state, though neither is without limitations. Whereas critics sometimes depict MMT programs as exemplary of the social control practices of the state, my analysis complicates this picture by pointing to the role of methadone both in facilitating the material requirements for autonomy and in challenging conventional notions of the relationship between embodiment, pleasure, and autonomy. My engagement with the service delivery practices entailed in NEPs draws out the value of user involvement and user-run service delivery; these forms of service delivery emerge as a site for the organization and politicization of typically marginalized individuals and groups. Moreover, they point to the complexity of what we understand as "the state," which (as discussed in the previous chapter) we can understand as comprising a collection of "loosely coupled" arms.[8] Here, one such arm ends up being the users themselves, as they deliver state-funded services. In each case, the particular interactions among physical or psychological addiction, dependence on the state, and extreme stigmatization presents a unique lens through which to view and complicate our understanding of a relationally conceived notion of autonomy and the various forms of harm that threaten to constrain it.

Harm Reduction: An Overview

As the accounts of MMT and NEPs in the following sections make clear, not all programs delivering (nominally) harm reduction services strictly subscribe to the "official" principles of harm reduction. Despite problems in practice, as a potential means to theorizing an embodied politics of recognition that effectively fosters autonomy, the *theory* of harm reduction presents some important clues.

Drug policy and treatment, particularly in North America, are politically charged realms. Harm reduction is an increasingly advocated alternative to the "moral model" approach favored by the dominant forces in public policy and administration today. Rooted in public health principles and emerging from advocacy among drug users themselves, harm reduction seeks to minimize the harms of drug use (and other risky behaviors) in our society, while acknowledging that complete abstinence may not be possible or desirable for any person at a given time. Examples of harm reduction initiatives include NEPs, MMT, safe injection and inhalation sites, safer-sex education, smoking reduction programs, controlled or moderate drinking programs, and a host of other programs for specific communities or issues. In addition to rejecting the moral model, harm reduction also diverges from the increasingly prevalent medical model of addiction. Although positive in that it "has the advantage of lifting the moral, or criminal, stigma from the deviant," this model is problematic for harm reductionists because it shifts the "control of deviance" from "legal authorities to the medical profession." Further, the medicalized approach primarily takes notice of individualized physiological factors, failing to acknowledge psychological, social, and cultural factors.[9]

In contrast, harm reduction programs emphasize the multiple axes of oppression to which a user may be subject; the user is seen not just in terms of her relationship to the treatment program or to a given drug, but also as an individual embedded in various relationships that are always structured by power dynamics. Rod Sorge, the late AIDS activist, explains, "Harm reduction focuses largely on the social and environmental aspects of drug taking, looking at the way that drug use is 'produced,' learned, experienced, organized, and controlled and then implementing interventions based on this information." Sorge claims that this outlook shifts the understanding of how to respond to the needs of drug users: "Because most drug users do not have the luxury of leaving their drug-using circumstances behind after or even during treatment, interventions are focusing more and more on helping them make use of their contexts and communities to survive."[10] The notion of "meeting people where they are" is often described as taking a low-threshold approach to service delivery; this is meant to reflect a nonjudgmental attitude and to expand access to a broader range of participants. Instead of adopting punitive measures when, for example, service users continue to use drugs or somehow deviate from certain relatively trivial norms (e.g., lateness, standards of "politeness"), as other treatment programs have traditionally done, low-threshold approaches focus on making contact with users and forging an ongoing relationship.[11]

An emphasis on "bottom-up" approaches to service development and delivery is often a feature of harm reduction programs. Whereas power differentials between providers and users have traditionally acted as barriers to genuinely assisting the user in better accessing the tools necessary to reduce harm, a growing number of harm reduction programs are run by or heavily involve users. When such user involvement is put in place, "those affected are accepted as partners who are capable of assuming responsibility for making personal changes in their behavior and helping others to do the same."[12]

Methadone, Social Control, and the Politics of Pain and Pleasure

Addiction has often captivated autonomy theorists, including theorists of rational choice, because the conventional understanding suggests that to be an addict is necessarily to act against one's own will.[13] By turning our attention to the physiological, phenomenological, and ideological nuances that characterize addiction, however, and the perceived harms with which it is associated, a more complicated picture emerges. Methadone is particularly illuminating as a site for such complication because it is at once a "treatment" for addiction and a physiologically addictive substance. Moreover, in its service delivery context, it presents unique configurations of dependence.

First discovered during World War II as an analgesic, methadone is a synthetic opiate used in "maintenance" treatment as a way to prevent withdrawal symptoms associated with cessation of the use of opiates (such as heroin and prescription opiates like Vicodin or OxyContin). At a high enough dosage, it blocks the euphoric effects of other opiates, ostensibly eliminating incentives to use these drugs. American doctors Vincent Dole and Marie Nyswander were the first to experiment with maintenance treatment in the mid-1960s. Dole and Nyswander, along with some other colleagues, published a significant amount of research reporting the findings of their studies.[14] Though harm reductionists have reconceived MMT as consistent with their philosophy, Dole and Nyswander applied a disease model to heroin addiction, arguing that the drug induces "a metabolic disorder that places patients in need of continued use of heroin or other opiates."[15] Dole, Nyswander, and Mary Jeanne Kreek explain: "Because of the short period of action of heroin, [the addict] oscillates between the limits of 'high' and 'sick' with insufficient time in the normal condition of 'straight' to hold a steady job. Addiction leaves little time for a normal life."[16] In contrast, methadone, which is usually taken once a day, was found to enable addicts "to redirect their time away from obtaining and using drugs."[17]

In this section, I argue that MMT provides a useful example of how an embodied notion of recognition, rooted in a relational conception of autonomy, can yield a form of service delivery conducive to the aims of an autonomy-fostering state. It does this while attending to some of the harms that follow from the experience of addiction in social contexts where dependence in general and illegal drug use in particular are stigmatized and pathologized. Recognition theorists emphasize the centrality of recognition to identity, specifically to the development of an *authentic* identity, one that enables us to be "true" to ourselves.[18] This authentic self is always socially constituted, and in turn, where social messages reflect a negative or disparaging image back on individuals or groups, they may experience profound damage and distortion to the self.[19] While some theorists emphasize the importance of relations of recognition to the psychical development of the individual[20]—her sense of self and ability to imagine herself as an individual worthy of dignity and rights— others suggest that a more structural, less individually focused theory of recognition, rooted in concerns about justice, is more appropriate.[21] These conceptions are obviously not unrelated; both share a sense that the structure of social relations (here relations of recognition) shapes one's identity and ability to act autonomously. Through this case, I want to suggest that in addition to attending to both the psychical and institutional aspects of relations of recognition—both of which constitute responses to forms of misrecognition, or, as we might view it, harm—we need to consider the *embodied* aspects of recognition as vital to the development and exercise of autonomy. The importance of viewing recognition from this vantage point emerges, then, on the bodies of the service users who depend on both methadone (the substance) and MMT (the service delivery model), and in the arguments of critics of both the substance and the service model.

Critiques of Methadone Maintenance Treatment

Despite findings suggesting that it is the only significantly successful manner of establishing abstinence from heroin,[22] MMT remains controversial. The relevant controversies typically fall into three categories. First, some critics argue that MMT simply substitutes one form of addiction for another: methadone is an addictive opiate, withdrawal from which causes painful and debilitating symptoms. Second, others worry that because methadone is an opiate, and for the non-opiate dependent (or for the opiate dependent under some circumstances) may have euphorigenic effects, some individuals may exploit the system to attain methadone for the purposes of "getting high" or seeking pleasure. Finally, a group of critics charges that MMT is a harmful disciplinary practice, seeking to normalize the criminalized addict and increase social control over those who do not conform to dominant bourgeois ideals.

Each of these categories of critique highlights, on the one hand, problematic conceptions of autonomy that conflate independence and autonomy, and on the other hand, a failure to attend to the implications of embodiment in the face of the necessarily constructed nature of the regulation of pain and pleasure. Building on one of the key insights of a relational conception of autonomy—the rejection of the dependence/autonomy opposition[23]—an analysis of the limitations of these critiques allows us to draw out the contours of an embodied notion of recognition, which I claim underpins the philosophy of this harm reduction service. Thus, despite these critiques—or rather, by way of them—MMT is recast as a potentially autonomy-fostering form of service delivery. But I do not dismiss the deeply problematic nature of MMT service delivery, in particular in the United States; the problems associated with this form of service delivery highlight the need for a multifaceted politics of recognition in the context of the autonomy-fostering state, a model further explored in the following section on NEPs.

A common mantra of those who criticize MMT for the physical and psychological dependence it is thought to perpetuate is that MMT users are "replacing one addiction with another." Peggy Peterson and colleagues note that both resistant politicians and some people who use drugs themselves express this sentiment: "The notion of maintaining a methadone dose level indefinitely is unappealing to some people, because participants are not truly 'drug-free.'"[24] Abstinence-oriented programs like Alcoholics and Narcotics Anonymous also generally reject methadone use, viewing it as an incomplete form of adherence to their programs. Philippe Bourgois describes one arm of the dependence-focused critique group as framing its resistance around notions of morality; he refers to these opponents as the "Just-Say-No camp." Members of this camp are "oblivious or else hostile to the 'addiction is a metabolic disease' discourse. . . . They exhort citizens to personal abstinence based on individual willpower and spirituality."[25]

Critics also express concern about the pleasurable effects of methadone. That is, if the drive for using heroin and other opiates in the first place is the pursuit of illegitimate pleasure—pleasure that extends beyond the "natural" and appropriate forms that are constructed as legal and legitimate in our society—the "treatment" for this unwieldy need for excessive pleasure ought not generate further pleasure. In fact, in opiate-dependent individuals, methadone does not have euphorigenic effects.[26] For those who are not dependent, however, such effects are present. As Bourgois notes, critics fear that those who are "not truly addicts will wheedle their way into methadone addiction—or worse yet, that individuals who actually enjoy methadone may become addicted to methadone for its latent euphorigenic properties."[27] Critics are also wary of the potential abuse of methadone in combination with other licit and illicit substances, a phenomenon documented forcefully in the documentary *Methadonia*, wherein many of the profiled MMT clients are seen to abuse benzodiazepines, a class of sedative drugs that enhance the effects of methadone, generating euphoria.[28] The methadone black market that exists in most jurisdictions where MMTs exist, with some clients receiving "take-home" doses (which need not be consumed in the clinic) and diverting them to the street, is further fuel for the fears of the "illegitimate pleasure" camp.

Perhaps the most pressing critique for the purposes of my argument falls into the "social control" category. This critique suggests that MMT is a vehicle for both state and other actors to exert control over those deemed "deviant"; by way of this form of service delivery, the deviant is disciplined, monitored, and reconstituted in the form of an idealized, "straight" subject. In fact, this critique incorporates several of the attributes found in the preceding two critiques, albeit in a different light. On the one hand, the dependence created by the substance and the form of service delivery is seen to undermine the service user's autonomy and, further, make the intrusion of disciplinary power into the user's life imminent. On the other hand, concerns about the regulation of pleasure are seen to embody the bio-power exerted by the state, as it produces and manages the particular bodily experiences of these subjects. Unlike the other two critiques, however, the social control critique is not concerned with the moral failings of the addict (and the failure of methadone to remedy these), or the potential for transgressors to exploit the program; instead, the critique is targeted at relations of domination that are perceived to emerge through the subtle manipulations of the service user—with these relations acting *on* and *through* the user via *his* or *her* agency.

In the case of methadone, the perceived medicalized approach of this service is seen as emblematic of the practices most concerning to those theorists who view the welfare state as necessarily involved in the project of social control. In particular, it is the embodied nature of the power relations present in these contexts that stands out. Writing critically about the structure of and meanings associated with MMT programs, Philippe Bourgois, Jennifer Friedman, and Marixsa Alicea draw on Foucault in order to conceptualize the problematic dynamics they observe in the clinics.[29] Bourgois claims that MMT is an example of the use of bio-power, Foucault's term for the ways that "historically entrenched institutionalized forms of social control discipline bodies."[30] According to Bourgois, the medicalization of methadone as drug treatment—as opposed to the nonmedical, criminal status given to heroin or other offending drugs, for which users must be alternately punished or treated—already suggests the ways that normal/abnormal and legitimate/ illegitimate come to be constructed via bio-power. Additionally, Bourgois points to the study of MMT by scientists and social scientists as a site for this configuration of power relations. Social scientific (and medical and juridical) accounts of methadone maintenance, he argues, focus on quantified data, failing to capture the imbrication of this "treatment" modality in "a Calvinist-Puritanical project of managing immoral pursuits of pleasure and of promoting personal self-control in a manner that is consonant with economic productivity and social conformity."[31] Debates over the adequate dosage of methadone, for example, are common in work produced by disciplines that study methadone; Bourgois sees this technical tinkering as masking the actual disciplinary functions of methadone, manifested differently at both high and low dosages.

Friedman and Alicea emphasize the way the medicalization of methadone treatment provides a language with which the service user is seemingly able to define herself (e.g., as having a "metabolic disease") in an apparently agentic manner, yet always through the lens provided by the "institution" of methadone. As they are transformed into "safe deviants" through methadone maintenance, the authors explain, the women are co-opted into the "machinery controlling themselves and others who fail to conform." They adopt a medicalized and therapeutic discourse rather than a political one, and, in turn, "learn to distrust their perceptions and doubt their critical assessments of the dominant culture."[32] This runs counter to the way Friedman and Alicea conceptualize (illicit) drug use. Women's heroin use, in their account, is a form of resistance, which they frame as a response to oppression, by virtue of which "women are often denied the vision and means to create their own subjectivities."[33] Though they acknowledge that heroin use is neither entirely an instance of resistance nor solely one of passive dependence, their emphasis is on the former. According to this narrative, the physical effects and aftermath of heroin addiction paint a picture of agency and self-government that is subsequently quashed by the methadone institution: "By scarring their body through needles, women refuse to accommodate patriarchal expectations of them and maintain control of their bodily self-expressions, gestures, and appearances. Through their own agency, these women transcend feminine passivity and invisibility."[34]

Refiguring Methadone: Autonomy, Embodiment, Recognition

Each of these critiques raises important and challenging questions for our consideration of the practices of an autonomy-fostering state, and for how we conceive of autonomy and recognition. The first two critiques figure largely in highly politicized public debates over MMT programs; the third critique is a significant site of contention in academic and activist discussions of methadone service delivery. I suggest that each critique presents, to varying degrees, impoverished notions of the relationality and embodiment that are pivotal to an adequate conception of autonomy.

Addiction situates questions regarding dependence and autonomy in a unique light. While it may be intuitive to imagine one who is addicted—one who physically and psychologically *depends* on some substance or behavior—as utterly lacking in autonomy, I want to suggest that such a view conflates independence and autonomy. The potentially (and at times actually) fruitful dynamics of methadone maintenance programs, in fact, suggest that there are conditions under which someone who is dependent in this way can be self-governing in many respects, enabling the individual to determine and pursue her life plans. Though this self-government or autonomy may be partial—it is determined in part by dependence on another substance, methadone—to discount it for this reason elides the fact that all human beings are dependent on at least some other persons or substances. Such dependence, as this case shows in particular, can actually be an enabling relational basis for the development and exercise of autonomy.

The arguments advanced by those who see MMT as simply substituting one addiction for another reflect the stigmatized and pathologized conception of dependence noted above, obscuring important aspects of what may aid in the development of autonomy. If we turn to these enabling aspects, a different picture of MMT emerges. If autonomy is developed in the context of enabling social relations, as I have suggested, one such relation, at the most functional level, must be that between the clinic and the methadone user; by responding to the physical and psychological need of the opiate-dependent individual, the clinic (and the service delivery system) affords her *part of* the recognition necessary for her autonomy competency. Taylor argues that the notion of equal dignity stems from a claim that all human beings deserve our respect because they possess what he refers to as *"universal human potential,"* which he interprets as "the potential for forming one's own identity."[35] Setting aside what may be (and often is) the inadequate respect afforded MMT clients in the clinic setting, the provision of the material benefits of this service itself reflects some respect for the service user's ability to develop her identity and live an autonomous life, despite her dependence on opiates. This form of recognition, then, is one component of the relational support necessary to foster autonomy.

Whereas recognition is a key component of endeavors to foster autonomy, misrecognition, I argue, is a distinctive type of harm that hinders autonomy on a number of levels. At the outset of this section, I noted the variation in scholars' approaches to recognition, with some theorists adopting an institutional approach and others taking up the psychical aspects of recognition. I suggested as well that a third dimension of recognition—an embodied one— ought to be highlighted. Harm can be inflicted at every junction: structural failures of recognition that impair participatory possibilities, psychical violence that weighs on the subjectivity of those who are misrecognized, or the failure to recognize the bodily needs, desires, and experiences of some subjects. By harm, we may mean limitations on political and social freedoms that exclusionary structures generate; we may mean the development of unfavorable relations-to-self that limit who we are, who we aim to be, and how we can achieve our life plans in a given society; or we may mean, in the two preceding interpretations, embodied forms of such harm, both institutionally and psychically located. These forms of harm resulting from misrecognition are certainly not discrete; rather, one always inhabits the terrain of the others. Remedies, therefore, must take note of each dimension.

MMT makes the importance of such an embodied approach to recognition more concrete: it is not just the recognition of need in an abstract sense that characterizes the dynamics of MMT programs, it is the recognition of actual, intense, bodily need. Methadone meets the physical needs of the opiate dependent; the fact that it can relieve the pain caused by withdrawal symptoms is uncontestable. Critics who are skeptical of providing a treatment that potentially provides forms of illegitimate pleasure to the user ignore the constructed nature of notions of pleasure, legitimate or illegitimate. Further, they assume a view of autonomy that *excludes* the body, locating it as yet another source of autonomy-limiting dependence. From the perspective of such critics, certain types of pleasure (either legal/legitimate pleasure, or pleasure that is not related to addiction/dependence) and certain types of pain relief (relief from pain that is not "one's own fault," or that is not caused by supposedly hedonistic excesses of pleasure) are seen as warranted and not necessarily compromising to autonomy. In contrast, in the case of addiction, these critics police the morality and legitimacy of pleasure, effectively denying that the bodily needs of methadone users are valid sites of recognition that must be attended to in order to adequately foster autonomy.

It may seem simplistic to consider the mere provision of a chemical substance as a form of recognition—indeed, as I will explain below, it is *insufficient* on its own in the pursuit of fostering autonomy. But the politically fraught nature of this substance—navigating the politics of pain and pleasure as it does—makes its provision more complicated than the provision of other substances (e.g., pharmaceuticals, nutritional products). Moreover, because this realm of pain and pleasure is deeply rooted in experiential knowledge that cannot necessarily be accessed through straightforward attempts at establishing moral respect, in particular those rooted in notions of taking up the other's position via some form of substitution,[36] MMT presents an opportunity to conceive of respect and recognition in a different manner—one that allows for difference that need not be transparent. Iris Young writes, "Through dialogue people sometimes understand each other across difference without reversing perspectives or identifying with each other." In moving away from the notion that we must entirely inhabit the rational thought processes or reasons of those around us in order to achieve reciprocity and avert misrecognition, another way of viewing and acknowledging "the other" moves into focus: in her capacity and sensitivity as an embodied agent.[37] Whereas theorists like Honneth and Taylor lay emphasis on the psychic needs associated with recognition ("feelings of discontent and suffering . . . coincide with the experience that society is doing something unjust, something unjustifiable"[38]), and Fraser emphasizes the institutional structures required for recognition ("institutionalized patterns of cultural value express[ing] equal respect for all"[39]), an embodied sense of recognition opens up an arena in which to contend with the highly subjective realm of such notions of pain and pleasure.

The distorted notion of pain and pleasure that some critics of methadone endorse—their failure to recognize the contingent phenomenology of these sensations—extends beyond the morality-based critiques to the social control critiques advanced by others. Bourgois argues that the social control function of methadone is advanced by its use as a tool to *deny* opiate users the pleasure they gain from using the substance for which methadone substitutes (i.e., heroin). The difference between the two drugs, he claims, turns entirely on the question of pleasure: "Ultimately, it can be argued that the most important pharmacological difference between the two drugs that might explain their diametrically opposed legal and medical statuses is that one (heroin) is more pleasurable than the other (methadone)." Methadone is thus "a biomedical technology that facilitates a moral block to pleasure."[40] But Bourgois, too, despite his effort to call into question the particular construction of pain and pleasure extant in the late capitalist liberal state, ends up freezing in place a static notion of pleasure (and ultimately identity) in advancing this claim. In claiming that methadone necessarily "blocks" the user's pleasure, Bourgois ascribes a narrow notion of pleasure to the drug user. It is as though by virtue of being an opiate user, one is necessarily interested only in a lifestyle that takes drug use as a primary, and perhaps its only, source of pleasure. Pleasure for the drug user as conceived by Bourgois must be "getting high," and not the stability—and ensuing lack of periodic discomfort associated with withdrawal—that methadone may bring, or the ability to pursue other life goals, as described, for example, by Lisa in the opening vignettes in this chapter. Such an argument, then, reinscribes the bourgeois notions of pain and pleasure that Bourgois wants to call into question in that it characterizes "addicts" as monolithically in pursuit of "deviant" pleasure.

In conceptualizing methadone as a tool for delegitimizing and denying addicts the pleasure of heroin, Bourgois may be understood to suggest that the pursuit of the heroin high is, at least in some significant part, an autonomous pursuit, one that users prefer, after reflecting on their own values and priorities, to the effects of methadone. In fact, in explaining this apparently autonomous preference and the context out of which it emerges, Bourgois' argument may seem to accord with the relational conception of autonomy I defend in this book, and the role played by recognition in structuring the relational context best suited to fostering autonomy. Bourgois argues that "the search for cultural respect" informs and shapes the dynamics of methadone on the streets.[41] Methadone, he explains, occupies an "unsatisfactory location in street-based status hierarchies."[42] Thus to be "recognized" as an equal or as legitimate on "the street" may preclude the use of methadone. Moreover, Bourgois adds, the problematic dynamics of the clinic (to which I return below), which may be degrading or unjust, also fuel antipathy toward methadone.

But both of these constraining factors—street-based respect and clinic climate—do not sufficiently show that methadone maintenance, as a treatment modality and as a source of embodied recognition, necessarily generates social relations that restrict autonomy. Moreover, as with the notion of pleasure Bourgois associates with users of heroin, the ideal of respect put forth also implies a static notion of the addict's identity.[43] It assumes that street-based respect is the only configuration of respect that the user values. In contrast, the provision of methadone in and of itself may signify a type of respect (for the needs and goals of the user) outside the realm of street respect. As well, the service users' broadened possibilities, afforded by methadone, may well open the door to other relations of respect and recognition. This is not to discount the ethnographic work that informs Bourgois's conceptualization of the "search for respect" that shapes the experience of the heroin user; rather, the point is to call into question "street respect" as a determinative structure for the addict's current and future life situation. Autonomy may be developed in the context of various types of relationships; no one set of relationships is necessarily ideal in this respect. But some contexts are better than others, and given the political and social climate in North America (i.e., the war on drugs and the ensuing criminal penalties for drug use and the extant social welfare system), the dynamics of (an ideal) MMT program may be better than those of "street respect" for the purposes of autonomy fostering.[44]

Like Bourgois, Friedman and Alicea's critique of the social control function of methadone relies on a limited view of the conditions under which autonomy and agency are developed and exercised by heroin users, in this case women heroin users. In Friedman and Alicea's account, because of the image of heroin as particularly destructive and deviant, women who use the drug conceive of themselves as transgressing particularly precipitous boundaries. They write, "By using heroin, [women] can break though the confining walls of objectification and envision themselves living beyond preestablished traditional gender boundaries." Imagining themselves—and imagined by society— as "wild" rather than manageable, women who use heroin resist the norms of passivity and silence expected of them, instead taking up the oppositional qualities of being "loud, critical, uncontrollable, and unpredictable."[45] Demonstrating this phenomenon, Friedman and Alicea quote "Jane," a client at a methadone clinic where they conducted interviews: "It made you feel like ya had confidence even though you didn't. You know what I mean? You didn't feel like that when you were straight because I never had any confidence in myself. I always felt stupid. So when I got high it made me feel like I was somebody, I guess, you know what I mean, in the beginning, anyway."[46] Friedman and Alicea situate the lack of confidence and other self-defeating feelings Jane describes as a function of, among other societal constraints, oppressive gender norms.

Although this account of women's heroin addiction is compelling, Friedman and Alicea's interpretation of their subjects' accounts of heroin use at times masks the *illusory* nature of the resistance in which they are engaged. Introducing Jane's comments, the authors write, "Free from the pressures of living up to traditional expectations, [women who use drugs] feel confident— an unlikely feeling for those who often are subjugated."[47] But, in fact, this analysis does not exactly convey the limited nature of the confidence, which is reflected in the direct quote from Jane above—that is, it is short-lived and its *contrast* to the reality experienced when "straight." Thus, when Friedman and Alicea shift to their critique of the methadone clinic, they rely on a potentially misleading counterpoint in order to conceptualize what they take to be the clinic's autonomy-constraining function.

Once they are "on the clinic," or begin a MMT program, the women "become 'safe deviants' by becoming dependent on social service systems, being processed through conventional institutions, and being watched by 'straight' people—clinic staff and doctors."[48] Disciplined yet infused with a sense of self-government that reflects the dominant norms of the methadone institution and the larger society, these women begin to "regulate their own behaviors," Friedman and Alicea write. Such regulation is the target of their criticism. Whereas the context of "resistance" out of which the women's heroin use emerges apparently reflects the capacity for autonomy, the authors claim that the methadone clinic creates relations of domination that constrain autonomy.

Again, there is no reason to believe that the particular conditions of the methadone clinic are not represented accurately in their account. Nevertheless, the contrast between, on the one hand, the *substance* heroin and the *social relations* of the "heroin world," and on the other hand, the substance methadone and the social relations of the methadone clinic, does not suggest that the latter is necessarily an arena where autonomy cannot be fostered. On the contrary, the autonomy that Friedman and Alicea ascribe to the women *while* they are in active heroin addiction assumes a static condition under which the "heroin addict" identity remains in place indefinitely, and the oppressive relations that contribute to the women's motivation to use drugs in the first place stay fixed. This is not to say that dependence on heroin rules out autonomy, but again, that a possibility for greater autonomy may be possible and to preclude the possibility of alternative and enabling relational contexts is to place a limit on the human potential of the subjects in question.

Recognition as Multifaceted: The Limits of Methadone

MMT presents an interesting case of a mechanism for fostering autonomy through relations of embodied recognition. In conceptualizing MMT this way, I want to call into question critiques that fail to consider the possibility that first, methadone as a substance (even as a substance on which one becomes dependent) may provide the embodied support (remedy to physiological harms) necessary to foster autonomy, and second, MMT as a service that *recognizes* bodily need may structure enabling relations of recognition that act as remedies to the harm of misrecognition—even if this remedy is admittedly incomplete. An ideal form of recognition (with regard to the aim of fostering autonomy) is not only an embodied, relationally attuned one, but also one that emerges from multiple locations—that is "multifaceted." As I will explain further in the next section, because autonomy is, at least in part, ascriptive, it matters both *if* one is recognized as autonomous and *who* is recognizing whom as autonomous. Unfortunately, though the provision of methadone itself may reflect a recognition of bodily need in a context of interdependence that allows for the development of autonomy, the often-problematic service provider–service user relationships, coupled with the social stigma attached to MMT services, make the recognition afforded by these programs highly impoverished. Ultimately, this limited form of recognition may be outweighed by the dignity-harming treatment that many experience in these settings.

There are a number of practical aspects of MMT service delivery that have been shown to improve the experience of service users: a "low-threshold approach" (see above), adequate dosing (for moralistic and financial reasons, as well as out of apparent ignorance, many clinics underdose clients, a self-defeating practice that results in a failure to effectively block the effects of other opiates and remove cravings), and improved therapeutic services, to name a few. But one category of remedies in particular speaks to the problems of recognition described above: user involvement. Involving users in service delivery may generate conditions under which a wider set of actors is "empowered" to ascribe autonomy to others and vice versa. Moreover, the experience of engaging peers and the community may be an important tool for both building wider relations of recognition (creating institutional change to enable participatory parity) and developing the skills and sense of self necessary to develop the capacity for autonomy (creating psychic change). As Suzy Croft and Peter Beresford write, successful attempts at involving users in service delivery "show us how there can be a much closer relation between people's needs and the services provided. They also offer insights into a different relationship between citizenship and human need."[49] Attending to needs, as I have argued, is critical to fostering autonomy; at the same time, allowing for opportunities for service users to create and define needs, as well as to participate in their satisfaction, is an important site for expanded participation. In the following section, I explore a model of harm reduction service delivery that adopts such an approach.

Needle Exchange and User-Run Service Delivery

NEPs are one of the most politically visible and controversial forms of harm reduction services. With the HIV/AIDS crisis coming into the public eye in the mid-1980s, the public health implications of injection drug use became particularly urgent. Further, with injection drug use as the fastest-growing risk factor for HIV infection, the need for strategies to reduce this risk cannot be overstated.[50] The first NEP was started in Amsterdam by a self-organized group of illicit drug users, the Junkiebond, which received support from municipal authorities despite official legal constraints on the distribution and sale of syringes in the Netherlands. In the United States, early NEPs were often formed as acts of civil disobedience, forging ahead despite legal restrictions. The first official NEP in the United States to receive support from its county health department after its establishment was located in Tacoma, Washington. Subsequently, NEPs have been established in many jurisdictions in the United States and around the world. Nevertheless, political opposition, social stigma, and limitations on resources have severely limited the availability and scope of NEPs in North America.

Like MMT programs, NEPs face a host of moral condemnations that both reject the validity of providing such services to the "deviant" population they are intended to reach, and fear that these services will result in increased drug use. Moreover, the establishment of the actual venues for needle exchange is difficult, with NIMBY politics prevailing in many instances. Political opposition to NEPs often flies in the face of statistical evidence pointing to epidemic levels of HIV/AIDS and the effectiveness of providing clean needles as a mechanism for halting the spread of this devastating disease. For example, in Washington, D.C., where an estimated *one in twenty* residents live with HIV, until July 2009 federal law prevented the investment of local tax dollars in NEPs.[51] Moreover, the political resistance to NEPs often limits the effectiveness of these services even where they do exist. Police interference (as described in the opening vignettes), limitations on the number of syringes exchanged, and limited hours of operation (among other factors) can severely restrict the number of people who can access this service.[52]

Where effective NEPs exist, they are sometimes user-run or heavily involve service users (and other community members) in their design and implementation. In this section, I explore user involvement in service delivery and user-run service delivery as mechanisms for fostering autonomy. The theoretical foundation for this analysis of user involvement is found in the notion of autonomy as ascriptive. In configuring the appropriate relations necessary to generate the embodied relations of recognition described above, individuals, groups, and institutions are engaged in the *ascription* of autonomy to certain individuals with various types of bodies and bodily needs. As Mika LaVaque-Manty describes, "Autonomy is . . . at least partly *ascriptive*: I am autonomous if someone ascribes self-authorization to me." Therefore, ascription of autonomy can be understood as a manifestation of recognition. But it is also intimately linked to the development of the actual capacities necessary for autonomy. LaVaque-Manty writes, "There is a complex interaction between acquiring the capacity for responsible agency and coming to be recognized (in one's closer and wider social environment) as capable of being responsible."[53]

That is, if others—especially those in positions of power—recognize me as autonomous, even if I lack some of the requirements associated with the capacity for autonomy (e.g., self-esteem or a sense of self-worth), the very ascription of autonomy may cultivate these requirements.[54] In turn, if others refuse to recognize me as a self-governing individual, I may be utterly incapable of conceiving of myself as such, and therefore lack (or continue to lack) the psychic and institutional resources necessary for the development of autonomy.

But who is responsible for such ascription? One aspect of the autonomy-fostering state, I argue, is the configuration of relational support via the delivery of social services in such a way that these ascriptive practices are overdetermined in favor of broad and meaningful relations of recognition. Such relations provide the tools for the development of autonomy. Service delivery models that allow for sites of recognition at multiple locations present ideal opportunities for such development. In the case of user involvement or user-run NEPs, the fact that state agents are not the only ascriptive bodies in relation to "clients" is key. Instead, clients, here reimagined as *citizens*, derive recognition as autonomous individuals from their peers and the wider community. Further, such relations take different forms, in accordance with the fact that recognition may follow from speech acts, recognition of bodily needs and provision of embodied forms of support, simple moments of symbolic respect, and so forth. To be effective, then, enabling relations of recognition must attend to a variety of potential and extant harms. Of particular importance to a multifaceted recognition politics is the need for participation by community members (including service users) in service delivery, advocacy, and support work with one another. Symmetrical reciprocity (substitution) is still not achieved (or desirable) because of the diversity of members of these groups. But shared experiences of identity or ascription of identity form one side of a community's ability to "[reason] about the connected implications of the actions and effects on one another that multiple narratives and critical questioning reveal to us."[55]

Below I look at the example of VANDU, a Vancouver organization of drug users engaged in various forms of service delivery, including an NEP. I then situate the successes of VANDU in the context of the politics of recognition that I have argued is most conducive to fostering autonomy. Despite the positive implications of this form of service delivery—many of which attend to the concerns raised by MMT in the preceding section—there are some tensions and questions that arise, which I also explore below.

A Case of User Involvement: VANDU

Advocates of user involvement, emerging particularly out of Britain (where this mode of service delivery has gained considerable traction), point to the practice's benefits for enhanced citizenship, inclusion in the politics of need interpretation, and individual empowerment. But even supporters of this approach have raised important critiques of the manner in which service users have been incorporated into the system; further, they have also questioned the effects of the institutionalization of the originating movements' agendas. The push for user involvement is not only a product of user-initiated activism. Suzy Croft and Peter Beresford point to right-wing critiques of the welfare state that look to user involvement as a way of *reducing* government intervention, situating it as an expression of their distaste for the "nanny state."[56]

Croft and Beresford divide approaches to user involvement into two main categories. First, from the Right, "consumerist" approaches shift the language of service provision to that of the market, no longer referring to service users or clients, but instead to "consumers." In addition to emphasizing the needs and wants of the consumer, this approach engages in a process of "converting [consumers'] needs into markets to be met by the creation of goods and services." Second, the "democratic" approach has emerged primarily from user groups and organizations, rather than from service providers, as is the case for the consumerist approach. Beyond just a focus on services and their delivery, this approach "is concerned with how we are treated and regarded more generally; with the achievement of people's civil rights and equality of opportunity."[57] Or, in other words, the democratic approach to user involvement is concerned with establishing a just politics of recognition.

A benefit of programs that take up this democratic approach, wherein we find the confluence of need satisfaction with a broader, more solidaristic attention to social justice, is that such programs are more likely to carefully consider the social context of the user in their design and implementation. For example, the widespread acknowledgment of the racism of drug policy in the United States is often a critical factor in how a program catering primarily to people of color will be structured. Thus successful user-involved programs consider the varying social pressures and layers of oppression in which users may be embedded. Further, by considering the user as not just a product of her relationship with the drug itself but as situated within a complex web of social relations, such programs are engaged with assisting the user in a holistic sense. Walter Cavalieri, an activist who runs a needle exchange program in Toronto, writes, "Workers here have pushed the limits to make our exchanges safe places to receive assistance, friendly help, good information, attention, validation, and so forth. We are involved with peoples' lives, not exclusively with their veins. With the whole person. With their families/communities. With the community as a whole."[58]

VANDU, the user-run organization introduced in the opening pages of this chapter, is a useful example of Croft and Beresford's notion of the democratic approach to user involvement; moreover, it embodies the contextualized, relationally aware approach to service delivery described above. VANDU was formed in 1997 by a group of local drug users, activists, and other community members who, in the face of the growing public health emergency that gripped the Downtown Eastside neighborhood in Vancouver, felt that something had to be done. Through posters and word of mouth, organizers organized a series of meetings from which they gathered information on the needs and issues of concern facing their peers. A report on the organization notes, "By bringing the meetings to drug users and allowing all to participate, no matter how high they were or how bizarre their behavior, the organizers were able to successfully document users' concerns using a low threshold format."[59]

VANDU eventually gained funding from the Vancouver/Richmond Health Board (and later from other government sources), a development that required certain features of the institution to become more formalized (e.g., registration as a nonprofit charity). But the organization remains true to its initial emphasis on user-run service delivery. The mission statement of VANDU reads, "The health of our participants is enhanced by including users and former users in decision-making and task fulfilling opportunities which build self-esteem, trust, informal networks of support, and a sense of community."[60] With this framework in mind, one of the key aims of the organization is to "[challenge] traditional client-provider relationships and empower people who use drugs to design and implement harm reduction interventions."[61] In order to maintain the emphasis of user-run service design and delivery, relatively fixed rules regarding participation are in place. VANDU includes full members (former or current drug users) and supporting members (those who are not former or current drug users). The latter group must not exceed 10 percent of membership and cannot vote, though such members are permitted to express their views and participate in other ways.[62]

With services like the NEP, as well as the provision of basic first aid, supervision of after-hours toilets, syringe recovery efforts in local low-income hotels, and so forth, one of the key features of VANDU is the decoupling of dependence, physical and social, from autonomy and choice more broadly. The report suggests that, "in realizing that drug users can make a difference through choice, members are able to reinvent or reframe themselves in a more positive and productive light that stands in stark contrast to the disabling stigma typically afforded to drug users by society."[63] Central to this stigma is the notion of the addict as overcome by her body, unable to resist its desires, and therefore capable of neither acting autonomously nor participating effectively in social and political life.[64] The use of the needle itself, because it violates the imagined boundaries of the body in what is perceived to be an unnatural manner, is particularly potent as a symbol of the self overcome by embodied existence; the barriers between body and world, inside and outside, no longer exist or are severely compromised.

This example, then, demonstrates that by minimizing the harm associated with drug use—in a manner that necessarily is concerned with attending to the needs of the body by making continued drug use safer—the services delivered by VANDU foster autonomy even in the face of dependence, including dependence that is deeply embedded in bodily need. NEPs enable users to make the choice to use clean needles, but they also make possible the autonomy gained by users *because* of the choice to use clean needles. The latter form of autonomy fostering is a function of not only the physical freedom associated with averting blood-borne diseases, but also the minimization of the *social* harms of failure to recognize the embodied and relational needs of, in this case, people who use drugs.

The manner in which user-run programs like the NEP, and organizations like VANDU, meet these relational needs is central to their distinction from the limited autonomy-fostering potential of the harm reduction program discussed in the previous section (MMT). In the case of MMT, the structure of the service delivery does not effectively enable ascription of autonomy, stopping short at meeting the bodily needs of the service user, an important but insufficient configuration of relations of recognition. In contrast, by cultivating an organization that attends to the needs of its members while developing their capacities for autonomy (as described by the members' accounts of their experiences of empowerment and personal growth via participation), the user-run structure of VANDU has allowed members to access a measure of *ascriptive* autonomy, as described in sections above. As it gained members, became increasingly organized, and effectively met the needs of its members, VANDU has become a key stakeholder for the local, provincial, and federal governments; the state recognizes VANDU members collectively as autonomous actors that provide key input regarding their own access to social services. Officials are known to pay particular attention to the voices of VANDU representatives when making and implementing policy decisions.[65] Moreover, media outlets turn to VANDU as a key source, while other community organizations regard it as an important partner. Thus relations of recognition are multifaceted: they extend from a variety of sources, fostering autonomy both through the actual acknowledgment of service users' autonomy and through the opportunities to develop the capacity for autonomy that ensue from the acknowledgment of these citizens' *potential* for autonomy. This acknowledgment is critically related to the fact that VANDU is run by users.

Limitations: Origins, Co-optation, and the Conflicting Imperatives of the State

Let me summarize the qualities I have attributed to user involvement in service delivery, in particular user-run service delivery, which might exist in an autonomy-fostering state. Such a service delivery model generates relations of recognition that are both attentive to the embodied nature of autonomy that extend from multiple locations to provide ideal *ascriptive conditions* for autonomy. In providing the resources necessary to meet the bodily needs of users—and more important, because of their ability to gain access to peers in a way that client-service provider hierarchies have traditionally thwarted—user-run organizations and programs like VANDU and NEPs, respectively, offer an embodied form of relational support. At the same time, through self-organization, both empowerment and development of capacities follow, presenting further opportunities for members of user-run organizations to gain ascriptive autonomy as others come to recognize these capacities. These, then, are qualities that offer a more complete model of harm reduction, and therefore an ideal basis for fostering autonomy. But as noted above, there are limitations to the possibilities of user-run service delivery and user involvement. First, some commentators point out that user-involvement schemes emerging out of social movements (rather than out of the service delivery sphere itself) are most likely to be successful, with the latter point of origination generally failing to achieve the desired goals. Second, though the state may make claims to support the values associated with user involvement, the power dynamics already embedded in our social structures (and underlying social control agendas) may impose discursive constraints that undermine the aims that a user-involvement model aspires to in the first place. In such cases, the result is a subtle co-optation and depoliticization of service users by the state. Finally, the multiplicity of the state—its various institutions, each with their own interests and imperatives—may result in conflicting goals and clashes of values that hinder rather than foster autonomy.

The first concern is, I think, difficult to overcome. It is an empirical question whether social movement–originated user involvement supersedes state-originated user involvement with regard to meeting the sorts of objectives described here. In their article on user involvement, Croft and Beresford note that the "political process" (they emphasize that it is political) of involving people in need definition and interpretation "has most often grown from political rather than welfare movements." They point out that "the gay switchboards, lesbian lines, rape crisis and women's centres have grown out of women's and gay liberation movements and not a social policy tradition."[66] Many NEPs and VANDU also largely emerged organically, though public health imperatives have fostered their continued existence (while other political forces have constrained them). If it is true that user involvement stemming from such organic social justice struggles is more likely to yield positive outcomes for users, one implication is that the state has an obligation to enable the social and political conditions out of which citizens can engage freely in such struggles; freedom of organization, freedom of speech, availability of public spaces in which to organize, and so on are all examples of the types of conditions that make such struggles possible. It is worth noting, however, that organization occurs even, and perhaps especially, where such conditions are *not* present.

A more complicated question is whether state actors should actively organize citizens (service users) to form user-run organizations or to lobby on their own behalf for user involvement. Indeed, if there is to be an autonomy-fostering state, one aspect of it might even necessarily require such intervention by the state. The second limitation highlighted above points to a potential problem with such state-initiated user mobilization. Some scholars argue that the power dynamics between state institutions/actors and service users, particularly marginalized and vulnerable service users, are so stark and so ingrained that it is impossible to create conditions under which free and equal participation by users will be possible. In a study that seeks to use "analysis of discourse [to shed] light on the politics of service user involvement," Suzanne Hodge finds that power dynamics are played out through subtle manifestations in "patterns of linguistic interaction that bound and discipline the shape of permitted discourse."[67] These findings seem to suggest that there are major obstacles to state-led user-involvement strategies.

Though the organization Hodge studies makes some self-conscious adjustments to its practices in order to contend with potential power disjunctures (e.g., having service users chair meetings), Hodge argues that the terms of the discourse in the forum she observes are still largely determined by a dominant normative framework that is not meant to be challenged. When users stray from this dominant framework, though they are not *prevented* from participating, they may have to overcome multiple attempts to divert discussion from controversial or challenging issues. In the case that she describes, where the hot-button issue of electroconvulsive therapy (ECT) is discussed, users challenge the legitimacy of this practice, yet an official tells Hodge that their view is not consistent with "current clinical practice [and] clinical evidence within health services." With this appeal to the expertise of professionals, the official suggests that discussions about the issue are not particularly fruitful. Hodge's interpretation of the official's comments suggests that "although, on [the official's] account, members are not prevented from raising the topic, there is no potential for it to become the subject of debate oriented to changing policy," because the forum is not set up "to be a mechanism by which contested norms such as the use of ECT would be opened to change."[68]

Despite these objections, it is not clear that even with such discursive boundaries in place, productive change, including change that ultimately fosters autonomy, cannot occur. The disorderly suggestions of users in the context of the resistant but not prohibitive forum may actually be part of the process of expanding the discursive boundaries or facilitating the shifts in thinking that are required of institutions. In this sense, while Hodge raises valid concerns, she does not acknowledge any possibility for the (admittedly frustrated) efforts of users to raise controversial issues and gradually shift the terms and substance of the discourse they are both engaged in and resisting. Though the immediate response is "no response," in fact it may be the pressure they exert on the discursive boundaries of the forum that is most important in expanding the scope and nature of relations of recognition in this context. Given this potential for gradual change in the face of the potential limitations of state-led user-involvement initiatives, I think it is hasty to dismiss such initiatives out of hand. Hodge ultimately suggests that user involvement that evolves from service-led initiatives is less productive than "independent, user-led organizations," which "engage with the kind of issues that are off the agenda for most user involvement initiatives"; the latter, she argues, should be "promoted," though she does not explore how such promotion works here.[69] While this may be true broadly speaking, it is misguided to eliminate the possibility for state- or service-led initiatives where user-led organizations do not exist at present. Even where the motivations of such state-led initiatives are not always consistent with the goal of fostering autonomy in service users, they may inadvertently have this effect.[70]

Yet, while sometimes, whether intentionally or inadvertently, the imperatives of the state align themselves with the goal of fostering autonomy and extending relations of recognition to further social justice aims, some commentators worry that at other times the *multiplicity* of the state and the resulting conflicting imperatives may thwart such progressive outcomes. The example given in the opening pages of this chapter helps to explicate the concern raised here: while one arm of the state (the provincial government) lends its support to the NEP and to the work done by VANDU members, the goals of another arm of the state (the criminal justice system) seem to run counter to this goal. With goals of harm reduction and prohibitionism espoused by different arms of the state (or by the same arm in different contexts or to different audiences), devastating outcomes sometimes follow: in this case, the increased police presence and ultimate crackdown at the NEP led to a substantial decrease in the number of clean needles accessed by users.[71] Both the bodily benefits of clean needles and the relational resources provided by user-delivered programming are lost in this case, at least over a period of time.

Despite the serious obstacles that such clashes pose for the aims of harm reduction and autonomy fostering more generally, user-run services may be particularly well equipped to handle the potentially conflicting messages directed at them by various arms of the state. The organization of VANDU, its connections to the community, and the dedication of its volunteers, among various other factors, served to bolster a strong response to the police crackdown. In fact, going further than the status quo, service users became frustrated with the slowness of the implementation of a long discussed safe injection site (SIS). Thus, describing the action as "a direct community response to the reallocation of 44 VPD [Vancouver Police Department] officers to the DTES [Downtown Eastside] . . . also intended to protest the government's failure to open a sanctioned SIS," a coalition of community organizations and individuals (including VANDU) opened an unsanctioned SIS.[72] Thomas Kerr, Megan Oleson, and Evan Wood describe the concurrent efforts of coalition members to document and protest police harassment. But despite the police presence and multiple efforts to force the SIS out of its quarters, the unsanctioned site was in operation for 181 days. According to Kerr and colleagues, "The injection drug users involved in this particular project organized themselves in the face of a police crackdown despite the health and legal risks associated with this type of action, and in doing so focused the attention of politicians and the public on the harmful effects of the police crackdown and the outstanding need for a sanctioned SIS within the DTES."[73] Despite the conflicting, discontinuous aims of the state in its multiplicity, the presence of user-run services, even when they come under attack, proves fertile ground for organizing against those interventions that threaten to limit autonomy. Moreover, the recognition already afforded service users by community organizations and community members in this case expanded as the public's attention was drawn to the unsanctioned SIS; surely, the police had the physical power to shut down the facility, but they did not make use of this power to its fullest extent for a long period of time. Finally, as I discuss in chapter 5, given appropriate coordination, state fragmentation can indeed produce conditions that foster autonomy.

Although there are obstacles to fully effecting the potential benefits of user involvement in service delivery as a means for fostering autonomy, there are many reasons to believe that the resilience of user groups is such that the benefits outweigh the threats. Moreover, even seemingly small shifts in the power dynamics of the traditional service provider–client relationship go a long way in addressing what emerge as the shortcomings of otherwise autonomy-enabling programs like MMT. By making space for a multifaceted politics of recognition—emerging from multiple sites to generate enabling ascriptive conditions for autonomy, and attending to the embodied nature of autonomy and the relational conditions this understanding points to—user involvement and user-run service delivery present a useful model for theorizing the autonomy-fostering state.

Conclusion

In an article criticizing what he takes to be the overemphasis on neutrality and cost-benefit analysis in current harm reduction rhetoric, Andrew Hathaway argues that this positivistic approach has hampered harm reduction as a *political* movement. He writes, "Discursive efforts to persuade based on strict rationality reinforce *endangerment* themes over drug use *entitlement* . . . unduly overlooking the deeper morality of the movement with its basis in concern for human rights." Hathaway is concerned that advocates of harm reduction are emphasizing the "cost" savings associated with the programs the movement encompasses—in terms of both economic resources and other measures, such as health and employment—while overlooking questions of marginalization, domination, and exclusion. Moreover, this approach, which often relies on scientific data to back up its claims, neglects one of the key tenets of harm reduction theory: "Harm reduction in principle recognizes that there are both costs and benefits to drug use, and is chiefly respectful of the motivation and decision to use drugs." Because, as I have discussed above, pleasure is not easily incorporated into our extant frameworks for evaluating autonomous behavior, this "benefit" side of drug use is particularly fraught. Ultimately, Hathaway's main concern is that the rhetoric of neutrality adopted by harm reduction means that its "underlying respect for human rights is sacrificed in exchange for an illusion of neutral standing." "Arguing for social change," he continues, "requires we make a choice between rival *traditions of argumentation*," here between prohibitionism and tolerance. The language of "harm," Hathaway argues, has been used in a way that prevents such normative claims making.[74]

By imbuing the notion of harm with the normative content provided by aspirations to fostering autonomy and remedying misrecognition, we can salvage, and perhaps even bolster, harm reduction as a political movement. Harm, as Hathaway's argument suggests, and as the complexities of the cases of harm reduction services discussed in this chapter demonstrate, cannot be conceived as existing in a zero-sum relationship to autonomy. It is not the notion of harm itself, but rather the failure to theorize and operationalize plural and contested notions of harms and their remedies that renders the rhetoric of harm reduction potentially impotent, as Hathaway worries.

In this chapter, I have argued that harm reduction may provide a useful model for theorizing the autonomy-fostering state, wherein a multifaceted, embodied politics of recognition serves to enable the social relations that best allow for the development of autonomy competency and the minimization of autonomy-constraining harms. Understood as a form of harm, misrecognition can be considered in light of both institutional and psychical concerns, with particular attention to the needs of the body and the regulation of pain and pleasure—aspects of harm that are often overlooked in contemporary accounts. As Hathaway notes, harm reduction, as is perhaps the case for all radical political movements, is constantly in danger of "cooption and negation . . . by competing mainstream interests."[75] But when its principles are used as the foundation for the development of service delivery practices that incorporate users and offer the material and physiological resources necessary to enable autonomy, it presents an instructive challenge to the stigmatized notion of dependence, thereby decoupling independence and autonomy. Even in this stark case of dependence, the ideal of the autonomy-fostering state offers possibilities for a more inclusive notion citizenship in the context of social service delivery.

7 CONCLUSION

A just state has an obligation to foster autonomy in its citizens, particularly its most vulnerable citizens. Although autonomy has conventionally been conceived of in individualistic terms, feminists (and, increasingly, mainstream political philosophers) have reconceived of autonomy as constituted through social relationships. Included among those social relations that can either foster or hinder the development and exercise of autonomy is the relationship between citizen and state. In turn, social service delivery serves as a central site for the negotiation of the terms of these state-citizen relationships; it is through service delivery that most citizens have their most direct interactions with the state, coming to understand themselves as citizens in part through these exchanges. Particularly in a society that stigmatizes and subordinates those constructed as "dependent," citizens who claim social welfare services are indeed among those who are most vulnerable. But such vulnerability need not lead to constrained autonomy; rather, in contrast to the meanings associated with welfare dependence in our society, the delivery of social welfare services can foster autonomy in such citizens.

Like this book itself, the preceding paragraph is a mixture of normative and descriptive claims: I have suggested both that the state *ought* to deliver services in an autonomy-fostering manner and that it *does* do so. Though the former is a premise for the investigation I undertake in this book, much of my argument has been founded not on such normative claims but on descriptive accounts and analyses of existing models of social welfare service delivery. I began this book with a series of questions that highlight the tensions and paradoxes that the aspiring autonomy-fostering state might encounter. I explored those tensions in the cases discussed throughout the book. In the chapters that have preceded this one, I looked to the survivors of domestic violence who find respite in a "coordinated fragmented" state that offers an often conflicting yet somehow enabling mix of service delivery practices and philosophies. I considered also people who are addicted to drugs yet who, as they participate in the delivery of services like needle exchange programs and receive embodied forms of support ranging from clean needles to methadone maintenance programs, gain access to the conditions necessary for autonomy competency *via* the state. Drawing on these empirical contexts, the descriptive claim I have made, then, is that it is not just that the state *ought* to be autonomy fostering, but rather that it *is* autonomy fostering.

Yet, earlier in the book, I looked also to the cases of citizens subjected to coercive and demeaning new paternalist programs, which were built on the assumption of service users' incompetence. I drew on the experiences of immigrants, cut off from vital services in an effort to discourage the arrival of other immigrants, who by no fault of their own were born into circumstances (shaped in part by American foreign policy) that prompted them to seek a better life outside their homelands. In these cases, even where program designers imagined that services would enhance autonomy—usually conflating autonomy and independence in making such claims—service users' were hindered in their pursuit and exercise of the capacity for autonomy. Moreover, their access to what I have suggested is a crucial ascriptive component of autonomy—the importance of recognition as autonomous individuals—was severely limited. These cases, then, suggest that the claim above is more precisely formulated as: *some* arms of *some* states *sometimes* effectively foster autonomy in *some* of their citizens through the delivery of social welfare services.

These qualifiers do not mean that the "quest" for an autonomy-fostering state is futile. Rather, the occasional instances of successful autonomy fostering provide the basis for a theory of an autonomy-fostering state. The questions I have tried to answer, then, are the following: What can we learn from these "sometimes" instances of effective autonomy-fostering social welfare service delivery? And, what can we learn from the more prevalent instances wherein the state fails to foster autonomy through service delivery? More specifically, what conceptions of autonomy, citizenship, and the state shape the successful cases, on the one hand, and the often deeply troubling unsuccessful examples, on the other? Following, I first summarize the elements of the autonomy-fostering state—and their theoretical implications—that I have derived from the cases I explore in this book. Second, I conclude by reflecting on the methodological approach I have taken up—what I refer to as an "empirically situated" approach to political theory. Such an approach, I want to suggest in this closing chapter, is necessary for theorizing the autonomy-fostering state if we acknowledge the political nature of both the "substance" of autonomy and the theory and practice of service delivery.

Autonomous Individuals

Consider the following individuals:

- The injection drug user who spends some afternoons distributing clean needles to fellow users at a user-run needle exchange program, and others injecting heroin or cocaine into an available vein, using the sterile needle she collected at that same program earlier that day.
- The survivor of domestic violence who, because of a no-drop policy, is not given the choice to "drop the charges" against her partner, as she might have done otherwise, but who is visited by an advocate after her partner's arrest, who not only provides support but also facilitates her search for housing and child care in the wake of her partner's removal.
- The opiate addict who, each morning, travels to a clinic that provides him with a dose of methadone, a legal substitute for heroin, morphine, and similar drugs, thereby staving off the intense and painful withdrawal symptoms that are inevitable were he to simply stop using illicit drugs "cold turkey" or fail to show up at the clinic one morning.
- A domestic violence survivor who is berated by the police officer who responds to a call she has placed, yet whose advocate assists her in challenging the demeaning treatment.

This is the unlikely cast of characters that gives shape to the model of "the autonomous individual" offered in this book. In fact, the paradoxes embodied by these subjects are perhaps the only elements that make this "model" cohesive in the traditional sense. Yet, if autonomy is the capacity to determine one's own ends, to live according to one's own life plans, the notion of a *model* of the autonomous individual seems itself to be paradoxical. Nonetheless, even if a model of autonomy fits awkwardly with the concept itself, in contexts of oppression our notion of autonomy must have some *content* if it is to be significant.

When conventional popular and political discourses produce of a model of the autonomous individual, it undoubtedly excludes all the figures described above: it is a model that hinges on an ideal of independence that is deeply gendered and racialized. If the atomistic, unencumbered individual is too much of a caricature to accurately represent what mainstream political theory conceives of as the autonomous individual, this still-prevalent popular ideal seeps into our political discourses and, in turn, our public policies.[1] In turn, the political discourses that are founded on such a notion of the autonomous individual fail to ascribe autonomy to large groups of stigmatized and marginalized citizens. The social welfare policies founded on this impoverished conception of autonomy reproduce and exacerbate the relations of domination and oppression that are often the reason why those affected by the policies are in need of services in the first place. Thus I have argued that a relational conception of autonomy is the necessary foundation of the autonomy-fostering state and its modes of service delivery. By drawing our attention to the structure of the relationship between state and citizens, a relational conception of autonomy prompts us to look specifically at the relations of *power* at work in such relationships. It also challenges us to rethink notions of privacy, responsibility, and dependence.

In contrast, built on flawed notions of autonomy, the cases described in chapters 3 and 4 offer pictures of welfare policies that fail to foster autonomy. First, the new paternalist model of service delivery presumes the incompetence of service users, negates the value of care work and care relations for individual women's practices of meaning making, and inaccurately presumes that work in the paid labor force (as opposed to the private sphere) will confer status on service users. Imposing measures of "conditionality" on welfare recipients, new paternalist programs fail to foster autonomy in large part because of the lack of respect they embody. At once devaluing the sorts of relationships that might foster autonomy and perpetuating those that limit autonomy, new paternalist programs offer dismal prospects to service users. Second, narrow conceptions of the motives of immigrants lead policy makers to place severe limitations on welfare services for noncitizens, many of whom migrate because of the global inequalities that the United States bears at least some responsibility for creating and perpetuating. Something like a "large-scale" denial of relationality allows policy makers to ignore the collective responsibility borne by Americans for the conditions under which human beings live elsewhere in the world. In turn, migrants, whose decisions to come to the United States may be autonomous if understood in a relational context, can exercise their autonomy in some cases only by making claims on the state to welfare. But because autonomy and dependence are seen as antithetical, the ideal of "taking responsibility" is held up as a reason for denying welfare rights. Instead, it is in attempting to lay claim to benefits that migrants take responsibility for themselves and, in turn, gain autonomy. Yet it is here that they are rebuffed.

In contrast to the autonomy-hindering effects of the programs and policies discussed in chapters 3 and 4, chapters 5 and 6 offered accounts of service delivery models that foster autonomy in users—in people like those described at the beginning of this section. Service users who benefit from the programs described in chapters 5 and 6—coordinated community response programs for domestic violence survivors, methadone maintenance programs, needle exchange programs, and so on—are not suddenly freed of all those aspects of life that hinder one's autonomy (e.g., discrimination and stigmatization, trauma and loss). Because these programs begin from the premise that human and institutional relationships must be organized in ways that foster autonomy, that these relationships *matter* for autonomy, service users are freed from some of the oppressive relations of power that emerge in programs like those described in the preceding chapters.

How does a relational account of autonomy inform these more successful programs? In both cases, the notion that social relations shape autonomy implies that it is not the absence of state intervention that will generate the most autonomy. This point is highlighted in the discussion of paternalism in chapter 3: there I argued that paternalism should be understood not simply as intervention, but as referring to forms of intervention into citizens lives that perpetuate relations of domination and oppression. In contrast to such paternalistic forms of intervention, the relationships that emerge from CCRs are, first, plural in their forms and, second, able to institute checks and balances that weed out the damaging power relations that mark unsuccessful programs. Moreover, a relational conception of autonomy calls into question the framing of discussions of state intervention into the arena of domestic violence as a debate over the loss of privacy, where such a loss is understood as necessarily leading to a loss of autonomy. Within such a frame, the debate is over whether such a loss is "worth" the protection granted. I argue instead that the conflation of privacy and autonomy within such a framework obscures the potential for relational conditions that enable autonomy while publicizing domestic violence (removing from it the cloak of privacy), which has been a key goal of feminist struggles.

This move away from the conflation of autonomy and privacy makes most sense when we think of relational autonomy as at least "weakly" substantive.

Theories of relational autonomy, I have noted, are often placed in two categories. Procedural or content-neutral theories of autonomy require individuals to subject their preferences or motives to certain procedures that are meant to demonstrate that these preferences are really "their own," but which do not specify whether certain types of decisions or actions are consistent with some value associated with autonomy. It is the capacity to choose for oneself that is most central to these theories, not the choice itself. But the case of domestic violence draws our attention to one of the shortcomings of this approach to theorizing autonomy: if women are subject to oppressive gender norms that lead them to internalize beliefs that erode their sense of self-worth and that shape their understanding of what constitutes a "good" wife, partner, mother, and so on, they may claim their decisions as their own even when these decisions are constituted by oppressive socialization.

Of course, if autonomy is relational, one's decisions must always be constituted in part by socialization. But, as I argue in this case of mandatory arrest policies within the context of CCR programs, we can and must distinguish between forms of socialization that reproduce oppressive norms and those that do not. Nonetheless, to draw lines between socialization that is and is not oppressive is a *political* process, which is figured in particular *contexts*. This is why I have suggested that we cannot "fix" the substance of autonomy in place; it is within a given context that the substance of autonomy must be worked out, negotiated, and challenged. For example, the women's movement against domestic violence reshaped the terms of debate over this issue in a way that has redrawn the line between public and private. With such a shift in place, we can observe when a choice to stay in an abusive relationship is produced by oppressive gender norms. In a context where domestic violence is widely seen as a public/political issue and where privacy can be distinguished from autonomy, decisions to risk one's life in an abusive relationship usually cannot be seen as autonomous. In turn, mandatory arrest policies *combined with* the provision of a coordinate set of services that include elements of both "impartial" justice and particularized care can be seen as autonomy fostering.[2]

Like mandatory arrest policies, some harm reduction programs—which aim to reduce the harm of risky activities, particularly drug use, without requiring abstinence—foster autonomy only or mostly when delivered in a particular way. I draw this distinction in my discussion of methods of harm reduction, methadone maintenance programs and needle exchange programs. In chapter 6, I argue that harm reduction programs offer a unique model of autonomy-fostering service delivery, potentially alleviating the harms of misrecognition (in addition to the physically rooted harms associated with criminalized drug use). When the state recognizes the needs of drug users by providing harm reduction services, as in the case of methadone maintenance, it in part alleviates the harms of misrecognition that often plague drug users in our society. By misrecognition I mean the failure to acknowledge and attend to the relationally constituted "authentic" self of some individuals or groups. The state recognizes drug users particularly by attending to the *embodied* needs of the user, which are so often seen as secondary in our society.

In addition to the damage caused by failing to recognize embodied need, misrecognition is destructive of autonomy, because autonomy is in part ascriptive. The status of "autonomous individual" is conferred by others when they recognize us as such, regardless of the actual capacities we may or may not have. In turn, those in positions of power are most likely to be able to ascribe autonomy in ways that have significant social consequences. If we contrast methadone maintenance programs to the new paternalist pregnancy-prevention programs, which fail to recognize material and relational needs of young women, the former programs' autonomy-fostering potential is evident. Like new paternalist programs, however, many methadone maintenance programs are delivered in ways that are demeaning and restrictive. Thus, though they meet crucial embodied needs, they do not always effectively foster autonomy; these programs recognize need but they often do not recognize autonomy. Thus the ascription of autonomy is intimately tied to the capacity for autonomy: being recognized as autonomous may grant me access to the relational and material resources necessary to develop the capacity for autonomy. In turn, being denied such recognition may hinder my capacities for autonomy by limiting these resources: the autonomy potentially enabled by meeting embodied needs through methadone maintenance programs may ultimately be eroded.

In contrast to methadone maintenance programs, which are frequently delivered in settings marked by hierarchy and disciplinary power, needle-exchange programs are sometimes user run. These user-run services, I argue, attend to embodied need *and* recognize or ascribe autonomy. It is through *multifaceted* relations of recognition that user-run needle-exchange programs effectively ascribe autonomy to users. First, by funding a program that is run by users (as in the case I describe in chapter 6), the state recognizes the capacity of users to effectively deliver services to fellow users. In addition, since service users must make an active choice to use clean needles, thereby reducing the harms associated with drug use and increasing autonomy, the provision of this service implies that the state *expects* that users will make the autonomous decision to participate. This expectation is especially interesting in light of the fact that addiction is often seen as incommensurable with autonomy. Yet the state suggests that even in the throes of addiction, a user may make the decision to use such resources—a decision motivated by the desire to pursue one's own ends, which we may assume include protection from blood-borne diseases transmitted through unclean needles. Finally, in the case described in chapter 6, drug users benefit from the public recognition they may receive as members of the community delivering services to peers. Together, these various forms of recognition mean that needle-exchange programs may create the conditions necessary for not only embodied recognition but also ascriptive autonomy.

In both the case of CCRs and harm reduction programs, the success of the autonomy-fostering state is partly a function of the fragmentation of the state. While it seems counterintuitive that fragmentation of the state's service delivery apparatus might make it more effective in enabling autonomy, in these cases we see that where fragmentation is coordinated, such success is possible. The analyses I provide in this book point to the fact that the state as a singular entity does not exist. Rather, the state has multiple arms that are, I argue (following Lynne Haney), "loosely coupled."[3] Some feminist theorists have argued that even when disaggregated, the state presents itself as a necessarily masculinist power, albeit one that exercises this power by a variety of techniques. But the fragmentation of the state, I find, means that the various arms of the state may have conflicting and divergent aims, some of which may enable feminist goals and others of which may not. Sometimes, as in the case of CCRs, the sites of difference and conflict actually serve to produce an immanent form of self-critique within service delivery practices. Though we may be critical of the potential lack of accountability that can ensue from state fragmentation, in the case of needle-exchange programs this argument is turned on its head when the users themselves act as an arm of the state in their roles as service delivery practitioners. Coordinated fragmentation, user involvement, and multifaceted forms of recognition characterize a potentially autonomy-fostering state.

When the state fosters autonomy, it also provides a crucial conduit to full citizenship for service users. Because my focus in this book is on the delivery of social welfare services, the social dimensions of citizenship are of particular interest. Traditionally, social citizenship has been understood as the status that grants one access to the basic resources necessary to exercise one's autonomy, and in turn, to exercise political and civil rights. Because basic resources are conventionally understood in terms of material conditions rather than social relational conditions, accounts of social citizenship often fail to notice the importance of service delivery practices. But such practices are crucial not only for generating the conditions necessary to act autonomously, but also because service delivery is a key site for citizens' political learning and claims making.[4] Thus, though some theorists have rejected the notion of social citizenship as overly focused on rights rather than obligations, or as a mechanism for the exercise of disciplinary power, I have argued that when we rethink social citizenship in a manner that places a relational conception of autonomy at its center, the concept remains important to a larger understanding of inclusive citizenship.

Though my focus is often on social citizenship, in chapter 4 I explored the effects of welfare reforms on noncitizens. Although legally the immigrants who were harmed by the 1996 welfare reforms in the United States were not citizens, in many ways the questions that those reforms raised are ones of citizenship. As Linda Bosniak notes, "Status noncitizens are, in fact, not always and entirely outside the scope of those institutions and practices and experiences we call citizenship." It is rather their "personhood and national territorial presence" that confer some of the benefits we conventionally associate with citizenship.[5] In the case of the welfare reforms that served to deny access to certain institutions, practices, and experiences, questions regarding obligations to noncitizens arise. I have argued that the adequate provision for the rights of noncitizens, who may identify psychologically with many aspects of citizenship despite not having legal standing, is an important facet of taking political responsibility for the role of American foreign policies in shaping the global economy. Moreover, to generate an inclusive community of citizens and noncitizens alike, immigrants should have the right to claim autonomy-fostering social welfare services *in order* to exercise their own political responsibility.

An Empirically Situated Approach

The theories of citizenship, the state, service delivery, and autonomy that I propose in this book, and which I have summarized above, are founded on analyses of cases wherein the state is successful or unsuccessful in its attempts to foster autonomy. In all these cases, I suggest that the ways that autonomy is theorized have an important effect on the policies that follow. It is easy to attribute policies to "factual" knowledge, as though they are based on prescriptions that must follow inevitably: the poor and welfare dependent are "not like you and me," but rather require paternalistic services to "direct" their behavior toward their own goals. Immigrants pursue a life in the United States because they want to shirk their responsibilities and "leech" off the system; this implies a need for welfare policies that act as deterrents to immigration. Mandatory arrest policies in domestic violence cases necessarily infringe on privacy and therefore cannot foster autonomy. People who are addicted to drugs cannot make autonomous choices; the only solutions to their problems are policies that facilitate abstinence. All these claims are based on overly individualistic and atomistic theories of autonomy and the self, not on expert knowledge that cannot be challenged. As Mark Bevir argues, "The intentions of actors derive in part from traditions, discourses, or systems of knowledge that are . . . social constructs."[6] Such is the case for those actors whose policies shape social service delivery practices. Thus, in both the cases that demonstrate a failure to foster autonomy and those that succeed, we must pay attention to what those traditions, discourses, and systems of knowledge are, what notions of autonomy they produce, and what their implications are for the vulnerable citizens who rely on welfare services. In trying to draw lessons from the various cases I have used in this book, I interrogate the theoretical foundations of social welfare policy in order to conceive of the elements of an autonomy-fostering state. Without such cases, I argue that such theorizing would be difficult if not untenable. For this reason, I conclude with some reflection on this method, which I understand as an empirically situated approach to political theory.

Joseph Carens defends what he calls a "contextual approach" to political theory by appealing to a number of reasons why engaging with specific cases is a fruitful way of "doing" political theory. He writes, "The underlying presupposition of this sort of contextual approach to theory is that actual social and political practices sometimes contain embedded wisdom. Societies may come over time to do the right thing in response to concrete problems without managing to articulate in theoretical terms why it is the right thing."[7] Indeed, it is the case that such "embedded wisdom" can be found in unique models of service delivery, such as those that I discuss in chapters 5 and 6. Though not necessarily articulated, however, what I understand as "the right thing" and what practitioners do in order to make it so is informed by particular conceptions of, in the case of my study, autonomy. That is, the right thing is not fact but interpretation. It makes sense, moreover, that practitioners of such models of service delivery—the street-level bureaucrats who I have suggested, follow-ing Lipsky, are crucial mediators of access to citizenship status and rights—do not, as Carens notes, manage to articulate in theoretical terms why such prac-tices are right. This might well be the case because they are engaged in a dif-ferent project altogether: while I have tried to use contextual analyses to inform a broader project of reconceptualizing autonomy, the state, citizen-ship, and service delivery itself, practitioners (who, we should not forget, may include service users themselves) have more immediate political and humani-tarian goals.

This distinction between my project and the aims of service delivery prac-titioners is important because it reflects another aspect of my theoretical and methodological approach: the feminist theoretical foundation of this book. Political theorists have often been criticized for failing to engage with empiri-cal realities and instead focusing on normative theories that take as their basis ideal conditions that are, to some extent, envisioned as outside politics. Ca-rens's work responds to this critique, as does some other recent work. In an article that examines the purpose and appropriate methods of the "theoretical endeavor" in the twenty-first century, Marc Stears notes that one response to questions regarding the appropriate relationship between empirical inquiry and normative political theory is a call for "a radical reconnection of the aims and methods of the theoretical academy with those of its empirical contempo-rary."[8] Though, as I note above, the aims of my project and those of practit-ioners may not be the same, that they are deeply intertwined reflects a move to the sort of "reconnection" to which Stears refers. One approach to methodol-ogy that may offer further insight into such a reconnection, and which in-forms my work, is found in some types of feminist scholarship.

Judith Squires and Wendy Martineau point to "the historically close con-nection between feminist scholarship and activism, the commitment to nor-mative goals and political change, and the attention paid by feminists to the epistemic issues surrounding empirical inquiry, knowledge production, and expertise."[9] While feminist scholars have not been plagued by the disconnect between theoretical and empirical work found in political science, their work is shaped by an ongoing critique of the "truth" value attributed to the findings of empirical inquiry. Feminist theorists tend to be "attuned to the power dy-namics entailed within certain positivist approaches."[10] Squires and Martin-eau, then, call for an approach to political theory that is dialogical and reflexive, that engages the subjects of the inquiry itself, and that is conscious of the struc-tural location and power dynamics that position the scholar herself in a given context.[11] Though the empirical nature of this project stops short of actually collecting primary data, I have engaged with the ethnographic work of other scholars in order to generate such a "dialogue" with the subjects of my inquiry—users of social welfare services.

Perhaps this is not enough. Does drawing on secondary ethnographic work for a case-based approach to political theory minimize some of the benefits of empirical engagement by virtue of its detachment from the field itself? I think there is merit to this concern and, indeed, I think political theorists, particularly feminist political theorists, may have much to gain from engaging in primary field research. Nonetheless, wherever our data come from, we should read them as we do texts—in an interpretive manner. Thus, just as I do not assign "truth value" to the quotations that the ethnographers whose work I draw on cite, instead using these quotations as sites at which to understand the nature and practices of meaning making, primary data should not be seen as "factual." Squires and Martineau argue that "the methodological contribution of feminist political theory therefore resides both in the rejection of normative theory as a source of moral commands that political theorists help to realise, and in its skepticism of positivist political science as a source of objective facts that political actors simply seek to disseminate."[12] Whether political theorists take up the approach I have in this book or go further to engage with primary data, be it qualitative, archival, or ethnographic, such skepticism must remain in place. In advocating an "empirically situated" approach to political theory, I am not at the same time gesturing toward a more positivistic political theory. I have tried to navigate the path between normative theories and empirical accounts in this book without appealing to such a positivistic paradigm. Rather, by highlighting the power relations within which our understanding and ascriptions of autonomy exist, I have emphasized not only the interpretive but also the political nature of defining service delivery and theorizing autonomy and citizenship.

Though not always explicitly addressed in the book, the political nature of service delivery never lurks far from the surface; whether it is in the context of debates over the role of the state in domestic violence survivors' lives or shifting interpretations of citizenship and migration, practices of social service delivery necessarily exist within shifting configurations of power relations. The structure, content, and aims of these services are always subject to contestation, challenge, and subversion. They emerge out of processes of negotiation, conflict, and sometimes cooperation. That social service delivery is a political realm should not be surprising given what is at stake in this realm. If there is a realm where questions of "who gets what, when, and how" are ever present, social service delivery is it. Such questions of distribution are at the heart of service delivery. They are also at the heart of "autonomy fostering," the mode of service delivery and the model of the state I have proposed in this book. In the preceding chapters, I have suggested that what is at stake in autonomy-fostering practices is not only the distribution of material resources (which are indeed necessary for the development and exercise of autonomy), but also the distribution of relational support—the configuration of appropriate social relationships that enable individuals to develop the capacity to be autonomous and to be recognized as such.

Conclusion

The state can foster autonomy. No one autonomy-fostering state exists, but in perhaps unexpected locations within various states, there exist innovative modes of social welfare service delivery that effectively foster individual autonomy. Moreover, they do so in citizens who are among the most vulnerable in our society—who are stigmatized and marginalized, who are dependent, and whose lives are cloaked in uncertainty and precariousness. To open our eyes to such instances of the autonomy-fostering state, we must rethink our conceptions of autonomy, citizenship, the state, and service delivery. I have endeavored to do this in each of the cases I have analyzed in the foregoing chapters. Looking not to an idealistic vision of the good society, but to existing practices—messy and incomplete as they sometimes may be—I have argued that several key elements enable the state to foster autonomy. Among these, I have pointed to the importance of user involvement; the value of a state that is at once fragmented and coordinated, opening up spaces for critique and contestation; the necessity of recognizing and attending to embodied needs; and the role of practices that generate appropriate ascriptive autonomy.

As I write this book, the economic crisis in the United States (and around the globe) has seen record numbers of people making claims on the state for the resources they so desperately need to keep themselves and their families afloat. At the same time, fears of "big government" and state intervention are stoked by the rhetoric of contemporary political debate. It is only when we can rethink our understanding of what it means to be dependent, when we can envision state intervention that enables autonomy rather than that which replicates relations of domination and oppression, that we will be able to meet people's needs without casting on them a stigmatizing light. Moreover, it is when members of our communities can access an autonomy-fostering state that they are most likely to come to understand themselves as citizens in the fullest sense, shaped by their rights, obligations, and duties.

Notes

....

CHAPTER 1

1. Among the many works that take up relational autonomy (some without using the term) are the following: Benhabib, *Situating the Self*; Benson, "Autonomy and Oppressive Socialization"; Christman, "Saving Positive Freedom"; Christman, *Inner Citadel*; Fraser and Gordon, "A Genealogy of Dependency"; Friedman, *Autonomy, Gender, Politics*; Kittay, *Love's Labor*; Mackenzie and Stoljar, *Relational Autonomy*; Minow, *Making All the Difference*; Nedelsky, "Reconceiving Autonomy"; Nedelsky, "Law, Boundaries, and the Bounded Self"; Young, *Justice and the Politics of Difference*.

2. Nedelsky, "Reconceiving Autonomy," 9.

3. Anderson and Honneth, "Autonomy, Vulnerability, Recognition, and Justice," 129.

4. Christman, "Saving Positive Freedom," 87.

5. Anderson and Honneth, "Autonomy, Vulnerability, Recognition, and Justice," 127.

6. Ibid., 132–37.

7. Mackenzie, "Relational Autonomy, Normative Authority, and Perfectionism," 525.

8. Anderson and Honneth, "Autonomy, Vulnerability, Recognition, and Justice," 130.

9. Friedman, "Autonomy and Male Dominance," 157.

10. Ibid., 162. In a situated that is *not* characterized by chronic domination, however, one might also be more likely to take advantage of needed protection, while maintaining the appropriate critical stance in relation to the source of protection. For example, in chapter 3, I explore potentially autonomy-enabling services for domestic violence survivors that can be understood as a form of protection.

11. Mackenzie and Stoljar, "Introduction," 13.

12. Friedman, *Autonomy, Gender, Politics*, 21.

13. Benson, "Autonomy and Oppressive Socialization," 385.

14. Benson, "Feeling Crazy."

15. Benson, "Feminist Intuitions and the Normative Substance of Autonomy," 133.

16. See Christman, "Relational Autonomy, Liberal Individualism, and the Social Constitution of Selves."

17. See Fallon, "Two Senses of Autonomy"; LaVaque-Manty, "Kant's Children."

18. Honneth, *Struggle for Recognition*; Taylor, *Multiculturalism and "The Politics of Recognition."* Nancy Fraser also discusses the effects and implications of misrecognition, but she focuses more on the institutional effect, expressing some wariness about exploring the psychic effects. This is discussed in more detail in chapter 3. See Fraser, "From Redistribution to Recognition?"; Fraser and Honneth, *Redistribution or Recognition?*

19. See LaVaque-Manty, "Kant's Children."

20. Marshall, *Citizenship and Social Class*, 6.

21. Ibid., 8.

22. Ibid., 15.

23. Gordon, "The New Feminist Scholarship on the Welfare State." See also Lister, *Citizenship*.

24. Bosniak, *The Citizen and the Alien*.

25. Ibid., 7.

26. Cohen, "Carved from the Inside Out," 33.

27. Lipsky, *Street-Level Bureaucracy*, 4.

28. Ibid., 162.

29. Ibid., 160.

30. Ibid., 178.

31. For a feminist critique of bureaucracy, see Ferguson, *Feminist Case Against Bureaucracy*.

32. Lipsky, *Street-Level Bureaucracy*, 183.

33. Ibid., 181.

34. The passage of PRWORA has some interesting implications for service delivery, which I will discuss in my book (e.g., the institution of conditional benefits that give rise to new sanctioning procedures, which may result in permanent loss of benefits for some recipients).

35. Lipsky, *Street-Level Bureaucracy*, 181.

36. Soss, *Unwanted Claims*, 153.

37. Ibid.

38. Ibid., 16.

39. At the time of Soss's study, "public aid," or what is generally known as "welfare," took the form of Aid to Families with Dependent Children (AFDC). As of 1996, AFDC no longer exists. In its stead, eligible individuals receive Temporary Assistance for Needy Families on the condition of meeting relatively stringent work requirements.

40. Piven and Cloward, *Poor People's Movements*; Piven and Cloward, *Regulating the Poor*.

41. Piven and Cloward, *Regulating the Poor*, 7.

42. Brown, "Finding the Man in the State."

43. Brown divides the state into its liberal, capitalist, prerogative, and bureaucratic dimensions.

44. Gordon, "The New Feminist Scholarship on the Welfare State," 22.

45. Ibid.

46. Cruikshank, *Will to Empower*, 67.

47. Ibid., 4.

48. Ibid., 90.

49. Chapter 3 presents an account of the loosely coupled arms of the state, drawn from work by Lynne Haney. See Haney's "Feminist State Theory" and "Homeboys, Babies, Men in Suits."

CHAPTER 2

1. Marshall, *Citizenship and Social Class*, 8.

2. Kymlicka and Norman, "Return of the Citizen"; Lister, *Citizenship*.

3. In Marshall's account, social citizenship is only one of three prongs of citizenship (civil, political, and social). While social citizenship is most immediately relevant to questions of social service delivery, the legal aspects of citizenship are also of immediate import in decisions about how one is entitled to services; indeed, the two must be understood as

mutually constitutive. I return to the legal aspects of citizenship and their relation to social citizenship in chapter 4.

4. Some programs advanced by particular arms of the state do reflect the model of social rights I propose in this chapter, such as the ones I discuss in the cases that appear in chapters 5 and 6. Nevertheless, I do not claim that any one state as a whole successfully offers social rights as defined in this chapter, as of yet.

5. Fraser, "Struggle over Needs."

6. Marshall, *Citizenship and Social Class*, 28.

7. Gorham, "Social Citizenship and Its Fetters," 27.

8. Ibid., 29.

9. Ibid.

10. Ibid., 36.

11. Piven and Cloward, *Poor People's Movements*; Piven and Cloward, *Regulating the Poor*.

12. In this sense, I am in a way *stipulating* that Piven and Cloward are offering a critique of social citizenship. While they might actually advocate for social citizenship broadly speaking, what I want to show is that their analysis of the current (and past) state of social citizenship in the United States highlights what social control–focused critiques of the *concept* of social citizenship have in mind. That is, Piven and Cloward argue that social citizenship, as it has been instantiated in the United States, fails because it has at its core an impetus to control or "regulate" the poor.

13. In chapter 3, I return to a discussion of the ways that "work" is conceived in welfare debates.

14. Piven and Cloward, *Regulating the Poor*, 6.

15. Ibid., 33.

16. Ibid.

17. Ibid., 35.

18. Kymlicka and Norman, "Return of the Citizen," 354–55.

19. Ibid., 356.

20. King and Waldron, "Citizenship, Social Citizenship and the Defence of Welfare Provision," 426.

21. Ibid., 428.

22. Ignatieff, "Citizenship and Moral Narcissism," 71.

23. Ibid., 70.

24. Ibid., 69.

25. Ibid.

26. Fraser, "Struggle over Needs."

27. Friedman, *Autonomy, Gender, Politics*.

28. Christman, "Saving Positive Freedom," 87.

29. See, for example, Lipsky, *Street-Level Bureaucracy*; Soss, *Unwanted Claims*.

30. Fraser, "Struggle over Needs," 200.

31. Ibid., 202.

32. Ibid.

33. Ibid.

34. Julie White provides a helpful analysis of the importance of a more participatory politics of need interpretation and care for democratic politics. See *Democracy, Justice, and the Welfare State*, 135–37.

35. Gorham, "Social Citizenship and Its Fetters," 36.

36. This is not to say that all attributes of conditionality that may be found in a given welfare system are disqualified. Only perhaps a system of guaranteed annual income would achieve this, but it would fail on other fronts I cannot discuss here. The point is simply that

any social rights must be evaluated not only on whether they provide material resources, but also on whether (in this case) the conditions accompanying these resources foster or hinder autonomy competency.

37. I do not mean to claim that certain classes or categories of people are "less autonomous" than others by nature, or even by virtue of their social location. In my account of autonomy, however, there is reason to believe that those who have been subject to recurring and sustained experiences of domination may be more likely to have been limited in their abilities to develop and exercise the capacity for autonomy. See Friedman, "Autonomy and Male Dominance."

38. Cruikshank, *Will to Empower*, 38.

39. Ibid., 41.

40. Ibid.

41. Ibid., 72, 86.

42. King and Waldron, "Citizenship, Social Citizenship and the Defence of Welfare Provision," 428.

43. Fraser and Gordon, "A Genealogy of Dependency," 19.

44. Minow, *Making All the Difference*, 293.

45. Ibid.

46. See the discussions of ascriptive autonomy in later chapters.

CHAPTER 3

1. For examples of "relational" feminist accounts of autonomy, see the following: Friedman, *Autonomy, Gender, Politics*; Mackenzie and Stoljar, *Relational Autonomy*; Nedelsky, "Reconceiving Autonomy"; Ben-Ishai, "Autonomy-Fostering State."

2. PRWORA is marked by an end to "entitlement," the imposition of work requirements, lifetime limits, sanctions, and narrowed eligibility. See Weaver, *Ending Welfare as We Know It*.

3. Such conceptions of paternalism are offered by White in *Democracy, Justice, and the Welfare State*, and Smiley in "Paternalism and Democracy."

4. Mill, *On Liberty*.

5. Dworkin, "Paternalism," 108.

6. Ibid., 117.

7. I take the notion of autonomy as a status, or as ascriptive, from LaVaque-Manty, "Kant's Children." See also Ben-Ishai, "Sexual Politics and Ascriptive Autonomy."

8. On the politics of recognition, see, for example, Fraser, "From Redistribution to Recognition?"; Honneth, *Struggle for Recognition*.

9. Dworkin, "Paternalism," 117.

10. Ibid., 125.

11. Smiley, "Paternalism and Democracy," 308.

12. Ibid., 309.

13. Ibid., 311.

14. Ibid., 314.

15. White, *Democracy, Justice, and the Welfare State*, 135–37.

16. Ibid., 136.

17. Dworkin, "Paternalism," 119.

18. White, *Democracy, Justice, and the Welfare State*, 136.

19. Mead, "Rise of Paternalism," 2.

20. Ibid., 5.
21. Ibid., 7–8.
22. Ibid., 9.
23. Smith, *Welfare Reform and Sexual Regulation*, 38.
24. Mead, *The New Paternalism*.
25. Schram, "Review," 671.
26. Mead, "Rise of Paternalism," 26.
27. Ibid., 27.
28. Schram, Fording, and Soss, "Neo-liberal Poverty Governance."
29. Smith, *Welfare Reform and Sexual Regulation*, 55.
30. Schram, Fording, and Soss, "Neo-liberal Poverty Governance," 19.
31. Mead, *Government Matters*, 158.
32. Ibid.
33. This was President Bill Clinton's pledge, and an oft-repeated phrase in discussions of welfare reform.
34. PRWORA requires recipients to work within two years of receiving aid in order to continue the receipt of aid. But states can avert this requirement if they demonstrate reduced caseloads of a certain level. Since the rolls have fallen dramatically in most states, work for welfare has not increased immensely.
35. Maynard, "Paternalism, Teenage Pregnancy Prevention, and Teenage Parent Services," 91.
36. Mead, "Welfare Employment," 64.
37. Wilson, *When Work Disappears*, 39.
38. Mead, "Welfare Employment," 49.
39. Smith, *Lone Pursuit*, 22. Thanks to Anne Manuel for directing me to this source.
40. Ibid.
41. Ibid., 30.
42. Maynard, "Paternalism, Teenage Pregnancy Prevention, and Teenage Parent Services," 91.
43. Edin and Kefalas, *Promises I Can Keep*.
44. Ibid., 34. They take the term "relational poverty" from Kaplan, *Not Our Kind of Girl*.
45. Ibid., 24.
46. For a much fuller discussion of the issue of care work and welfare, see the first four essays in Hirschmann and Liebert, *Women and Welfare*.
47. Pateman, "Another Way Forward," 36.
48. Mead, "Welfare Reform and Citizenship," 188.
49. Smith, "Sexual Regulation Dimension of Contemporary Welfare Law."
50. Mead, "Welfare Reform and Citizenship," 189.
51. For a discussion of the role of work in conceptions of American citizenship, see Shklar, *American Citizenship*.
52. This is not meant to perpetuate a claim that the poor are somehow "different from the rest of us." Rather, values are always contextually formed and forming, and may lack consistency or, at times, be opposed to one another—even in autonomous individuals. It is the ways that inconsistencies and oppositions are managed that are most revealing in the long run.
53. Edin and Kefalas, *Promises I Can Keep*, 182.
54. Ibid., 34.
55. Ibid., 206.
56. See Westlund, "Selflessness and Responsibility for Self."
57. Kaplan, *Not Our Kind of Girl*, 11.

58. Ibid., 181.

59. See recent debates about middle-class professional mothers who "opt out" of successful careers in favor of caring for their children full-time. The original article that sparked this debate is Belkin's "The Opt-Out Revolution."

60. Edin and Kefalas, *Promises I Can Keep*, 205.

61. Ibid., 206.

62. Some studies make claims about the value of low-wage jobs, despite middle-class perceptions of their fulfillment value. See, for example, Newman, *No Shame in My Game*.

63. Beem and Mead, "Introduction."

64. Mead, "Summary of Welfare Reform," 177.

65. For more on the two-tiered welfare system, see Soss, *Unwanted Claims*.

66. Mead, "Summary of Welfare Reform," 177.

67. Ibid., 178.

68. Mead, "Welfare Reform and Citizenship."

69. King, "Making People Work," 74.

70. Ibid.

71. Soss and Schram, "A Public Transformed?," 111 (quoting E. E. Schattschneider).

72. Cited in ibid., 112–13.

73. Ibid., 120.

74. Dyck and Hussey, "End of Welfare as We Know It?"

75. King, "Making People Work," 74.

76. Wilson, "Paternalism, Democracy, and Bureaucracy," 341.

77. Ibid., 340.

78. White, "Social Rights and the Social Contract." 515–16.

79. Kaplan, *Not Our Kind of Girl*, 184.

80. Ibid., 190.

81. White, *Democracy, Justice, and the Welfare State*, 136.

82. Mead, "Rise of Paternalism," 28.

CHAPTER 4

1. See Marshall, *Citizenship and Social Class*.

2. Fujiwara, *Mothers Without Citizenship*, 25.

3. Shachar, *Birthright Lottery*; Young, "Responsibility and Global Labor Justice."

4. Ibid., 3.

5. Young, "Responsibility and Global Labor Justice," 381.

6. Fujiwara, *Mothers Without Citizenship*; Marchevsky and Theoharis, *Not Working*.

7. Tumlin and Zimmermann, *Immigrants and TANF*, 2.

8. Marchevsky and Theoharis, *Not Working*, 22.

9. Fujiwara, *Mothers Without Citizenship*, 41.

10. Ibid.

11. Tumlin and Zimmermann, *Immigrants and TANF*, 15.

12. See Hero and Preuhs, "Immigration and the Evolving American Welfare State."

13. Fujiwara, *Mothers Without Citizenship*, 41.

14. See Zimmermann and Fix, *Declining Immigrant Applications for Medi-Cal and Welfare Benefits*.

15. Marchevsky and Theoharis, *Not Working*, 163.

16. Borjas, *Impact of Welfare Reform on Immigrant Welfare Use*. "Public charges" are immigrants who are likely to depend on the government for subsistence.

17. Borjas and Hilton, *Immigration and the Welfare State*.

18. See references provided in Fix and Passel, *Scope and Impact of Welfare Reform's Immigrant Provisions*, 8.

19. Fujiwara, *Mothers Without Citizenship*, 44.

20. Ibid.; Marchevsky and Theoharis, *Not Working*.

21. Shachar, *Birthright Lottery*, 1.

22. Mackenzie and Stoljar review the varieties of procedural and substantive accounts of autonomy in the introduction to their edited volume on relational autonomy. See Mackenzie and Stoljar, "Introduction." In the next chapter, I argue in support of a particularly framed substantive account of autonomy.

23. Benson, "Feeling Crazy," 73.

24. Ibid., 83.

25. Sassen, "America's Immigration 'Problem,'" 829.

26. Fujiwara, *Mothers Without Citizenship*, 44.

27. Ibid.

28. The decision to come to the United States is mischaracterized as a "free" choice, insofar as one makes the decision in a particular context and as one must be granted permission to act on that decision. Fujiwara notes that "access by noncitizens whose migration is due to economic necessity as a result of neoliberal policies" has also been limited. Ibid.

29. Sassen, "America's Immigration 'Problem,'" 813–14.

30. Ibid., 819.

31. Marchevsky and Theoharis, *Not Working*, 17.

32. Ibid., 27.

33. Ibid., 67.

34. See Harvey, *Condition of Postmodernity*.

35. Marchevsky and Theoharis, *Not Working*, 18.

36. Inda, "Flexible World," 90.

37. For an example of the former argument, see Macedo, "Moral Dilemma of U.S. Immigration Policy." Ryan Pevnick argues against the assertion of Macedo and others that there is a necessary trade-off between the provision of redistributive programs for citizens and liberal immigration policies. See Pevnick, "Social Trust and the Ethics of Immigration Policy." Young cites Hannah Arendt's conception of political responsibility as a model for her own, but moves away from the citizen/membership approach on which Arendt also relies. See Arendt, "Collective Responsibility."

38. Young, "Responsibility and Global Labor Justice," 376.

39. Ibid., 381.

40. Ibid., 376.

41. See Marshall, *Citizenship and Social Class*.

42. Bosniak, *The Citizen and the Alien*, chap. 3.

43. *Plyler v. Doe*, 457 U.S. 202 (1982).

44. Bosniak, *The Citizen and the Alien*, 66.

45. Ibid., 67.

46. Quoted in ibid.

47. Shachar, *Birthright Lottery*, 7, 3.

48. Ibid., 36, 37.

49. Ibid., 37–38.

50. Ibid., 165.

51. Ibid., 169.

52. Young, "Responsibility and Global Labor Justice," 373.

53. That is, if we assume that there remain constraints on who is permitted to enter the country lawfully. This is not to say that the current constraints on immigration are ideal,

but that they allow for at least some limits on the extent of responsibility. Were those constraints to change, the extent of responsibility and the best ways to discharge it might also shift.

54. Young, "Responsibility and Global Labor Justice," 381.

55. Fujiwara, *Mothers Without Citizenship*, 57–61.

56. Ibid. (quoting Ong, *Buddha Is Hiding*).

57. For a discussion of the "gratuity principle" in welfare policy, see Reich, "New Property."

58. Fujiwara, *Mothers Without Citizenship*, 63.

59. Ibid., 74.

60. Ibid., 85.

61. Ibid., 88.

62. Bosniak, *The Citizen and the Alien*, 68.

63. Fujiwara, *Mothers Without Citizenship*, 92.

64. Marchevsky and Theoharis, *Not Working*, 153–55.

65. For more on the "chilling effect" of welfare reform on immigrant welfare claims, see Fix and Passel, *Scope and Impact of Welfare Reform's Immigrant Provisions*.

66. Marchevsky and Theoharis, *Not Working*, 163.

67. Ibid., chap. 5.

68. Young, "Responsibility and Global Labor Justice," 387.

69. Of course, as Fujiwara notes, the Southeast Asian veterans were not granted the same status as American-born veterans. But for the public and media who took up their cause, this connection may have been helpful.

70. See Lipsky, *Street-Level Bureaucracy*.

71. Soss, *Unwanted Claims*, 61.

72. Marchevsky and Theoharis, *Not Working*, 27.

CHAPTER 5

1. A recent, prominent example of new feminist theorizing of the state is Cruikshank, *Will to Empower*.

2. See Haney, "Feminist State Theory."

3. For discussions of "care," see, for example, Chodorow, *Reproduction of Mothering*; Gilligan, *In a Different Voice*; Kittay and Feder, *Subject of Care*; Noddings, *Caring*; Tronto, *Moral Boundaries*; White, *Democracy, Justice, and the Welfare State*.

4. Brown, "Finding the Man in the State."

5. Pence and McMahon, *Coordinated Community Response to Domestic Violence*, 1.

6. Thelen, *Advocacy in a Coordinated Community Response*, 3.

7. For a critique of this model, see Nedelsky, "Law, Boundaries, and the Bounded Self."

8. Friedman, *Autonomy, Gender, Politics*, 13.

9. Haney, "Feminist State Theory," 659.

10. Brown, "Finding the Man in the State," 8.

11. Ibid., 7.

12. This disaggregation of the meanings of protection is parallel in some ways to the redefinition of paternalism discussed in chapter 3. There, I followed other theorists in arguing that paternalism should be understood not simply as intervention into the lives of individuals, but also as intervention that perpetuates relations of domination and inequality. In a similar sense, some forms of protection can be understood as the exertion of masculinist

state power where gendered relations of unequal power are reproduced and exacerbated, but it need not be understood as such.

13. Haney, "Homeboys, Babies, Men in Suits," 773.

14. For an interesting discussion of the links between theories of "new governance" and the policy reforms in Britain that led to fragmentation of the state (and attempts to remedy this fragmentation), see Bevir, *Democratic Governance.*

15. Pence and Shepard, "Introduction," 5.

16. Shepard and Pence, *Coordinating Community Responses to Domestic Violence,* 2.

17. Pence and McMahon, *Coordinated Community Response to Domestic Violence,* 11.

18. Pence and Shepard, "Introduction," 13.

19. The research on the efficacy of increased arrest and prosecution with regard to deterring future violence is ambiguous. A small selection among the many studies showing that pro-arrest policies are effective (in terms of reduced deterrence and reduced levels of violence) includes the following: Dutton et al., "Arrest and the Reduction of Repeat Wife Assault"; Zorza, "Must We Stop Arresting Batterers?"; Buel, "Recent Development"; Hanna, "No Right to Choose." Studies and analyses showing evidence to the contrary (i.e., *increased* recidivism or failure to deter some groups of batterers) include the following: Hirschel, Hutchison, and Dean, "Failure of Arrest to Deter Spouse Abuse"; Sherman and Smith, "Crime, Punishment, and Stake in Conformity"; Davis, Smith, and Nickles, "Deterrent Effect of Prosecuting Domestic Violence Misdemeanors"; Mahoney, "Legal Images of Battered Women."

20. On the genuine risks of "leaving" and the motivation for not doing so, see also Mahoney, "Legal Images of Battered Women."

21. Coker, "Crime Control and Feminist Law Reform in Domestic Violence Law," 826.

22. Friedman, *Autonomy, Gender, Politics,* 146. Below I will return to whether such beliefs and the actions that follow from them are actually autonomous.

23. Hanna, "No Right to Choose."

24. This parallels the larger structure of criminal law. Hanna writes, "The criminal justice systems serves the state; thus, prosecutors should not consider the individual wishes of abused women if those wishes conflict with community goals. Under this rationale, mandated participation would be justified in any case in which prosecution is in the state's interest," as it would be in any type of case that reflected "the state's interest." Ibid., 1872.

25. Ibid., 1870.

26. Friedman, *Autonomy, Gender, Politics,* 151.

27. Ibid., 150.

28. See note 19 above.

29. Miccio, "House Divided," 269.

30. As one reviewer of this book's manuscript noted, the proceduralist view does not commit theorists to saying that mandatory policies *always* undermine autonomy; if women endorse intervention, they can be seen as autonomous in this view. But it is the cases wherein women do not endorse intervention that require the most explanation. I suggest that in some cases, even where such endorsement is lacking, the state's policy (and the "state," in turn) may be autonomy fostering (and substantive).

31. For an example of the procedural account, see Friedman, *Autonomy, Gender, Politics.* See also Mackenzie and Stoljar, "Introduction." "Self-reflection" is an oversimplification of the proceduralist account.

32. Benson, "Feeling Crazy."

33. I am grateful to my colleagues and mentors at the University of Michigan for their suggestions in formulating this approach to substantive autonomy. In particular, Mariah Zeisberg provided valuable feedback on this issue.

34. Of course, entirely free choice is mythological, but I use the term to echo the rhetoric that such claims take up. Rather, the distinction is between always relationally situated decision-making processes, some of which are more or less constraining than others.

35. For one feminist account of substantive autonomy, see Stoljar, "Autonomy and the Feminist Intuition."

36. Oshana, *Personal Autonomy in Society*, 59. Oshana is referring to the case of a "subservient wife" who "chooses" her position. The case is different insofar as physical violence is different from subservience (thought not necessarily exclusive of it).

37. Christman, *Politics of Persons*, 172.

38. Friedman, *Autonomy, Gender, Politics*, 145.

39. U.S. Department of Agriculture, *Domestic Violence Awareness Handbook*.

40. See Friedman, *Autonomy, Gender, Politics*.

41. Raz, *Morality of Freedom*. Raz's account of "the hounded woman" provides a relevant account of the limitations that threats to survival pose to autonomy. See also LaVaque-Manty, "Food, Functioning, and Justice."

42. See, for example, Coker, "Crime Control and Feminist Law Reform in Domestic Violence Law"; Miccio, "House Divided."

43. This example is based both on my experience as a volunteer advocate in a CCR in Washtenaw County, Michigan, and on examples given in Shepard and Pence, *Coordinating Community Responses to Domestic Violence*, and Thelen, *Advocacy in a Coordinated Community Response*.

44. Brown, "Finding the Man in the State," 10.

45. Thelen, *Advocacy in a Coordinated Community Response*, 1.

46. SafeHouse Center, *SafeHouse Center Training Manual*, 20.

47. Thelen, *Advocacy in a Coordinated Community Response*, 2.

48. Ibid., 5, 9.

49. Ibid., 9.

50. Ibid., 12.

51. Gamache and Asmus, "Enhancing Networking Among Service Providers," 79.

52. The system also attempts to take into account the potential and extant power inequalities within the CCR system itself through a variety of mechanisms, including the use of private meetings (excluding criminal justice officials) to gather feedback from community members, ongoing training and education of officials in the justice system, flexibility in problem-solving strategies, and so on. See ibid., 80–82.

53. Coker, "Crime Control and Feminist Law Reform in Domestic Violence Law," 811.

54. The concept of "mestiza autonomy" recently proposed by Edwina Barvosa-Carter (2007) may be a helpful way of theorizing the experience of minority women or women who lack racial and class privilege, and the multiple commitments and loyalties they may have in their communities.

55. Haney, "Feminist State Theory," 659.

56. See, for example, Coker, "Crime Control and Feminist Law Reform in Domestic Violence Law"; Fraser, "Struggle over Needs"; Miccio, "House Divided."

57. See also McDermott and Garofalo, "When Advocacy for Domestic Violence Victims Backfires."

58. Piven, "Ideology and the State," 250.

CHAPTER 6

1. Negroponte, *Methadonia*.

2. Kerr et al., *Responding to an Emergency*, 33.

3. Wood et al., "Impact of a Police Presence on Access to Needle Exchange Programs," 116.

4. Ibid.

5. Human Rights Watch, *Abusing the User.*

6. Some methadone clinics in the United States are public, while increasingly more are privately owned and require clients to pay much higher dispensing fees. Regardless of whether it actually administers the "treatment," however, the state intervenes in methadone treatment insofar as it regulates the legality of and conditions under which methadone can be dispensed.

7. On ascriptive autonomy, see also LaVaque-Manty, "Kant's Children"; Fallon, "Two Senses of Autonomy."

8. Haney (drawing on other scholars' work) uses this notion of the loosely coupled arms of the state. See chapter 5 for further explanation. See also Haney, "Feminist State Theory."

9. Erickson, "Introduction," 6.

10. Sorge, "Harm Reduction."

11. Compare to new paternalist programs. See chapter 3.

12. Marlatt, "Basic Principles," 55.

13. See, for example, the essays in Elster, *Addiction*; Elster and Skog, *Getting Hooked.*

14. See, among others, Dole and Nyswander, "Medical Treatment for Diacetylmorphine (Heroin) Addiction"; Dole, Nyswander, and Kreek, "Narcotic Blockade"; Dole, Nyswander, and Warner, "Successful Treatment of 750 Criminal Addicts."

15. Tapert et al., "Harm Reduction Strategies," 152.

16. Dole, Nyswander, and Kreek, "Narcotic Blockade," 305. It is interesting to note this emphasis on work (labor market participation) as a primary source of meaning, or at least order, in one's life. See my discussion of work in chapter 5.

17. Tapert et al., "Harm Reduction Strategies," 152.

18. Taylor, *Multiculturalism and "The Politics of Recognition,"* 30.

19. Ibid., 25.

20. See, for example, Fraser and Honneth, *Redistribution or Recognition?*; Honneth, *Struggle for Recognition*; Taylor, *Multiculturalism and "The Politics of Recognition."* Taylor also points to the work of Fanon as demonstrating particularly poignantly the psychical effects of misrecognition. See, for example, Fanon, *Black Skin, White Masks.*

21. See Fraser and Honneth, *Redistribution or Recognition?*, 29.

22. See citations in Peterson et al., "Harm Reduction and HIV/AIDS Prevention," 154.

23. On the construction of the notion of dependence, see Fraser and Gordon, "A Genealogy of Dependency." Addiction provides a particularly poignant window into this pathologization.

24. Tapert et al., "Harm Reduction Strategies," 155.

25. Bourgois, "Disciplining Addictions," 173.

26. Bourgois claims that "a significant number of addicts actually managed to enjoy the methadone high," either by requesting higher doses than needed for "maintenance purposes" or because of the variations in the effects of methadone depending on one's metabolism. Ibid, 181. At the appropriate dose, however, most sources suggest that euphoria is minimal to nonexistent in dependent individuals. See Dole, Nyswander, and Kreek, "Narcotic Blockade," and Fiellin, Friedland, and Gourevitch, "Opioid Dependence."

27. Ibid., 175–76.

28. Negroponte, *Methadonia.*

29. Bourgois, "Disciplining Addictions"; Friedman and Alicea, *Surviving Heroin.*

30. Bourgois, "Disciplining Addictions," 167.

31. Ibid., 168.

32. Friedman and Alicea, *Surviving Heroin*, 130–31.

33. Ibid., 88.

34. Ibid., 91.

35. Taylor, *Multiculturalism and "The Politics of Recognition,"* 41–42.

36. The most well-known version of this is found in Habermas's theory of communicative action. See, among others, *Reason and the Rationalization of Society.* Seyla Benhabib also takes up a substitution model, though she is more attentive to the role of difference. See *Situating the Self.*

37. Young, *Intersecting Voices*, 39, 50. Young writes, "While comparing the situation and desert of agents according to some standard of equality is ultimately necessary for theorizing justice, prior to such comparison there is a moment of respect for the particular embodied sensitivity of the person."

38. Honneth, "On the Phenomenology of Experiences of Social Injustice," in Fraser and Honneth, *Redistribution or Recognition?*, 129.

39. Fraser, "Integrating Redistribution and Recognition," in ibid., 36.

40. Bourgois, "Disciplining Addictions," 167, 169.

41. Ibid., 189. See also Bourgois, *In Search of Respect.*

42. Bourgois, "Disciplining Addictions," 189.

43. Patchen Markell suggests that in all instances of recognition—as it is defined both by those who, following Taylor and Honneth, focus on the psychic consequences of misrecognition, and by those who, following Fraser, focus on the institutional consequences—a problematic aspiration for sovereignty over the self emerges. "Invoking identity as a *fait accompli* precisely in the course of the ongoing and risky interactions through which we become who we are (or, more precisely, who we will turn out to have been)," he writes, "[the politics of recognition] at once acknowledges and refuses to acknowledge our basic condition of intersubjective vulnerability." *Bound by Recognition*, 14. I do not agree that all forms of recognition require this type of limited notion of identity. Instead, I suggest that some forms of recognition can attend to identity as a flexible, relationally constructed, unfixed entity, while still—adopting something like a time-slice approach—attending to the institutional and psychic needs of the subjects whose ability to achieve autonomy, I believe, still depends on some form of recognition.

44. This distinction between contexts that are more ideal or less ideal for the development of autonomy reflects the weak substantive view of autonomy that I adopt. I discuss this notion of autonomy—as opposed to the procedural view of autonomy, which would likely make no normative distinction between street respect and alternative forms of respect and recognition as contexts for the development of autonomy—elsewhere in the book.

45. Friedman and Alicea, *Surviving Heroin*, 89.

46. Ibid., 90.

47. Ibid., 91.

48. Ibid., 130.

49. Croft and Beresford, "User-Involvement, Citizenship and Social Policy," 16.

50. Peterson et al., "Harm Reduction and HIV/AIDS Prevention," 230.

51. See the PreventionWorks! website, http://www.preventionworksdc.org/.

52. See, for example, Wood et al., "Impact of a Police Presence on Access to Needle Exchange Programs."

53. LaVaque-Manty, "Kant's Children," 369.

54. See Ben-Ishai, "Sexual Politics and Ascriptive Autonomy."

55. Young, *Intersecting Voices*, 59.

56. Croft and Beresford, "Politics of Participation," 31.

57. Ibid., 32.

58. Cavalieri, "Working with Lives and Not Just Veins," 15.

59. Kerr et al., *Responding to an Emergency*, 10.

60. Ibid., 15.

61. Ibid., 16.

62. The report on VANDU notes that although the organization is indeed user-run, the (paid) program director, Ann Livingston, is not a current or former user. But members interviewed in the King report claim that Livingston's actions are guided by the users. As an advocate for users who are subject to the illegality of drug use in Canada, Livingston has the advantage of increased stability and some immunity from the various risks that drugs users face, which may at times compromise the consistency of their service. Though outsiders have raised some questions about this dynamic (e.g., the propriety of being led by a nonuser), internally the group is supportive of her role. Ibid., 21.

63. Ibid., 33.

64. Erving Goffman describes the Greek conception of stigma as closely related to "bodily signs designed to expose something unusual and bad about the moral status of the signifier." While he claims that the modern notion of stigma is less concerned with bodily evidence and more focused on "the disgrace itself than [to] the bodily evidence of it," his further analysis of stigma still demonstrates the key role of the body in generating such disgrace. See *Stigma*, 1–2.

65. Kerr et al., *Responding to an Emergency*.

66. Croft and Beresford, "User-Involvement, Citizenship, and Social Policy," 16.

67. Hodge, "Participation, Discourse, and Power," 165.

68. Ibid., 168.

69. Ibid., 177.

70. See chapter 5, where I explore the fragmented state's potential for creating space for fostering autonomy where it is not necessarily intended. In this case, Hodge notes, "the impetus for [the forum's] creation came primarily from the key statutory mental health agencies in the locality which need to be seen to be promoting user involvement." Ibid., 166. But even if the motivation was driven by statutory requirements, this does not rule out progressive implications.

71. Wood et al., "Impact of a Police Presence on Access to Needle Exchange Programs."

72. Kerr, Oleson, and Wood, "Harm-Reduction Activism," 14.

73. Ibid., 17.

74. Hathaway, "Shortcomings of Harm Reduction," 125, 128, 134 (italics in original).

75. Ibid., 135.

CHAPTER 7

1. Marilyn Friedman argues that feminist critiques of mainstream philosophers' overly individualistic conceptions of autonomy are now obsolete; many philosophers acknowledge the role of social relationships in the constitution of the autonomous self. My concern in this book has not been primarily to criticize philosophical conceptions of autonomy, but rather to critique scholarly and popular notions of social welfare service delivery and the state that are shaped by an overly individualistic conception of the autonomous self. Friedman, *Autonomy, Gender, Politics*, 91.

2. As I note in chapter 5, if mandatory arrest is instituted *alone*, without the necessary supportive services that constitute CCRs, this may not be the case.

3. Haney, "Feminist State Theory."

4. See Lipsky, *Street-Level Bureaucracy*; Soss, *Unwanted Claims*.

5. Bosniak, *The Citizen and the Alien*, 3.
6. Bevir, *Democratic Governance*, 60.
7. Carens, "Contextual Approach to Political Theory," 121.
8. Stears, "Vocation of Political Theory," 326.
9. Squires and Martineau, "Addressing the 'Dismal Disconnection,'" 1.
10. Ibid., 11.
11. Ibid.
12. Ibid.

Bibliography

Anderson, Joel, and Axel Honneth. "Autonomy, Vulnerability, Recognition, and Justice." In *Autonomy and the Challenges of Liberalism: New Essays*, edited by John Philip Christman and Joel Anderson, 127–49. Cambridge: Cambridge University Press, 2005.

Arendt, Hannah. "Collective Responsibility." In *Amor Mundi: Explorations in the Faith and Thought of Hannah Arendt*, edited by James W. Bernauer, 43–50. Boston: Martinus Nijhoff, 1987.

Barvosa-Carter, Edwina. "Mestiza Autonomy as Relational Autonomy: Ambivalence and the Social Character of Free Will." *The Journal of Political Philosophy* 15, no. 1 (2007): 1–21.

Beem, Christopher, and Lawrence M. Mead. "Introduction." In Mead and Beem, *Welfare Reform and Political Theory*, 172–99.

Belkin, Lisa. "The Opt-Out Revolution." *New York Times Magazine*, October 26, 2003.

Benhabib, Seyla. *Situating the Self: Gender, Community, and Postmodernism in Contemporary Ethics*. New York: Routledge, 1992.

Ben-Ishai, Elizabeth. "The Autonomy-Fostering State: 'Coordinated Fragmentation' and Domestic Violence Services." *Journal of Political Philosophy* 17, no. 3 (2009): 307–31.

———. "Sexual Politics and Ascriptive Autonomy." *Politics & Gender* 6, no. 4 (2010): 573–600.

Benson, Paul. "Autonomy and Oppressive Socialization." *Social Theory and Practice* 17, no. 3 (1991): 385–408.

———. "Feeling Crazy: Self-Worth and the Social Character of Responsibility." In Mackenzie and Stoljar, *Relational Autonomy*, 72–93.

———. "Feminist Intuitions and the Normative Substance of Autonomy." In *Personal Autonomy: New Essays on Personal Autonomy and Its Role in Contemporary Moral Philosophy*, edited by James Stacey Taylor, 124–42. Cambridge: Cambridge University Press, 2005.

Bevir, Mark. *Democratic Governance*. Princeton: Princeton University Press, 2010.

Borjas, George J. *The Impact of Welfare Reform on Immigrant Welfare Use*. Washington, D.C.: Center for Immigration Studies, 2002.

Borjas, George J., and Lynette Hilton. *Immigration and the Welfare State: Immigrant Participation in Means Tested Entitlement Programs*. Cambridge, Mass.: National Bureau of Economic Research, 1995.

Bosniak, Linda. *The Citizen and the Alien: Dilemmas of Contemporary Membership*. Princeton: Princeton University Press, 2006.

Bourgois, Philippe. "Disciplining Addictions: The Bio-politics of Methadone and Heroin in the United States." *Culture, Medicine, and Psychiatry* 24, no. 2 (2000): 165–95.

———. *In Search of Respect: Selling Crack in El Barrio*. 2nd ed. Structural Analysis in the Social Sciences. Cambridge: Cambridge University Press, 2003.

Brown, Wendy. "Finding the Man in the State." *Feminist Studies* 18, no. 1 (1992): 7–34.

Buel, Sarah M. "Recent Development: Mandatory Arrest for Domestic Violence." *Harvard Women's Law Journal* 11 (1988): 213–26.

Carens, Joseph H. "A Contextual Approach to Political Theory." *Ethical Theory and Moral Practice* 7, no. 2 (2004): 117–32.

Cavalieri, Walter. "Working with Lives and Not Just Veins." *Harm Reduction Communication*, Spring 1998.

Chodorow, Nancy. *The Reproduction of Mothering: Psychoanalysis and the Sociology of Gender.* Berkeley: University of California Press, 1978.

Christman, John, ed. *The Inner Citadel: Essays on Individual Autonomy.* New York: Oxford University Press, 1989.

———. *The Politics of Persons: Individual Autonomy and Socio-historical Selves.* Cambridge: Cambridge University Press, 2009.

———. "Relational Autonomy, Liberal Individualism, and the Social Constitution of Selves." *Philosophical Studies* 117, nos. 1/2 (2004): 143–64.

———. "Saving Positive Freedom." *Political Theory* 33, no. 1 (2005): 79–88.

Cohen, Elizabeth. "Carved from the Inside Out: Immigration and America's Public Philosophy of Citizenship." In *Debating Immigration*, edited by Carol M. Swain, 32–45. New York: Cambridge University Press, 2007.

Coker, Donna. "Crime Control and Feminist Law Reform in Domestic Violence Law: A Critical Review." *Buffalo Criminal Law Review* 801, no. 4 (2001): 1–56.

Croft, Suzy, and Peter Beresford. "The Politics of Participation." *Critical Social Policy* 35, no. 4 (1992): 20–44.

———. "User-Involvement, Citizenship, and Social Policy." *Critical Social Policy* 16, no. 1 (1989): 5–18.

Cruikshank, Barbara. *The Will to Empower: Democratic Citizens and Other Subjects.* Ithaca: Cornell University Press, 1999.

Davis, Robert C., Barbara E. Smith, and Laura B. Nickles. "The Deterrent Effect of Prosecuting Domestic Violence Misdemeanors." *Crime and Delinquency* 44, no. 3 (1998): 434–42.

Dole, V. P., and M. E. Nyswander. "A Medical Treatment for Diacetylmorphine (Heroin) Addiction: A Clinical Trial with Methadone Hydrochloride." *Journal of the American Medical Association* 193, no. 8 (1965): 646–50.

Dole, V. P., M. E. Nyswander, and M. J. Kreek. "Narcotic Blockade." *Archives of Internal Medicine* 118, no. 4 (1966): 304–9.

Dole, V. P., M. E. Nyswander, and A. Warner. "Successful Treatment of 750 Criminal Addicts." *Journal of the American Medical Association* 206, no. 12 (1968): 2708–11.

Dutton, Donald G., Stephen D. Hart, Les W. Kennedy, and Kirk R. Williams. "Arrest and the Reduction of Repeat Wife Assault." In *Domestic Violence: The Changing Criminal Justice Response*, edited by Eve S. Buzawa and Carl G. Buzawa, 111–28. Westport, Conn.: Auburn House, 1992.

Dworkin, Gerald. "Paternalism." In *Morality and the Law*, edited by Richard A. Wasserstrom, 107–26. Belmont, Calif.: Wadsworth, 1971.

Dyck, Joshua J., and Laura S. Hussey. "The End of Welfare as We Know It? Durable Attitudes in a Changing Information Environment." *Public Opinion Quarterly* 72, no. 4 (2008): 589–618.

Edin, Kathryn, and Maria Kefalas. *Promises I Can Keep: Why Poor Women Put Motherhood Before Marriage.* Berkeley: University of California Press, 2005.

Elster, Jon, ed. *Addiction: Entries and Exits.* New York: Russell Sage Foundation, 1999.

Elster, Jon, and Ole-Jşştorgen Skog, eds. *Getting Hooked: Rationality and Addiction*. Cambridge: Cambridge University Press, 1999.

Erickson, P. G. "Introduction." In *Harm Reduction: A New Direction for Drug Policies and Programs*, edited by P. G. Erickson, D. M. Riley, Y. W. Cheung, and P. A. O'Hare, 1–30. Toronto: University of Toronto Press, 1997.

Fallon, Richard H. "Two Senses of Autonomy." *Stanford Law Review* 46, no. 4 (1994): 875–905.

Fanon, Frantz. *Black Skin, White Masks*. London: MacGibbon & Kee, 1968.

Ferguson, Kathy E. *The Feminist Case Against Bureaucracy*. Women in the Political Economy. Philadelphia: Temple University Press, 1984.

Fiellin, David A., Gerald H. Friedland, and Marc N. Gourevitch. "Opioid Dependence: Rationale for and Efficacy of Existing and New Treatments." *Clinical Infectious Diseases* 43, suppl. 4 (2006): S173–77.

Fix, Michael, and Jeffrey Passel. *The Scope and Impact of Welfare Reform's Immigrant Provisions*. Washington, D.C.: Urban Institute, 2002.

Fraser, Nancy. "From Redistribution to Recognition? Dilemmas of Justice in a 'Postsocialist' Age." In *Justice Interruptus: Critical Reflections on The "Postsocialist" Condition*, 11–39. New York: Routledge, 1997.

———. "Struggle over Needs: Outline of a Socialist-Feminist Critical Theory of Late-Capitalist Political Culture." In Gordon, *Women, the State, and Welfare*, 199–223.

Fraser, Nancy, and Linda Gordon. "A Genealogy of Dependency: Tracing a Keyword of the U.S. Welfare State." In *The Subject of Care: Feminist Perspectives on Dependency*, edited by Eva Feder Kittay and Ellen K. Feder, 14–39. Lanham, Md.: Rowman & Littlefield, 2002.

Fraser, Nancy, and Axel Honneth. *Redistribution or Recognition? A Political-Philosophical Exchange*. New York: Verso, 2003.

Friedman, Jennifer, and Marixsa Alicea. *Surviving Heroin: Interviews with Women in Methadone Clinics*. Gainesville: University Press of Florida, 2001.

Friedman, Marilyn. *Autonomy, Gender, Politics*. Studies in Feminist Philosophy. Oxford: Oxford University Press, 2003.

———. "Autonomy and Male Dominance." In *Autonomy and the Challenges of Liberalism: New Essays*, edited by John Philip Christman and Joel Anderson, 150–76. Cambridge: Cambridge University Press, 2005.

Fujiwara, Lynn. *Mothers Without Citizenship: Asian Immigrant Families and the Consequences of Welfare Reform*. Minneapolis: University of Minnesota Press, 2008.

Gamache, Denise, and Mary Asmus. "Enhancing Networking Among Service Providers: Elements of Successful Coordination Strategies." In Shepard and Pence, *Coordinating Community Responses to Domestic Violence*, 65–87.

Gilligan, Carol. *In a Different Voice: Psychological Theory and Women's Development*. Cambridge: Harvard University Press, 1982.

Goffman, Erving. *Stigma: Notes on the Management of Spoiled Identity*. Englewood Cliffs, N.J.: Prentice-Hall, 1963.

Gordon, Linda. "The New Feminist Scholarship on the Welfare State." In *Women, the State, and Welfare*, 9–35.

———, ed. *Women, the State, and Welfare*. Madison: University of Wisconsin Press, 1990.

Gorham, Eric. "Social Citizenship and Its Fetters." *Polity* 28, no. 1 (1995): 25–47.

Habermas, Jürgen. *Reason and the Rationalization of Society*. Vol. 1 of *The Theory of Communicative Action*. Translated by Thomas McCarthy. Boston: Beacon Press, 1984.

Haney, Lynne. "Feminist State Theory: Applications to Jurisprudence, Criminology, and the Welfare State." *Annual Review of Sociology* 26, no. 1 (2000): 641–66.

———. "Homeboys, Babies, Men in Suits: The State and the Reproduction of Male Dominance." *American Sociological Review* 61, no. 5 (1996): 759–78.

Hanna, Cheryl. "No Right to Choose: Mandated Victim Participation in Domestic Violence Prosecutions." *Harvard Law Review* 109, no. 9 (1996): 1849–910.

Harvey, David. *The Condition of Postmodernity: An Enquiry into the Origins of Cultural Change.* Cambridge, Mass.: Blackwell, 1990.

Hathaway, Andrew D. "Shortcomings of Harm Reduction: Toward a Morally Invested Drug Reform Strategy." *International Journal of Drug Policy* 12, no. 2 (2001): 125–37.

Hero, Rodney E., and Robert R. Preuhs. "Immigration and the Evolving American Welfare State: Examining Policies in the U.S. States." *American Journal of Political Science* 51, no. 3 (2007): 498–517.

Hirschel, J. David, Ira W. Hutchison III, and Charles W. Dean. "The Failure of Arrest to Deter Spouse Abuse." *Journal of Research in Crime and Delinquency* 29, no. 1 (1992): 7–33.

Hirschmann, Nancy J., and Ulrike Liebert, eds. *Women and Welfare: Theory and Practice in the United States and Europe.* New Brunswick: Rutgers University Press, 2001.

Hodge, Suzanne. "Participation, Discourse, and Power: A Case Study in Service User Involvement." *Critical Social Policy* 25, no. 2 (2005): 164–79.

Honneth, Axel. *The Struggle for Recognition: The Moral Grammar of Social Conflicts.* Cambridge, Mass.: Polity Press, 1995.

Human Rights Watch. *Abusing the User: Police Misconduct, Harm Reduction, and HIV/AIDS in Vancouver.* New York: Human Rights Watch, 2003.

Ignatieff, Michael. "Citizenship and Moral Narcissism." *Political Quarterly* 60, no. 1 (1989): 63–74.

Inda, Jonathan Xavier. "A Flexible World: Capitalism, Citizenship, and Postnational Zones." *Political and Legal Anthropology Review* 23, no. 1 (2000): 86–102.

Kaplan, Elaine Bell. *Not Our Kind of Girl: Unraveling the Myths of Black Teenage Motherhood.* Berkeley: University of California Press, 1997.

Kerr, Thomas, Dave Douglas, Wally Peeace, Adam Pierre, and Evan Wood. *Responding to an Emergency: Education, Advocacy and Community Care by a Peer-Driven Organization of Drug Users: A Case Study of Vancouver Area Network of Drug Users (VANDU).* Ottawa: Centre for Infectious Disease Prevention and Control, 2001.

Kerr, Thomas, Megan Oleson, and Evan Wood. "Harm-Reduction Activism: A Case Study of an Unsanctioned User-Run Safe Injection Site." *HIV/AIDS Policy and Law Review* 9, no. 2 (2004): 13–19.

King, Desmond S. "Making People Work: Democratic Consequences of Workfare." In Mead and Beem, *Welfare Reform and Political Theory,* 65–81.

King, Desmond S., and Jeremy Waldron. "Citizenship, Social Citizenship and the Defence of Welfare Provision." *British Journal of Political Science* 18, no. 4 (1988): 415–43.

Kittay, Eva Feder. *Love's Labor: Essays on Women, Equality, and Dependency.* Thinking Gender. New York: Routledge, 1999.

Kittay, Eva Feder, and Ellen K. Feder, eds. *The Subject of Care: Feminist Perspectives on Dependency.* Feminist Constructions. Lanham, Md.: Rowman & Littlefield, 2002.

Kymlicka, Will, and Wayne Norman. "Return of the Citizen: A Survey of Recent Work on Citizenship Theory." *Ethics* 104, no. 2 (1994): 352–81.

LaVaque-Manty, Mika. "Food, Functioning, and Justice: From Famines to Eating Disorders." *Journal of Political Philosophy* 9, no. 2 (2001): 150–67.

———. "Kant's Children." *Social Theory and Practice* 32, no. 3 (2006): 365–88.

Lipsky, Michael. *Street-Level Bureaucracy: Dilemmas of the Individual in Public Services.* New York: Russell Sage Foundation, 1980.

Lister, Ruth. *Citizenship: Feminist Perspectives.* 2nd ed. New York: New York University Press, 2003.

Macedo, Stephen. "The Moral Dilemma of U.S. Immigration Policy." In *Debating Immigration*, edited by Carol M. Swain, 63–84. New York: Cambridge University Press, 2007.

Mackenzie, Catriona. "Relational Autonomy, Normative Authority, and Perfectionism." *Journal of Social Philosophy* 39, no. 4 (2008): 512–33.

Mackenzie, Catriona, and Natalie Stoljar. "Introduction: Refiguring Autonomy." In Mackenzie and Stoljar, *Relational Autonomy*, 3–34.

———, eds. *Relational Autonomy: Feminist Perspectives on Autonomy, Agency, and the Social Self.* New York: Oxford University Press, 2000.

Mahoney, Martha R. "Legal Images of Battered Women: Redefining the Issue of Separation." *Michigan Law Review* 90, no. 1 (1991): 1–94.

Marchevsky, Alejandra, and Jeanne Theoharis. *Not Working: Latina Immigrants, Low-Wage Jobs, and the Failure of Welfare Reform.* New York: New York University Press, 2006.

Markell, Patchen. *Bound by Recognition.* Princeton: Princeton University Press, 2003.

Marlatt, G. Alan. "Basic Principles and Strategies of Harm Reduction." In Marlatt, *Harm Reduction*, 49–68.

———, ed. *Harm Reduction: Pragmatic Strategies for Managing High-Risk Behaviors.* New York: Guilford Press, 1998.

Marshall, T. H. *Citizenship and Social Class, and Other Essays.* Cambridge: Cambridge University Press, 1950.

Maynard, Rebecca A. "Paternalism, Teenage Pregnancy Prevention, and Teenage Parent Services." In Mead, *The New Paternalism*, 89–129.

McDermott, M. Joan, and James Garofalo. "When Advocacy for Domestic Violence Victims Backfires: Types and Sources of Victim Disempowerment." *Violence Against Women* 10, no. 11 (2004): 1245–66.

Mead, Lawrence M. *Government Matters: Welfare Reform in Wisconsin.* Princeton: Princeton University Press, 2004.

———, ed. *The New Paternalism: Supervisory Approaches to Poverty.* Washington, D.C.: Brookings Institution Press, 1997.

———. "The Rise of Paternalism." In *The New Paternalism*, 1–38.

———. "A Summary of Welfare Reform." In Mead and Beem, *Welfare Reform and Political Theory*, 10–33.

———. "Welfare Employment." In *The New Paternalism*, 39–88.

———. "Welfare Reform and Citizenship." In Mead and Beem, *Welfare Reform and Political Theory*, 172–99.

Mead, Lawrence M., and Christopher Beem, eds. *Welfare Reform and Political Theory.* New York: Russell Sage Foundation, 2005.

Miccio, G. Kristian. "A House Divided: Mandatory Arrest, Domestic Violence, and the Conservatization of the Battered Women's Movement." *Houston Law Review* 42, no. 2 (2005): 237–323.

Mill, John Stuart. *On Liberty.* Edited by Elizabeth Rapaport. Indianapolis: Hackett, 1978.

Minow, Martha. *Making All the Difference: Inclusion, Exclusion, and American Law.* Ithaca: Cornell University Press, 1990.

Nedelsky, Jennifer. "Law, Boundaries, and the Bounded Self." *Representations* 30 (Spring 1990): 162–89.

———. "Reconceiving Autonomy: Sources, Thoughts, and Possibilities." *Yale Journal of Law and Feminism* 1, no. 7 (1989): 7–36.

Negroponte, Michael, dir. *Methadonia*. DVD. New York: First Run Features, 2006.

Newman, Katherine S. *No Shame in My Game: The Working Poor in the Inner City*. New York: Knopf and the Russell Sage Foundation, 1999.

Noddings, Nel. *Caring: A Feminine Approach to Ethics and Moral Education*. Berkeley: University of California Press, 1984.

Ong, Aihwa. *Buddha Is Hiding: Refugees, Citizenship, the New America*. California Series in Public Anthropology. Berkeley: University of California Press, 2003.

Oshana, Marina. *Personal Autonomy in Society*. Burlington, Va.: Ashgate, 2006.

Pateman, Carole. "Another Way Forward: Welfare, Social Reproduction, and a Basic Income." In Mead and Beem, *Welfare Reform and Political Theory*, 34–64.

Pence, Ellen, and Martha McMahon. *A Coordinated Community Response to Domestic Violence*. Duluth, Minn.: National Training Project, 1997.

Pence, Ellen, and Melanie Shepard. "An Introduction: Developing a Coordinated Community Response." In Shepard and Pence, *Coordinating Community Responses to Domestic Violence*, 3–24.

Pevnick, Ryan. "Social Trust and the Ethics of Immigration Policy." *Journal of Political Philosophy* 17, no. 2 (2009): 146–67.

Piven, Frances Fox. "Ideology and the State: Women, Power, and the Welfare State." In Gordon, *Women, the State, and Welfare*, 250–64.

Piven, Frances Fox, and Richard A. Cloward. *Poor People's Movements: Why They Succeed, How They Fail*. New York: Vintage Books, 1979.

———. *Regulating the Poor: The Functions of Public Welfare*. 2nd ed. New York: Vintage Books, 1993.

Raz, Joseph. *The Morality of Freedom*. New York: Oxford University Press, 1986.

Reich, Charles A. "The New Property." *Yale Law Journal* 73, no. 5 (1964): 733–87.

SafeHouse Center. *SafeHouse Center Training Manual*. Ann Arbor, Mich.: SafeHouse, 2006.

Sassen, Saskia. "America's Immigration 'Problem.'" *World Policy Journal* 6, no. 4 (1989): 811–32.

Schram, Sanford F. "Review: The New Paternalism." *Journal of Public Administration Research and Theory* 9, no. 4 (1999): 667–72.

Schram, Sanford F., Richard C. Fording, and Joe Soss. "Neo-liberal Poverty Governance: Race, Place and the Punitive Turn in U.S. Welfare Policy." *Cambridge Journal of Regions, Economy and Society* 1, no. 1 (2008): 17–26.

Shachar, Ayelet. *The Birthright Lottery: Citizenship and Global Inequality*. Cambridge: Harvard University Press, 2009.

Shepard, Melanie, and Ellen Pence, eds. *Coordinating Community Responses to Domestic Violence: Lessons from Duluth and Beyond*. Sage Series on Violence Against Women. Thousand Oaks, Calif.: Sage Publications, 1999.

Sherman, Lawrence W., and Douglas A. Smith, with Janell D. Schmidt and Dennis P. Rogan. "Crime, Punishment, and Stake in Conformity: Legal and Informal Control of Domestic Violence." *American Sociological Review* 57, no. 5 (1992): 680–90.

Shklar, Judith N. *American Citizenship: The Quest for Inclusion*. The Tanner Lectures on Human Values. Cambridge: Harvard University Press, 1991.

Smiley, Marion. "Paternalism and Democracy." *Journal of Value Inquiry* 23, no. 4 (2004): 299–318.

Smith, Anna Marie. "The Sexual Regulation Dimension of Contemporary Welfare Law: A Fifty State Overview." *Michigan Journal of Gender & Law* 8, no. 2 (2001): 121–218.

———. *Welfare Reform and Sexual Regulation*. New York: Cambridge University Press, 2007.

Smith, Sandra Susan. *Lone Pursuit: Distrust and Defensive Individualism Among the Black Poor*. New York: Russell Sage Foundation, 2007.

Sorge, Rod. "Harm Reduction: A New Approach to Drug Services." *Health/PAC Bulletin* 21, no. 4 (1991): 70–99.

Soss, Joe. *Unwanted Claims: The Politics of Participation in the U.S. Welfare System.* Ann Arbor: University of Michigan Press, 2000.

Soss, Joe, and Sanford F. Schram. "A Public Transformed? Welfare Reform as Policy Feedback." *American Political Science Review* 101, no. 1 (2007): 111–27.

Squires, Judith, and Wendy Martineau. "Addressing the 'Dismal Disconnection': Normative Theory, Empirical Inquiry, and Dialogic Research." *Political Studies Association Roundtable, "European Political Science,"* April 2010.

Stears, Marc. "The Vocation of Political Theory: Principles, Empirical Inquiry and the Politics of Opportunity." *European Journal of Political Theory* 4, no. 4 (2005): 325–50.

Stoljar, Natalie. "Autonomy and the Feminist Intuition." In Mackenzie and Stoljar, *Relational Autonomy*, 94–111.

Tapert, Susan F., Jason R. Kilmer, Lori A. Quigley, Mary E. Larimer, Lisa J. Roberts, and Elizabeth T. Miller. "Harm Reduction Strategies for Illicit Substance Use and Abuse." In Marlatt, *Harm Reduction*, 145–217.

Taylor, Charles. *Multiculturalism and "The Politics of Recognition": An Essay.* Edited by Amy Gutmann. Princeton: Princeton University Press, 1992.

Thelen, Rose. *Advocacy in a Coordinated Community Response: Overview and Highlights of Three Programs.* Clearwater, Minn.: Gender Violence Institute, 2000.

Tronto, Joan C. *Moral Boundaries: A Political Argument for an Ethic of Care.* New York: Routledge, 1993.

Tumlin, Karen C., and Wendy Zimmermann. *Immigrants and TANF: A Look at Immigrant Welfare Recipients in Three Cities.* Washington, D.C.: Urban Institute, 2003.

U.S. Department of Agriculture. *Domestic Violence Awareness Handbook.* Washington, D.C.: U.S. Department of Agriculture, 2002.

Weaver, R. Kent. *Ending Welfare as We Know It.* Washington, D.C.: Brookings Institution Press, 2000.

Westlund, Andrea C. "Selflessness and Responsibility for Self: Is Deference Compatible with Autonomy?" *The Philosophic Review* 112, no. 4 (2003): 483–523.

White, Julie Anne. *Democracy, Justice, and the Welfare State: Reconstructing Public Care.* University Park: Pennsylvania State University Press, 2000.

White, Stuart. "Social Rights and the Social Contract: Political Theory and the New Welfare Politics." *British Journal of Political Science* 30, no. 3 (2000): 507–32.

Wilson, James Q. "Paternalism, Democracy, and Bureaucracy." In Mead, *The New Paternalism*, 330–43.

Wilson, William Julius. *When Work Disappears: The World of the New Urban Poor.* New York: Knopf, 1996.

Wood, Evan, Thomas Kerr, Small Will, Jim Jones, Martin Schechter, and Mark Tyndall. "The Impact of a Police Presence on Access to Needle Exchange Programs." *Journal of Acquired Immune Deficiency Syndromes* 34, no. 1 (2003): 116–17.

Young, Iris Marion. *Intersecting Voices: Dilemmas of Gender, Political Philosophy, and Policy.* Princeton: Princeton University Press, 1997.

———. *Justice and the Politics of Difference.* Princeton: Princeton University Press, 1990.

———. "Responsibility and Global Labor Justice." *Journal of Political Philosophy* 12, no. 4 (2004): 365–88.

Zimmermann, Wendy, and Michael Fix. *Declining Immigrant Applications for Medi-Cal and Welfare Benefits in Los Angeles County.* Washington, D.C.: Urban Institute, 1998.

Zorza, Joan. "Must We Stop Arresting Batterers? Analysis and Policy Implications of New Police Domestic Violence Studies." *New England Law Review* 28 (1994): 929–90.

Index

....

www.ingramcontent.com/pod-product-compliance
Lightning Source LLC
Chambersburg PA
CBHW021904020426
42334CB00013B/470